AMERICAN DAUGHTER
GONE TO WAR

AMERICAN DAUGHTER GONE TO WAR

On the Front Lines
with an Army Nurse in Vietnam

Winnie Smith

WILLIAM MORROW AND COMPANY, INC.
New York

It is the policy of William Morrow and Company, Inc., and its imprints and affiliates, recognizing the importance of preserving what has been written, to print the books we publish on acid-free paper, and we exert our best efforts to that end.

Library of Congress Cataloging-in-Publication Data

Smith, Winnie.
    American daughter gone to war : on the front lines
        with an Army nurse in Vietnam / by Winnie Smith.
        p.   cm.
    ISBN 0-688-11188-2
    1. Vietnamese Conflict, 1961–1975—Fiction.   I. Title.
PS3569.M5396 C3   1992
813′.54—dc20   91-32138
                                                                                        CIP

Printed in the United States of America

First Edition

1   2   3   4   5   6   7   8   9   10

BOOK DESIGN BY PAUL CHEVANNES

This book is dedicated in loving memory to my parents, Kenneth George and Pearle Jeanette Robinson, who died during its writing. And to my son, Kenneth James Smith, who was born during its writing.

Acknowledgments

There are many people to thank for their contributions to this work.

Firstly, I hope the book demonstrates how profoundly I appreciate those people I worked with and who became my friends while I was in Vietnam: especially the corpsmen, my warrior buddies, and our casualties.

I must also thank Lynda Van Devanter for her book, *Home Before Morning,* that opened the door for me; and Rose Sandecki, former director of the Concord Vet Center, who led me through it.

When I told my father I had decided to write this book, he gave me an electric typewriter. That typewriter and his confidence in me went a long way toward making my decision a reality.

I have also been fortunate to have had thoughtful and constructive readers in the early stages of my writing, who were very helpful in offering suggestions and direction: especially Bob Britton, Katy Butler, Steve Dresner, and Peter Carroll.

Most of all I'm grateful to Doris Ober, an independent editor in the Bay area, who helped me with my writing. We worked closely together for nearly a year, and she was always wonderfully sensitive and perceptive—we even shared tears while talking about the book—and I came to recognize those qualities as a big part of her extraordinary talent. In the end, we had a publishable manuscript.

During the year that we worked on the book's revision, my agent, Lisa Bankoff, kept in touch, reiterating her interest and confidence in it, which was great encouragement. Since we finished the book, my editor at William Morrow, Liza Dawson, has also been very supportive and insightful in her editorial suggestions.

My final acknowledgment goes to the readers of this book. Their interest shows a concern for what happened to us in Vietnam, and by extension an effort to understand how any war affects those who go.

Contents

9

Contents

Author's Note

The book's chronology is not exact, but I've reconstructed when events occurred as best I could.

Except for my parents, the celebrities, and my friends Retta Stanley and Sheila Murphy, I have changed the names of the people I knew in the Army and the names of my family to protect their privacy.

There are others, particularly people I knew at Fort Dix and Camp Zama, who have been left out of the book in the interest of readability. I hope we will meet again, perhaps for the dedication of the Women's Vietnam Memorial statue near the Wall in Washington.

INTRODUCTION

ONE DECEMBER DAY, 1966: Saigon, Vietnam

IT has been a week since the rainy season ended, and the street in front of our villa has turned from mud to dust. Mud that seeped through cracks in my leather nursing shoes has dried to an orange powder under my feet, and puffs of dust rise with each step I take, coating the shoes and my stockings. A passing Jeep whips up a yellow cloud that sticks to my skin, making me look a shade tanner than I really am. In spite of mama-san's hard scrubbing and ironing, my starched white uniform is already dingy and beginning to droop.

For the thousandth time since I came to Saigon two months ago, I think how absurd it is for us to wear white duty uniforms. The supply room doesn't carry them, and there's no place to have them repaired; we wind up using adhesive tape to patch underarm seams and hemlines. The Army store carries nothing especially for women, much less white nylons or shoes. I wrote to my mother two weeks ago asking her to send shoes and nylons along with deodorant and tampons, and she wrote back asking what brands. It takes a week for letters to reach their destinations, so it will take the better part of this month to get one lousy pair of shoes and a box of hose. I wish I were almost anywhere else in Vietnam. As far as I know, there are only three other hospitals here where nurses wear these dumb duty uniforms.

Three blocks later I turn onto a path alongside main street, which is usually a relief as the street is paved. But today the flow of Vietnamese traffic has been overridden by a convoy of American tanks and armored personnel carriers, rumbling and spewing noxious fumes. I hold my breath as I pick my way through bicycles, motorcycles, and pedicabs. When they see me, the young soldiers in the backs of the trucks whistle and cheer. I'm about fed up with all the attention an American woman attracts in this country, but I dutifully smile and wave back. Thank goodness the hospital is only a block away.

I step onto the red and white tiles of the main corridor, relishing the shade of its adobe cover and a slight breeze that fans my face— the first I've felt all day. As much as I hate this uniform, I appreciate the fact that the Third Field Hospital was once a school for wealthy French children. It is well designed and constructed and one of the coolest places around. Adobe walls insulate us from the blazing sun, and high windows allow hot air to escape. This open corridor is the best of all, capturing the slightest movement of air to funnel it through the buildings.

As is my habit when I'm working the evening shift, I've come early for a reprieve from the sweltering heat before I face the ward. When I reach the triage area, I find a show in progress. It's the first I've seen, although the upcoming holidays have chased celebrities out of the woodwork. Everyone from Cardinal Spellman and Billy Graham to Roy Rogers and Rock Hudson has been here lately.

They descend at Tan Son Nhut Air Base and then are royally escorted to our showcase hospital less than a mile away. They are diverted from triage if there are incoming wounded, to spare them the sight of bodies caked in blood and dirt and the jagged edges of missing parts. They traipse through our spick-and-span wards converted from gracious old French classrooms, admire our spanking white adobe walls and shiny floors, find just the right touch of war zone glamour in our MPs and their M–16s that guard the sandbagged gates. I can guess what these superstars are thinking. Our boys have the best of everything, even nurses decked out in starched whites.

They nod, smile, shake hands, sometimes do a little song or dance, and leave. Then, no doubt, they retire to a comfortable hotel room with hot running water and air conditioning. I resent their magnanimous welcome and solicitous treatment. I resent the camera crews and journalists trotting doggedly after them. Resent everyone's acting as though it were a big deal for them to spend a few days or weeks entertaining the troops.

But this celebrity is an exception. I know she's special when I read the insignia on her fatigues, the silver leaf and caduceus of a lieutenant colonel in the Army Nurse Corps. She is Martha Raye. And she is great. Without benefit of microphones or props or a big audience, she performs a full-length show, her jokes and songs bringing smiles to our faces. I look at the crowd, mostly patients in blue pajamas. Those in wheelchairs are in front; a man with two casted arms uses the armrests of the wheelchairs on either side of him. His neighbor is a man whose dressings start at his nipple line and disappear under his pants. Holding on to this soldier's arm is a man with Kerlix wrapped around his head, covering his eyes. Many patients lean on crutches; many have arms in slings; others are variously bandaged. Martha Raye nods toward her audience, says how proud she is to be here, and calls our fighting men our nation's honored heroes. Of course, we know about the antiwar demonstrators, and she speaks of them derisively. "Those people aren't good enough to lick your boots!" she exclaims, expecting applause.

Instead, there's awkward silence. Scattered through the audience are amputees, some missing both legs, who will never again wear boots. The comedian stammers through a few rehearsed lines and then abruptly stops. "Please forgive me." Her voice cracks; she turns to leave.

First one, then another, and yet another begin to clap. One calls out, "Come back!" and all join in applauding, calling her back.

She wipes away tears with the back of her hand. "Anyone who

says American boys aren't the best in the world doesn't know what they're talking about!"

It rankles them to be called boys, but she's forgiven. After all, she's old enough to be any of our mothers.

Yes, I silently agree, these are the greatest guys in the world. In my heart, they always will be.

Turning to go to work, I think back to when I first cared for them at Fort Dix. That was only a year and a half ago, but it seems much longer. Indeed, it feels as though I've known them all my life.

CHAPTER ONE

MAY–OCTOBER 1965: Fort Dix, New Jersey

They were not called patients. They were called casualties.

They were not there when I arrived in May. At first they came in ones and twos, so we reserved a four-bed room for them. When the pace quickened, we reserved a six-bed room for them. When they came in larger numbers, we used both rooms.

They were the war wounded, evacuated from places I did not yet know—Tan Son Nhut, Bien Hoa, Da Nang, Cam Ranh Bay. They had passed through Clark Air Force Base in the Philippines and Travis Air Force Base in California, and they came to Fort Dix from nearby McGuire Air Force Base—en route to final destinations close to their hometowns.

They came with air evacuation cards, tags rather than charts that recorded name, rank, serial number, date of injuries, operations performed, and information for their care. Their stories appeared in capital letters, cryptic abbreviations ubiquitous in wartime medicine: MFW RLE for "multiple fragment wounds of the right lower extremity"; MGSW LUQ for "multiple gunshot wounds of the left upper quadrant"; BKA BLE for "below-the-knee amputation of both lower extremities"; AEA for "above-the-elbow amputation."

Long after other patients were fast asleep, casualties remained wide-awake. Some lay in their bed talking—about families and sweethearts, about the "good things in life" from apple pies to red-light sex. Others paced the hallway or squatted on their haunches against the wall. Some roamed the hospital until it was time for pain medicines, antibiotics, or dressing changes or until they were told they were off limits and ordered back to the ward. A few joined me in the nursing station to smoke cigarettes and shoot the breeze.

At first I attributed their sleeplessness to the time difference, then to the excitement, or anxiety, of being on their way home, then to their just wanting to talk. Not until I knew them better did I understand how a darkened hospital room full of unknown shadows taunted their war zone instincts, how, when they did fall asleep, they sometimes awakened in terror from soft sounds they didn't recognize.

They spoke little of these things to me. They supported one another, protected one another's secrets. No matter what troubles they may have had or what hardships lay ahead, they were home now. Safe, if not sound.

Though most of these men were with us for only a few days, we cared for them with long-range goals in mind. To wean them from morphine and stave off addiction, we switched most to codeine for pain. For some, we were too late; trembling and sweating from withdrawal, they begged for the "other pain medicine." I steeled my heart. I knew the sooner they overcame their addictions, the sooner they could go home. Next we took down their dressings, to assess the wounds and plan their management.

Though casualties were a small part of the fifty-bed ward, care of their wounds became a major part of my work. Every four hours, after completing rounds on the rest of the ward, I rolled the dressing cart into their room. They were always pleased to see me—the only woman around—but they dreaded the cart. They knew that the dressings had to be changed, that dead tissues breed infection, but that didn't make it any less painful. And they had to endure it every day and every night, day after day and night after night.

Mostly we cared for wounds to arms and legs—some so deep that bone was exposed. Those with minimal pus or dead tissue required only wet-to-dry dressings—damp gauze applied to dry out on the wound. By the next dressing change, removing the stuck-on gauze would debride—rip away—pus and dead tissue. Wounds that produced too much pus required swabbing with hydrogen peroxide. Pus that resisted swabbing was scrubbed with a bristle brush. Dead tissue that resisted scrubbing was cut out with a scalpel.

Care of infected abdominal wounds was less painful but no less disturbing. Squirting syringes of sterile solution into the cavity flushed out pus, and its sickly sweet smell permeated the room as it drained into a basin. Men with such wounds stared in stony silence as the foul secretions spilled out of them.

Amputations are surgical wounds—seldom infected and easily re-dressed. For those casualties, the emphasis shifted to physical therapy. Watching the terror of a man with one leg take his first steps on crutches or the frustration of a man with one arm trying to spread butter on a piece of bread, I had to fight my urge to do everything for them. But they would have to learn sometime, and the sooner the better, for their wounds would not heal.

So I told them about my father who had lost his leg in World War II and how I had bragged to my classmates that he could take it off. I described conventions I'd been to for disabled veterans and how well men managed with wooden legs and hooks for hands. I never mentioned that my father refused to go to the beach without long pants to hide his artificial leg or his terror that he might one night awaken to the house on fire and be unable to get his leg on fast enough to escape.

We seldom witnessed family reunions. The Army didn't pay transportation costs or provide housing for such visits, and more distant families couldn't afford the trip—especially in light of such short stays. Among those casualties from nearby hometowns, many didn't call home to say where they were, putting off that moment of truth for as long as possible.

On the day shift my duties included discharging casualties for

19

the last leg of their journeys to hospitals nearer their homes. One was a twenty-three-year-old whose nose and one side of his face had been blown away and replaced by patchwork grafts. The morning of his release I found him crying in bed. Lightly touching his shoulder, I asked what was wrong.

"I want to die!" he blurted. "If I can't die, at least don't send me home!"

I wanted to say everything would be okay, that plastic surgery could do marvels, but I didn't know that for sure. I wished I could let him stay, but I was the one who had to send him home.

I was raised to believe that freedom, our way of life, must be protected at all costs. The price, I was learning, could be very high.

We didn't need official information to be aware of our growing involvement in Vietnam. Even if there had been no casualties, Fort Dix was an infantry training center, and many of the officers I met hoped to be going soon. They were excited by the prospect of proving their skills, their courage, their patriotism, themselves. Their greatest fear was that the war would end before they had the chance.

The closest I could get as a woman was a war zone hospital, but I was no less excited at the prospect. My plan was to request Vietnam as soon as my six months were up—the required stay before putting in for transfer—but I never got the chance. I received orders to a duty station bearing a San Francisco APO number, the Army's equivalent of a ZIP code.

I come from a long line of warriors, at least back to the Civil War, when my mother's great-great-grandfather served as a bugle boy for the Confederacy. My uncle Edward, a policeman deemed more valuable on the home front, always seemed to me to have regretted not having served in World War II. And my uncle Lee has kept his Army uniform hanging in his closet ever since, now going on twenty years. I used to sneak into his room to touch it, as if the pride and honor it represented might somehow rub off on me.

As a small child I lived with Lee and his sister Jenny and their mother—my grandmother—in North Carolina. My mother grew up there as well, then entered nursing school in New York City, where she married my father. He was a Boston Yankee, a career Navy man decorated for bravery during World War II. But following the loss of a third ship in shark-infested Pacific waters, he suffered from "battle fatigue" and was discharged from the Navy. Convinced he was a jinx and would bring my mother and me bad luck, he left us when I was barely one.

His abandonment devastated my mother. I was not yet two when, after a failed attempt at suicide, she left me with my grandmother in North Carolina and returned to New York to rebuild her life.

I was happy in the South. Nearby, my uncle Edward and aunt Sarah lived with their two daughters—my cousins Christine and Beth. Summers we went on picnics in the Blue Ridge Mountains, where my grandmother had been born and raised and stolen away at age fourteen by a traveling salesman.

Winters were happy as well, tough as they were without central heating or running hot water, and so cold that we kept an old coffee can next to the bed for middle-of-the-night calls of nature. My grandmother rose before the sun to stoke up an old potbelly stove in the kitchen. We practically lived in that room, the rest of the house was so shivering cold.

Mother remarried when I was four, but not until I was six and started school did I begin to wonder why I wasn't with her and my stepfather, as if I were unwanted by them and unworthy of a traditional family. When I was nine, they brought me to New York to live with them, and I was thrilled. My stepfather was a boisterous New Yorker. He took some getting used to after my soft-spoken family in the South, but he won me over with his warm heart and generosity. He was the only father I had ever known, and I felt grateful to have him.

New York with my parents was an easier life, with all the modern conveniences, but it was lonely. My mother worked as a nurse on the evening shift. Most days she was still in bed when I left for school and still at the hospital when I went to bed. My father managed an artificial limb shop and frequently fitted patients or went to meetings in the evenings. It wasn't unusual for me not to see him for more than a few minutes a day several days in a row.

Over the years I learned he was born and raised by an Irish mother on the Lower East Side of Manhattan. He carries the name of Robinson, but every St. Patrick's Day he clips on a green bow tie, hits the Irish bars, and speaks in a convincing brogue. I also learned that he had received wounds to his right leg in France during World War II and that two years and many operations later he had lost it to gangrene. When he was home on the weekends, he watched every World War II movie shown on TV—no matter how many times he had seen them—clearly proud of his part in the war, although he never discussed it.

When I was fourteen, my parents bought a red-shingled house in New Jersey. It was a dream come true for them, but my mother never went back to work, and by then I had grown accustomed to a lot of independence, to doing what I wanted to do when I wanted to do it. Now she decided what time I came home, what time we ate, and what we watched on TV. She never learned to drive, so we never went anywhere. We spent our evenings in front of the TV, hardly saying a word while she read newspapers and magazines and I did my homework. In time I started hiding out in the bathroom, where there were piles of comic books and *Readers Digest*s. In more time I just stayed in my room. It was a relief when weekends rolled around and my father took her to flea markets or shopping malls, and I had the house to myself. When I left for nursing school at age seventeen, I was glad to be on my own again.

In the fall of 1963, my senior year, an Army recruiter came and spoke to our class. She showed pictures of young nurses who looked proud and prestigious in uniforms with insignia on their lapels. She showed more pictures of nurses dining at swank officers' clubs and sight-seeing around the world. I was nineteen, and I wanted to travel. I joined the Army that month.

Two years later I visited my parents from Fort Dix to tell them I might be headed for Vietnam. It never occurred to me that they might not want me to go, so I was stunned by their reaction.

"War's no place for a girl," my father said, adjusting his artificial leg with both hands as I had seen him do so many times. "It's hard enough on men."

"What about the men who need nurses to take care of them?"

"There are plenty of other nurses," my mother answered, tight-lipped.

They couldn't change my mind about going, but as it turned out, they didn't have to. Three days after my orders arrived, I learned my destination was Japan. Though disappointed I was not to be a combat nurse, I had dreamed of going to Japan since junior high school.

The Army gave three days off duty to "clear." I cleared payroll so I would get paid and personnel so my files would arrive before I did. I got my mandated vaccinations and medical clearance and had my car sticker scraped off at the MP station. Then I cleared headquarters, where I was instructed to take my duffel bag with full field gear aboard the plane, and the adjutant's office, where I appointed my father my power of attorney and named my parents to inherit my life insurance should I get knocked off.

Did they know something I didn't know? Was this some kind of secret buildup that would take me to Vietnam after all?

Oh, I hoped so!

CHAPTER TWO

NOVEMBER 1965–
AUGUST 1966:
Camp Zama, Japan

CAMP Zama could have been Any Base, U.S.A., a hodgepodge of one-story green wooden buildings from World War II and three-story gray cement buildings of more recent times. There was even a stone barbecue pit under a stand of pine trees that looked as if it belonged more in upper New York State than in Japan. But I had only to step through the compound gate to reach the real Japan, a world in which I was a giant at five feet nine, odd woman out with curly blond hair and light eyes. Here spacious lawns on base exploded into crowded streets with no room to spare for sidewalks. Soldiers gave way to students in sailor uniforms, men in business suits and women in kimonos (some with babies strapped to their backs), and children playing in streets where cars seldom passed. Small shops offered wares I had never seen before: abacuses, futons, magazines printed in columns, and incense of every shape and color. And there were foods with English names I didn't recognize: kelp, abalone, squid, and sea urchins.

Tokyo and Yokohama were an hour's train ride away. Old

Japan was even closer, a coastline of fishing villages with unpainted buildings, unpaved streets, and wooden fishing boats with big eyes and toothy smiles that dotted the beaches.

The Army gave us one day a week to explore that world. The other six I worked on the dependents ward, located in one of the old World War II buildings. I liked its pervasive woody smell, its paned windows, and the sense of history it held. But with a war going on, I was an Army nurse caring for women and children— mostly women, many of whom complained about the creaky hallway, stained sheets, and having no choice in meals. I missed the casualties at Fort Dix, missed their brave smiles and appreciation for just being alive.

My fondness for those men carried over to off duty hours at our officers' club, where I joined patient-officer-warriors. They were here for medical care that would be completed before their tours were up—in other words, they would return to Vietnam— and viewed their time at Camp Zama as nothing short of playtime. Most hospital officers considered them too rowdy and socialized exclusively with one another. But the warriors' air of bravado and cocky self-assurance fanned my notions about war, and their zest for fun drew me out of my natural shyness. Most of all, I was drawn to the strong kinship among them, a sense of family that eased the loneliness of being so far from home. They were my buddies.

From them I learned that soldiering is not only dangerous but hard on the body. "Humping the boonies" with heavy packs and ammunition causes hernias. Persistent diarrhea and "no place to go" lead to hemorrhoids. Jumping off helicopters in "hot landing zones" means knee injuries. Enemy weapons cause "minor" wounds, and enemy mosquitoes bring cases of malaria. They all made the war seem much closer.

We spent most evenings at the club in the cocktail lounge—in a special corner cozily outfitted with a couch, chairs, coffee table, and two slot machines. The room was noisy with cheers for the clatter of falling nickels, groans for the near big wins, and the sound of leather cups thumping our games of liar's dice or ship captain, mate, and crew. Daytime hours at the club were quieter.

Then we forsook the cozy corner for the bar, built of American oak that reminded us of bars in American westerns although this one was tended by a smiling, bowing Japanese man. Overhead, appropriately enough, the television broadcast John Wayne westerns in Japanese (without subtitles) or another favorite form of Japanese entertainment, samurai movies.

More intriguing to me were the yarns our warriors spun, no matter that fantasies and half-truths were woven into the telling. Many of the storytellers were southerners whose easygoing, soft-spoken narratives appealed to my North Carolinian upbringing. Mississippi Cal was one, a clean-cut twenty-five-year-old helicopter pilot who loved cracking jokes, who almost always smiled and never complained, who was easy to talk to. He was someone I would have loved to date; only he had a son and a wife expecting at any minute.

Most of the soldiers were married, and a few kept it secret. Some expressed a romantic interest, but none pressured me. It was enough just to have an American woman to talk to, a "round-eye" to remind them of home and why they were fighting a war.

From their stories I learned the fighting outfits in Vietnam and their insignia—the Horse's Head of the 1st Cavalry, the Big Red One of the 1st Division, the Lightning Bolt of the 25th Division, the Screaming Eagle of the 101st. And I learned where they were based—An Khe, Bien Hoa, Cu Chi, and Tay Ninh. I learned the different kinds of choppers—Hueys, slicks, Cobras, and Bubbles—and the difference between grunts, Green Berets, fixed-wing and chopper pilots. It was like learning to distinguish one football team from another: their names, emblems and team colors, the cities they represent, and the kinds of players—quarterbacks, fullbacks, wide receivers, and linemen.

In less than a month these warriors felt like family to me. By Thanksgiving eve the topic of greatest discussion in this family was the live broadcast by Armed Forces Radio of the Army-Navy game—*the* game. In Japan that was during the wee hours of the morning. This posed no problem for me, a lowly second lieutenant, as my butter bar signified, working nights on a quiet ward; but my warrior buddies grumbled about getting up at such an ungodly hour to listen to it. We were gathered around the table in our corner of the officers' club, smoking cigarettes and drinking our various brands of booze.

"High time you got back into training," I quipped. It was the first time I ever dished out some of what I have always taken from them—teasing.

They roar approval. "Watch out!" shouts Mississippi Cal over their hoots and hollers. "The little nurse is coming in for the kill!"

This elicits moans and groans as everyone pretends to be dying. "Hey, Nurse! Help me! I'm bleedin' bad!" somebody calls. "I'm gonna die if I don't get a nurse!"

More whoops. Finally I get the double entendre and blush. "Watch it, officer," I say, failing miserably to sound offended. In any case, it is almost 2300 hours, time for me to go to work.

"Stay a little longer!" they protest. "The fun's just beginning!"

"No way," I say with mock seriousness. "This nurse has no time for boys. I have sick women to attend to."

"Tell 'em *you're* sick!"

"Tell them you're needed for moral support of the troops!"

I leave smiling. Hours later, hunched over a portable radio for the static-filled broadcast, I wonder if any of them have actually managed to wake up for the game.

"There she is! The killer lieutenant!" they whistle and cheer when I enter the dining room after work. I blush at the stares this accolade inspires, but I am pleased.

They had, I learn, stayed up all night rather than risk missing the game. So over breakfast on Thanksgiving Day we review it play by play. When we reconvene in the afternoon, Thanksgiving seems like yesterday. Dinner has been prepared by a Japanese cook, who has not yet mastered an American breakfast, much less the trimmings for our holiday feast—there is no cranberry sauce, no candied sweet potatoes, no persimmon pudding, no pumpkin pie—but it doesn't seem to matter. I am happy, truly happy, with my warrior family around me.

A week later Mississippi Cal receives orders to fly back to Vietnam. Others soon follow, and any hope of a Christmas spirit dissipates as more in our group receive orders to fly.

Shortly after Christmas, in midafternoon on a wintry day, I join our dwindling band in the cozy corner. Rising slightly until I am seated, they are uncharacteristically quiet.

Mississippi Cal, they inform me solemnly, is on the "list"—the weekly account of those who have been killed in action.

The cocktail lounge seems oddly quiet—no sound of nickels dropping into the machines, no thumping leather cup. "We'll Sing in the Sunshine" is playing on the jukebox, the familiar refrains filling the room. Everyone stares into his drink.

Peering at their faces, I see none of the despair I feel. I think of Cal, always cracking jokes. I think of his wife at home, expecting a baby who will never know him.

"Why?" I hear myself ask.

"Don't think about it," someone says. "Just think about the good times we had."

"Let's drink to that," someone else puts in. "And to all the VC he took with him." We raise our glasses.

Everything is back to normal in two days. Once in a while something will still remind us of him, but none of us speaks about it. New men are arriving, and Cal's face starts to fade.

The new year, 1966, brings me a new assignment to a new wing of the hospital, an orthopedic ward with fifty beds on either end and ten more in rooms along the connecting corridor. Similar wards above and below mean this new building holds more than three hundred beds. Evidently that isn't enough. Nearby the Army is building two more hospitals.

The ward's traditional ribbon-cutting ceremony ends with a punctuality to warm the most military heart. The first ambulance rolls in soon after, and we run to the windows to cheer its arrival. The sight of the green box with its big red cross sends a chill down my back; it is the same as those in the old war movies I watched with my father as a child. While the ambulance is being unloaded, the first dustoff helicopter—a big green bird with a big red cross—swoops down to the hospital lawn.

When I report for duty this night, there are seventy patients on our ward. Clark Air Force Base in the Philippines must be bursting at the seams.

A night nurse wears rubber-soled shoes to pass quietly through the night. She makes her rounds silently, checking IVs, dressings, or circulation to a limb. She whispers softly if she must wake a patient, so not to startle those who are asleep. That nurse is not caring for combat wounded.

In the field, where the war is silent after sundown, warriors sleep with one ear cocked and one eye half open. For them, soft footsteps could mean an enemy slipping through the lines. For them, a hospital ward is ominously quiet and dangerously dark.

It is around two or three in the morning, when patients are finally drifting off to sleep, that I step softly toward a newly casted leg to check circulation and then turn on my flashlight.

"Hit the dirt!" the soldier cries in alarm, diving to the floor where his cast hits with a loud thud. My flashlight, kicked out of my hand, clanks to the floor an instant later.

Urgent whispers and shouts erupt on the ward—"What is it?" "What's going on?"—as more soldiers hit the dirt, crashing from hospital beds to tiled cement.

"At ease! This is Japan!" someone yells.

One of our corpsmen turns on the lights. The whole ward is awake with half the patients out of bed. As we help them back, they joke about it, assuring me it is good to be kept on their toes, to keep their war zone reflexes in good working order.

I no longer pass quietly in the night, but there is no precaution against the alarms their own nightmares cause, the cries of "Hey! Where the fuck is everybody?" or "Doc! Over here!" or a shrill "Gooks!" piercing the night.

Reassuring calls answer, "It's okay, man. Nothing's happening." Or "Relax, soldier. This is Japan." If a man tries to apologize, he is told by everyone, "Don't sweat the small stuff."

When a casualty has been with us long enough to feel safe on the darkened ward, his sleep-deprived body frequently falls into slumber so profound that it resists being awakened. My first lesson in this is when I shake a man's shoulder and get socked in the chest. The next time I shake a leg and get kicked in the stomach. Wake-up rounds, I maintain, should fall under hazardous duty pay.

Days the place hops with more than a hundred patients coming and going for everything from operations and X rays to physical therapy and cafeteria meals. Because we have only two nurses and three corpsmen, we depend on "fit" patients to help with much of the work. One good arm with two good legs can refill water pitchers or ferry supplies around the hospital. One good leg with two good arms can deliver meal trays or paper work from a wheelchair. A few complain, but not many. They are helping their buddies.

The third week I rotate to the evening shift—1500 to 2300 hours. I begin to grow comfortable being the only woman amid a hundred men and then begin to know them as men instead of wounds. During these hours they are awake, have no appointments or chores to take them elsewhere in the hospital, and no matter how minor their problems—often just a casted limb—they are confined to the ward. Enlisted men, even sergeants held accountable for men's lives in battle, are presumed too irresponsible to leave the hospital.

They don't just lie down and take this insult; any way of getting around such regulations is considered fair play. There are times I feel more like a warden than a nurse, guarding against those who need bed rest "borrowing" crutches and tracking down those who fail to show up for their antibiotics.

Their greatest challenge lies in concealing forbidden drugs—everything from beer in the ice machine to, on rare occasions, marijuana in a bedside stand. On the other hand, everyone can have Darvon and Seconal at 2200, lights-out hour, a pattern set by other evening nurses. Even though these drugs are not held to be highly addictive—they are not counted with narcotics—it bothers me to hand them out like salt tabs in the jungle. But any effort to discourage their use brings loud and unanimous dissent.

One of my patients at this time is a city boy called Red who was thrown by a rocket and landed squarely on his right shoulder. His arm is in traction. Filling a glass for him from his water pitcher, I nod that he should swallow the pills in front of me—a cardinal rule of nursing.

Everyone is watching, but that isn't so uncommon. It's the suppressed laughter that makes me suspicious.

"Whoo!" Red gasps, fanning his mouth with his one good hand as the cubicle breaks into laughter.

Sure enough, there is the unmistakable odor of vodka in his water pitcher.

I flush at the ruse. "I don't have time for this game," I say, meaning it.

"Water," Red gasps at me.

I hesitate only a moment before pouring him another glass from his pitcher and glare at those who dare another round of laughter.

"Now that you've had your laughs," I say when they have quieted, "you'd better figure out who's going to stay awake to watch him breathe!"

"No problem, Lieutenant," Red's immediate neighbor answers, smiling. "We know all about guard duty."

"Then see to it," I say, and leave.

I never blow the whistle on them. I think I might act the same as them if I were cooped up on a ward.

There is another drug with chemical bondings closely resembling alcohol that we give to kill Vietnamese worms—intestinal ova and parasites that freeload trips to Japan in unsuspecting soldiers. We flush them out with routine checks on stools, then dose their gleeful hosts for five days with the drug. For those soldiers it means a five-day high without having to hide it. It isn't hard to figure out why cases of wormy stools occur in many men at once. One afflicted soldier fills specimen cups for all his buddies, who then take the five-day high as well.

Our crowd at the club is at least as party-minded as the patients are. By February Retta Stanley has arrived and become part of our group of merry pranksters. A few years older and a full head shorter than me, she has full lips, dark, wide-set eyes, and brown hair cropped to a near pixie. Flamboyant, exuberant, and famous for off-color innuendos, she is very different from my quieter self. But we are kindred spirits, in love with Japan and our warriors. On top of that she arranged for the Army to ship over her VW bug. Warrior buddies heretofore restricted by heavy casts or dressing changes now mobilize with us. When there are too many of us, they overflow onto the roof and hood. Wherever we go, we are almost always wild and rowdy—flying high, if not blowing two sheets to the wind.

Three of our best buddies are Weed, a lieutenant "ground pounder" with the Big Red One infantry; Irish, a chopper pilot with ice blue eyes, coal black hair, and a musical Boston accent; and Gung Ho Man, another chopper pilot who is stockier than most warriors and who keeps his crew cut so short that his head looks shaved. Although he has been a warrior too long to be truly gung ho, he belongs to the First Cavalry, which is renowned for its zealousness. Only the Marines are held to be more fervent, and they are widely held by Army types to border on crazy.

All three fly back to war on the same day. The night before, Retta and I meet them in our club's cozy corner. We're joined by Carolyn, a Red Cross worker who isn't a part of our clique but whom we all like and appreciate for her sarcastic humor.

Our first stop for our buddies' farewell evening is the massage parlor at a nearby base, Atsugi. The guys plead for us to take our saunas with them, but we decline; we're embarrassed just to be naked with our masseuses. After fifteen minutes in a steam sauna, fifteen minutes in a huge tub with *hot* water, and thirty minutes of knot-kneading massage at the strong hands of a young Japanese woman, we go to the Sagamihara striptease show—something Retta and I have heard a lot about.

Forget the tease part in a Japanese strip show. Moving to tinny phonographic music, a beautiful Eurasian dancer takes everything off. Japanese men in the audience watch sedately while American GIs go crazy. I'm caught completely off guard when the dancer unceremoniously squats and spreads her legs for the audience— to the wild cheers of Japanese men and a suddenly silent gallery of GIs.

When the lights come back on, everyone smiles and bows at us girls, clearly wondering what we thought of the show. Carolyn waves and grins as if to say "Great stuff!" Retta gives a thumbs-up. I can't say or do anything.

Dinner at the Tachikawa Air Force Base is followed by hot toddies at its bar. At closing time we make toasts to long life and good health while the jukebox plays the Ramsey Lewis Trio's rendition of "The 'In' Crowd." In the parking lot we exchange warm hugs and kisses with our departing warrior buddies, acutely aware that it will be a long time before they see another round-eye woman.

Watching their retreating figures, we wonder aloud if we will ever hear from them again. Silently we wonder if they'll make it back home in one piece. Silently, because our warriors have taught us that it's unlucky to speak of such things.

My birthday falls a day after the vernal equinox. This March 22, I am twenty-two.

Work has picked up. Increased action in the war has brought us increased numbers of casualties and more critical cases. To accommodate the changing times, additional beds are placed in the dayrooms on either end of the ward and in private rooms along the corridor. And we begin working twelve-hour shifts—save our head nurse, who continues working days only, and our clinical specialist, who continues working evenings only, functioning more as a nurse than a corpsman.

From early morning until lights out at 2200 radios on the ward are a constant background to our work. Nineteen sixty-six is the year that "The Ballad of the Green Berets" is popular. Whenever it comes over the air, patients stop whatever they are doing, and the ward of more than a hundred soldiers falls uncannily quiet and still. The men's eyes become distant, returning to places in their past, and the collective sadness is almost palpable. It is all I can do not to cry.

But mostly there is an untiring determination by patients to have a good time. The limit of my tolerance is met once at 0400 hours, when I discover a patient with a Japanese prostitute under his sheets. I am outraged in spite of the "red-blooded American boy" defense. At work the following night I have calmed down enough to compromise. Prostitutes will not be permitted on the ward, but from 2400 hours to 0400 hours no unauthorized absences will be reported. Anyone missing after 0400 will be presumed AWOL and so reported, and anyone returning in a disorderly state will have the book thrown at him.

That change in policy comes on the heels of another. No Seconal until 0100 hours. Now that patients are staying longer, I have a greater concern regarding addiction. I give permission for those who cannot sleep to gather in the atrium between the banks of elevators, where couches and chairs were placed after the day-rooms were converted to bed space.

The first week about a dozen patients party nonstop in the atrium until 0100 hours, when I dispense the Seconal, making so much racket I suspect a conspiracy to change my mind. But eventually the men come to enjoy the nonnarcotic hours filled with long discussions punctuated by peals of laughter. In more time some come to refuse the Seconal altogether—even at 0300 hours when I try to get them to sleep.

During one period on the ward a patient splurges on a hand-held tape recorder and begins using those early-morning hours to simulate the sounds of war. The idea catches on, and a group of men join him every night, practicing until they are pleased with their roles as incoming and outgoing mortars, high and low chop-pers, artillery and small-arms fire, machine guns, and grenades. One provides the short, sharp directions of a radio operator; others whisper to check their buddies' positions; yet others mimic the delirious kills and the cries of wounded. One by one the men relive their experiences in the heat of battle.

When a tape is finished, they invite me to hear the results and identify the different sounds: the *thwoop* of mortars, the *whoosh* and *kaboom* of artillery, the *whop-whop* of helicopters. All of it is impressive, but it is the terrified whispers of wounded calling for "Doc," that drives home the message for me.

Retta and I get three days off for the Easter weekend and travel to Atami for the cherry blossom season. The city, called the Riviera of Japan, is built on hills overlooking an azure sea. Its streets are lined with pink cherry trees in full blossom, and it bustles with pedestrians in kimonos.

We spend one afternoon feeling very much at home at an amuse-ment park; the rides are just like those we enjoyed as children. When we catch two Japanese girls following us, we ask them with gestures and laughter to join us on the Ferris wheel. Many rides later we buy them cotton candy and say good-bye.

The hotel has "European-style" beds, and the dining-room tables are laid with triple sets of silverware—very Western in flavor, but not so much as to include a bathtub. In the hotel basement, built over a natural hot spring, there is a public bath big enough to swim in. It's a huge room with smoked glass windows, where everyone is naked but acts perfectly natural, the kids splashing around while husbands and wives wash each other's backs. We're too shy to join them, so we take private baths in small chambers with sliding smoked glass doors. We wash and rinse from a wooden bucket and then soak for as long as we like in a sunken tiled tub. It is simply fantabulous.

It is now early May. I've made many good friends who have returned to war and yet more friends who are still with us. We always have fun, and they are always there when I need help, but being everybody's buddy and nobody's sweetheart is getting old. And though I am by now at ease with their constant attention, I'm wary. It is impossible to separate who and what we are from when and where we are, to know how we would feel if we were back home.

When Tom Jamison appears at our club, none of that matters. He is handsome in a classically rugged way—he looks like a park ranger—but it is the contagion of his smile and the light in his eye, his quiet self-assurance and easygoing sense of humor that drew me the most. And he is from North Carolina. Like myself, he played Ain't No Bears Out Tonight on tree-studded lawns, sipped iced tea from tall glasses, and sat on front porch swings to watch fireflies and listen to crickets on warm summer evenings.

A First Cavalry man, Tom feels lucky to make a living doing what he loves—flying choppers. I'm very curious about what he does in Vietnam, but only once does he consent to talk about it. "Ferry grunts in and out of the field," he says. "Rain fire when they need help. Once in a while jump the fence to take in commando groups." He pauses. "That's what I hate most. If you get your tail shot down over there, nobody's gonna come take it out for you."

The fence is what warriors call the Cambodian border. I have heard them speak of enemy supplies and of troops being moved over the Ho Chi Minh Trail and of heavy bombing in the area to stop them. But this is the first time I've heard mention of our men actually crossing the border.

Tom's gunshot wound to the leg will not get him stateside, but he says he doesn't mind. He is glad to serve his country and proud of his Silver Cross for bravery. Most of all, he is a war zone pilot, and his buddies in Vietnam still need him.

He is married and has two little girls, something I brush aside although I can't forget. I wish I could. We know that our relationship will end when he goes back to Vietnam and that he will return to his wife and children when his tour ends. But in a world where the future holds no guarantees, I choose to have and lose true love rather than risk never having it at all. It is my first season of love, so long awaited.

It is during this time that my orders come through for Saigon—not where I want to be, which is where my warrior buddies are.

The Gung Ho Man has written not to count on my orders, that many orders are changed when you report in-country. He also wrote that he is glad I'm coming, but Tom is furious about it, nagging me to get the orders changed. As it turns out, he can't nag for long. Chopper pilots are in short supply and high demand. June is just around the corner when he receives surprise orders to fly.

"I want you to forget me," he says the night before heading back. "Love another man as soon as one good enough comes along."

As he speaks, I can't shake what I have heard, that half the pilots in Vietnam die and only 17 percent finish a full tour. Tom already has two Purple Hearts.

We fall silent. Johnny Cash croons from my stereo in the darkened room. Then Tom says, without fear or anger, not even regret, "I don't think I'll make it out this time."

Two weeks later his crew chief writes. Nine days after returning to duty, their chopper ran into enemy fire in what was supposedly a cleared area. Tom got zapped.

I had prepared myself for his departure but not for this. On the outside nothing is changed. On the inside everything is different. Every time I walk into the club, I think of the time I spent there with Tom. When I drink with my warrior buddies, I no longer think of them as heroes but as survivors. Caring for patients at work reminds me of Tom's wounded leg and how Tom no longer exists. To escape the reminders, I go to the empty barbecue pit in the corner of the compound not far from the gate. It is the only place I can be alone. I spend long hours there, singing to myself and playing my guitar.

It seems much longer than three months since the Weed, Irish, and Gung Ho Man left. And it is much harder to be buddies with warriors after so many farewells.

After Tom, time passes by two clocks.

One marks time at Camp Zama, faithfully recording the rise and fall of suns on a calendar. After Tom, I go from club to work to bed or from work to club to bed. The war brings in casualties and takes away friends. Nothing changes but the numbers and the faces ebbing and flowing across the Tropic of Cancer. I no longer wonder how the war is going or if it will soon end. Time simply passes in the circle of work, club, and sleep.

The other clock marks time on the other side of the gate where the war ends and Japan begins, where the passing of hours and days with the rise and fall of the sun has meaning, where what I do and who I meet changes with the passing of these things. It is a huge relief to keep time by this other clock. I use it as often as I can.

There is a train, called the bullet, that covers three hundred miles in less than three hours, and the ride is so smooth you hardly know you are moving. Outside, farmers plant rice as they have for centuries, plucking shoots from wooden wheelbarrows along earthen levees and driving them into the ground.

Three weeks after Tom has ceased to exist, Retta and I take that train to Osaka. We sit through a tea ceremony—my legs cramped with the effort to sit Japanese style—where a geisha serves green tea that is as thick as soup and so bitter I can't get it down. We watch cloisonné jewelry being crafted, a delicate pouring of molten glass into copper channels. We take a nighttime boat ride where baskets of fire are hung over the sides of the boat to attract fish. Cormorant birds with leashes around their necks—tied just tight enough that they can swallow only small fish—then dive into the water. When they catch a large fish, they are pulled back to the boat by the fishermen and given a small fish as a reward.

All of it is beautiful and exotic, but after Tom, my heart isn't in it. I'm better off on base, where I can sit and get drunk, not think or feel anything. Or be alone at the barbecue pit and cry as much as I want.

In July a whole new bunch of officer patients arrive. Among them is Peter Carrington, an artillery butter bar with curly blond hair, blue eyes, powerful shoulders—and a way of smiling that makes you feel as if he were asking a question. And he is looking my way.

No longer so shy about such things, I strike up the usual conversation. He is, I learn, with the Twenty-fifth Division. His tank was blown up, and he has been sent to Camp Zama for a perforated eardrum.

We laugh. How did he manage to get to Japan for that? I nod toward his West Point ring. "A ring knocker."

Soon we're laughing about marching in parades, New Year's Eve dances, and Army-Navy games. For a moment our speaking about those years takes away the war. Careful, Smith, I tell myself. He's not married, but he is going back to Vietnam.

Yes, I answer myself, so there's no time to waste.

The time we spend together feels like freedom. Maybe because I know the danger of putting too much faith in the future, I can live the present with fewer regrets or expectations. Or maybe it's because Peter is not given to lazy hours at the club and we spend our time exploring the world beyond the gate. I lead him through mazes of Japanese streets and railroad stations, to the daibutsu in Kamakura and to fishing villages with views of Mount Fuji. We seldom even dine on base, preferring the noodle houses on mountain roads or restaurants in small towns, where we sit on tatami mats and eat with chopsticks.

Once we borrow Retta's car and drive to a remote seaside resort. Barefoot, we dare the waves to catch us and shriek and laugh like children when they do. Hand in hand we stroll the deserted beach as the sun goes down. Though we know each day brings us closer to the day the war will part us, we pretend that it doesn't matter.

From the war the Gung Ho Man writes: "One of my best friends just entered Special Forces school at Fort Bragg, so I imagine it won't be long and he will be over here also. Another guy who was a year behind me in high school is now stationed at Qui Nhon, and this makes three people from my hometown who are stationed here."

When the future arrives, Peter's orders to fly in hand, we head to Hakone for a pretend honeymoon. We go by train, and a young Japanese child across from us stares in fascination at our matching blond hair and light eyes. When her mother gestures apologetically, we nod and smile to say we don't mind. I avert my eyes from Peter, fearful he'll see my surge of emotions. I'm beginning to fantasize about one day having a child with him.

We can see Mount Fuji from our hotel, and there is a swimming pool—perfect for make-believe honeymooners, because no one else is ever there. We have a laughing fit at Peter in my bathing cap to protect his perforated eardrum. (We laugh a lot.) We snap pictures of each other in our hotel kimonos. We order dinner with champagne and caviar.

Back at Camp Zama Peter's farewell party doubles as my promotion party, though he isn't thrilled that I've been promoted to first lieutenant before him. When the party is over, I fight sleep as long as I can, not wanting the night to end. When I awaken, he is dressed and shaking me for one last kiss. Clutching my robe against the chill morning air, I watch him step through the door and close it softly behind him. From my window I watch him walk past the barbecue pit and disappear beyond the gate. Tears blur his image. I will them to stop.

"It's the Weed! Hey, Weed!" I cry in sudden recognition.

"Shit! I don't believe it!" Retta says. "What happened this time?"

He flashes us a big grin, his strong arms easily holding him on a pair of crutches for his right leg—casted to mid-thigh, I note, with wound drainage seeping through around the calf. "Nothin' much." He shrugs. "Had a little run-in with a VC who thought I could use some R and R."

His remark is greeted with chuckles, claps on the back, and handshakes. Though none of the other warriors in the dining room know him, he is welcomed as a long-lost buddy.

"Do you believe they wanted to send me to another hospital?" He pauses significantly, giving me a big wink. "I told 'em I had a fiancée at Camp Zama, and it'd sure mean a lot to me if we could pass this time together!" After settling into his chair, he asks if I've heard from the Gung Ho Man.

"He's in An Khe," I say, "flying VIPs around. Says things could be better, but he's not complaining."

"He'd be green with envy if he could see me now!"

We laugh at the Gung Ho Man thinking that the Weed is still humping the boonies with the Big Red One.

This second wound gets the Weed back to the States. In late July he writes about his flight home to Philadelphia: " . . . I tried commercial lines, but they didn't have time to bother with a soldier's problems with all that prime money floating around from civilians. I gave up and went down to Travis to hop a flight. . . . I made it home tired, hungry, and unloved.

"Remember I'd like to see you when you're home on leave. How about a trip to the beach? I still don't dig the hill country after my last expedition. . . . "

Not long after Weed's departure a fixed-wing pilot offers to take me to South Korea, and I accept. What I see shocks me: populations of homeless with children bathing in mud puddles and begging in the streets; five- and six-year-olds carrying their baby brothers and sisters on their backs. Shortly before the midnight curfew, strictly enforced by police, the scores of homeless families search for a place to sleep—in doorways, against buildings, on the sides of streets.

Back at the club my warrior buddies say Korea is easy street compared with Vietnam. It's hard to believe.

After that trip I begin to fantasize about how I might help the people, especially the children, once I am in Vietnam. I could scrounge up milk and food at the mess hall, medical supplies at work, clothes and blankets from churches back home. The fantasy feels real, as though I really could do something for those people. But when I share it, my warrior buddies shake their heads. Chris Hansen, yet another 1st Cavalry chopper pilot, wags his finger at me. "Make no mistake, little lady. It's those same sorry-looking people who sneak through the night to plant land mines. Crawl through jungles to ambush us. Rig their kids with satchel charges to blow us up. Stay away from those gooks, or you're liable to find yourself in some dark alley with a knife in your back!"

Of all the warriors, Chris is the one I least expected to be so bitter. A midwestern farm boy with sandy blond hair and pale blue eyes, he grew up dreaming of being a chopper pilot. He says he is happier than he ever has been and is itching to get back into the war. Since he was in Vietnam for only one month before being wounded, he still has most of his tour to go. That means he'll be there when I arrive in October. And that being the case, he promises to take me for a ride in one of those magnificent machines at the first opportunity.

CHAPTER THREE

SEPTEMBER—OCTOBER 1966: The Third Field Hospital, Saigon

BEFORE reporting to duty in Saigon, I take a month's leave back home in New Jersey. Nothing there is as I remembered.

Our red-shingled house looks the same but feels strange, as if it belongs in the far past. Even my parents seem like strangers. The things they hold important—house, yard, and shopping trips—no longer interest me. After I've shown my slides of Japan and told the stories that go with them, we have little to talk about. They once mention Tom, whom I had written about, but all I can say is that "he was a long time ago." I never tell them about Peter, knowing they would ask if we have future plans, which would raise the uncertainty of his making it out of Vietnam alive—something I don't want to think about. Nor do I mention my warrior buddies, worried that my parents couldn't understand our special friendships. Even the subject of Vietnam is taboo, for they still don't want me to go and act betrayed because I'm going against their wishes.

Home and family aren't the only uncomfortable parts of being stateside. At a party much like those I attended before joining the Army, I feel as if I were in a country where I have never been before. Everyone seems so phony in glitzy clothes, so out of shape and unattractive, so immature. It kills any desire I might have to visit other friends from the good old days.

I think about calling the Weed for that trip to the beach but never do. My parents would make a big deal out of it—assume a romance and hound me to confess. So I just sleep late and sit around.

It is a relief, when my leave ends, to grab a flight from McGuire Air Force Base, New Jersey, to Travis Air Force Base, California. But getting to Saigon isn't so simple. I spend four days waiting in the Travis terminal for space available. My third night a pilot who has noticed me for several days asks if I would mind a cargo plane. I jump at it.

After takeoff the navigator offers me a small seat between the pilot and copilot. It opens up a fascinating world of dim red instrument dials and brilliant stars beyond, but three nights of catnapping soon catches up with me. I sleep in the navigator's bunk, drifting off to the drone of engines.

I awaken as we are setting down to refuel at Guam. We resume our journey at sunrise, and I watch the world metamorphose into light blue sky and dark blue water. Nearer to our destination I catch my first sight of Vietnam, an emerald land in azure waters. From up here it is hard to believe there's a war going on.

Our descent relegates me to the windowless cargo area, strapped to the hull like everything else. Not a comfortable seat in any case, and our landing doesn't help—lurching and swerving madly. I clutch my seat, vainly striving not to bang into the hard hull at my back and staring in alarm as huge cargo crates in the center of the craft strain against thick straps. No sooner do we stop than beads of sweat pop out all over me; thank goodness I'm not wearing makeup.

"You must warrant a warm welcome." The navigator grins, extending a hand to help me from the low-slung seat.

"It *is* hot," I agree. "These winter greens are definitely out of order."

He chuckles. "I'm talking about that little VC welcoming party."

I smile, having been warned by warrior buddies that in-country veterans like to scare newcomers—part of the initiation rite.

"No joke," the captain assures me. "They must've known we're carrying some mighty precious cargo."

Tan Son Nhut is hardly out in the boonies, and it's broad daylight. Besides, if the base is under attack, why are we just standing here?

"Phew," I gasp, swiping at my forehead. "It's an oven in here."

"Welcome to Vietnam," the navigator says wryly as he pushes open the door and disappears outside in a single bound.

I could do with a breath of fresh air and am set to follow him. I stop three feet from the door. Here the blazing heat of a tropical noonday sun blasts back from the tarmac. My skin feels on fire. Rivulets of sweat pour through my hair and under my arms, soaking my blouse in an instant. And there's an awful stench, like a giant outhouse on a hot summer's day.

Pushing ahead into the furnace, I gape at the ground, which must be two stories down. There's no way for me to follow the navigator's nonchalant leap; it's risky in any case and unthinkable in high heels and tight skirt.

A wolf whistle draws my attention from the ground to the sidelines, where scores of men have stopped to stare at me. When I look up, they start whistling, cheering, and waving. Dazed by the sweltering heat, I brave an embarrassed smile and wave back, then realize they're looking up my skirt. Blushing furiously, I stumble back from the door.

The pilot comes to my rescue, his appearance in the doorway putting a stop to the catcalls. The copilot radios to request a ladder. I wince at the prospect, but that being the case, the sooner the better. My wool uniform, raunchy from the wait at Travis, is getting hotter and smellier by the minute. I long to take a bath, change into a cool cotton dress, and guzzle a tall glass of iced tea.

The ladder comes first, of course, and I wish every rung of the way that I were wearing pants. Touching down, I turn to glare at the gawkers. Some grin sheepishly; some shrug and go back to work; some keep right on staring. The captain stands next to me with hands on hips to say cease and desist. When they do, he turns to inspect damages to the plane. Eager as I am to get inside the terminal, I'm curious to see what he'll find.

Sure enough, we've been hit. How can it be? Hit on approach but now perfectly safe to stroll around as if we were on vacation.

Some vacation. An outhouse with coals under my feet. I must get off the tarmac, out of the blazing sun, and away from the leering men. I thank the crew and assure them that I can manage alone. As I have since basic training, I sling my pocketbook over my left shoulder and drag my duffel bag with my left hand, leaving my right hand free to salute. Only no one so much as hints at saluting.

The Tan Son Nhut terminal is a long one-story affair, a veritable beehive of soldiers buzzing noisily as they wait in innumerable, interminable lines. I'm the queen bee—the only woman in sight and the center of everyone's attention.

A private first class behind the counter looks at my orders dubiously. He's never heard of the Fifty-first Field Hospital although he recognizes the APO as being in Saigon. He hands the orders over to someone else behind the counter, then nods at me to take a seat while they figure out where it is.

My heart sinks. How long before I can get out of this uniform, this endless sea of men? Settling down on one of the long wooden benches that stretch through the terminal, I tuck my skirt tightly around my knees and my legs under the bench.

There's nothing to do but watch men file up to the counter and be on their way. How I envy their cool jungle fatigues! My wool jacket is an inferno, but I don't dare take it off; my sodden blouse would be sure to attract more attention. Even taking off my shoes seems out of the question.

Two hours later, on about my tenth trip to the counter, I'm informed that the Fifty-first Field has been located. It's attached to the Third Field Hospital, less than a mile away. The PFC has notified the hospital of my arrival, and someone's coming to pick me up.

I nod with relief and return to my seat. My bladder is demanding attention, but I'll wait until I'm at Third Field before answering it. The thought of a thousand eyes following me in and out of the ladies' room here is something I don't want to face.

So I wait. And wait. And wait. When I can no longer deny nature's call, I circle the terminal in search of a women's latrine. Three trips around, and I suspect the dreadful truth. There is none. I have no choice but to go back to the all-powerful PFC.

Leaning over the counter in hopes that no one will overhear, I ask the mortifying question: "Can you direct me to the ladies' room?"

His look suggests he never knew women did such things, so I give him a look to assure him we do. Glancing helplessly around, he blurts, "Let me ask someone about that, Lieutenant."

"Please do," I say, a cross between a command and plea that must reflect my rising anger and despair of this place.

In three hours I have not even seen another woman. I feel like a freak with legs sticking out from under a skirt, ready to pass out from wearing a wool jacket to hide the fact that I have breasts. And now the PFC who sends men far and wide across Vietnam can't even direct me to a ladies' room.

Returning, he tells me there's a single-holer outside the main building where I can go if I have to.

I have to. Once my bladder is appeased, my attention turns to my parched throat. I return to the counter and ask where I might find some water. The PFC shakes his head to say there is none. I blow up. Who's running this place? And isn't there some other way to go a lousy mile in this country? Can't I just walk?

"No, ma'am. It might not be safe. There aren't too many American women in these parts."

I glare at him. Does he think I haven't noticed? In the end I take a Lambretta—something I'll try never to do again. Shaped like a tiny flatbed truck, it has a cab built for one person and only one small wheel in front. Boards that serve as passenger seats are so low that I must angle my knees to keep them from sticking up in the air. The Vietnamese must be even smaller than the Japanese, and they have their own brand of kamikaze pilot, I see, as my driver ruthlessly attacks every hole in the road. With each one, my backbone slams into a strip of wood that keeps passengers from falling overboard.

I pay a hundred piasters, roughly one buck. It's a rip-off though I do not yet know that. Nor does it matter. I would have paid ten times as much just to get out of that terminal.

The Third Field Hospital, with its whitewashed adobe walls and polished tile floors, serves as the showcase hospital of Vietnam. No Quonset huts or fatigues for me.

The private at Tan Son Nhut didn't know about the Fifty-first Field Hospital, but the chief nurse major at Third Field sure knows about me. No sooner has she returned my salute than she presents me with depositions from the bank and PX in Japan, saying I owe them money. She ignores my pleas of innocence, warning that such monetary problems are unacceptable for officers and that I'm off to a bad start under her command.

A chewing out. Just what I need after the past four hours.

Tomorrow I'm to report to the placement center and sign in-country. The day after I'm to report for duty on the medical ward.

So much for being a combat nurse.

One more thing. My hair is too long to be in a uniform.

Shit. Everywhere I go, somebody tells me to cut my hair.

"That's all, Lieutenant." She pointedly waits for my salute.

A Jeep and driver take me to my quarters. Turning onto the main street in front of the hospital, we're thrown into the middle of a mad stampede of traffic. Bicycles in attack-force numbers, some outfitted with two-cycle engines that sputter blue smoke like old lawn mowers, wheel through clouds of dust. Skinny old men with legs of steel pump on pedicycles—updated rickshas with seats that accommodate one American or two Vietnamese-size passengers. Motorcycles, Lambrettas, old carts pulled by water buffalo, and Army vehicles—Jeeps, armored personnel carriers, trucks, ambulances, and tanks—vie for position in the narrow two-lane road.

My driver adds his two cents to the bedlam, honking his horn whenever smaller, slower vehicles get in our way—virtually every vehicle save other Army types. Dust and fumes are so thick that they hang in the air like a pall, and even stronger than at Tan Son Nhut is the odor of human excrement.

When we turn onto a narrow side street, traffic shifts to mostly nonmotorized bicycles and pedestrians who swiftly move out of our way. This soldier must have gone to the same driving school as my Lambretta driver, hurtling through potholes with a vengeance. Forsaking the horn, he yells at children in the street, "Dirty little bastards! Get out of my way!"

They stare at him blankly, raising my hope that no one understands the swearwords, a hope dashed by the cold glare of a woman that clearly says she does. When she sees me looking at her, she lowers her head, never missing a step.

Then it dawns on me that she's wearing black pajamas, which my warrior buddies in Japan said were Vietcong uniforms. And, I now notice, so are many other Vietnamese. Either the warriors were wrong or there's an army of VC walking the streets of Saigon.

We jolt to a stop in front of a makeshift kiosk—a board thrown over two waist-high fifty-five-gallon steel drums—manned by an MP playing peekaboo with a dozen or so skinny, raggedy children. Behind the kiosk stands a wrought-iron fence, about six feet tall and supported by stucco pillars. Added to that is a steel framework with a wire mesh fence, about fifteen feet tall and topped with concertina wire. Beyond the fence is a villa, iron bars on the windows. It looks a lot like a prison.

Not until my driver dumps my duffel bag in the road do I realize this is my home. Awkwardly climbing out of the Jeep in my tight skirt, I look around. The architecture is French; the buildings are two or three stories high with an outer fence or wall, similar to this villa but without iron bars or concertina wire. Many have big chunks of stucco missing and boarded-up windows. A few have lean-tos—constructed from scrap wood, corrugated steel, and cardboard—attached to their walls. All are badly in need of paint.

The Pied Piper MP grants me a casual salute and the first genuine smile I've seen since leaving the cargo captain and crew. I smile back into brown eyes that do not waver and a face so smooth I vaguely wonder if he has started to shave. He picks up my bag.

"Thanks, but I can handle it." I can handle it, but it must have gained twenty pounds since Travis. Travis! How long ago was that? Can it really be only a day?

I am to share the middle upstairs room with a Captain Cruz. Quick peeks along the corridor reveal one smallish room with a couch and chairs for entertaining. All the rest are crammed with cots, dressers, duffel bags, heaps of dirty laundry, and lines strung up for hand washables.

Our room is barely big enough for two bunk beds and one dresser. It has one open window, too high to see out of and too tiny to let in any light. But, I will discover, it's plenty big enough to drench us in driving monsoon rains or bury us in clouds of dust from the street. Both failures are forgiven in light of our having our own bathroom with a Vietnamese-size shower stall, a tiny sink, and a pre-pull chain toilet (to flush, you turn the handle on and off). The bathroom light is our only light, for there is no electrical outlet in our room. There is no hot water in the villa. And no telephone for personal use anywhere, save for emergency calls at the USO. No way to call Peter although he's only twenty miles away.

Water from the tap is tepid, but I'm so thirsty it hardly matters. I gulp down one glass and refill it. The second glass is at my lips when a first lieutenant nurse walks in.

She asks if it came from the faucet.

I nod.

"You'll be sorry," she says, and is gone without so much as a smile to welcome me aboard.

Bathed in a puddle of sweat, I awaken from a nap to the stirrings of my new roommate. Captain Cruz appears to be about thirty-five and speaks with a Spanish accent, an unlikely candidate for the Army Nurse Corps from what I've seen. Nor does she seem happy with the role, much less with me. For starters, she hasn't shared this room before me and doesn't appreciate having to do so now. Grumbling in Spanish, she starts emptying the bottom drawer of our dresser.

Clearly she's in no mood for conversation. I decide to get something to eat at the officers' club, four blocks away.

Nodding to a new MP at the villa gate, I step into Vietnam. It rained while I was napping, and the tropical night air feels refreshingly cool, especially after our stuffy room, but the odor of sewage is much stronger out here.

My roommate said to watch out for mud puddles, that even the small ones can be knee-deep, but they're hard to see in my shadow, cast by floodlights at the gate. Beyond the villa there is no light at all, not even a streetlight, so I must check with each step that my foot is on firm ground before putting my weight down. At least I'm not worried about getting lost; I can hear the sputtering and rumbling of traffic on main street from here. As I pick my way, my disappointment at not following warrior buddies into a combat area begins to waver despite the rankling noises and raunchy smells—or maybe because of them. It's a new world, fascinatingly different from anywhere I've been. Yet, I realize, I feel more as if I belong here than I did in New Jersey.

Saigon must be twenty years behind Seoul. Main street has no stores or so much as a food stand for the throngs of people. But there is a Texaco gas station, the familiar logo seeming oddly out of place here. I've heard that the population of Saigon has swollen from five hundred thousand to three million in the past five years. People must be fleeing the countryside faster than the city can accommodate them.

On the other side of the hospital perimeter wall is a guarded gate that leads to an alley. The alley ends at a wood-framed screen door opening into the Redbull Inn officers' mess. Checker-clothed tables in the dining room are crowded with officers in fatigues and khakis. Vietnamese waitresses serve drinks and trays of food. They dress in ao dais, snugly fitted silk dresses with long sleeves and ankle-length skirts side slit up to the waist over white satin pants. Their long black hair blows softly around their faces as ceiling fans like those in the movie *Casablanca* circle overhead. The bar is in a separate room, dimly lit, reeking of alcohol, packed with fatigue-clad officers served by Vietnamese bar girls. Through another screen door is a patio where naked card tables have been pushed aside for dancing. Only no one is dancing. There is a definite minority of round-eyed women; the few I see are shared at tables crowded with uniformed men.

Food takes forever, but I'm used to that after Japan. I'm not used to the unceremonious plopping down of dishes or a Vietnamese waitress who never so much as looks at me, much less smiles or bows. And what she plops down makes the meals in Japan look like gourmet feasts. I'm starved, but this fare isn't worth seconds.

In the bar I join dustoff chopper pilots stationed at Tan Son Nhut. On duty they enter the fray of battle to bring out wounded. Off duty they come to the Redbull Inn to play. What a strange life it must be, knowing as they sit for drinks that they might get shot down in the morning.

Though I'm tired, I'm no longer bone-weary. Though I'm still hungry, I'm not starved. But the stench in the streets and rivulets of sweat pouring off me are unmitigated. This will be the way of life here.

My night's sleep isn't long in the making when the Saigon tap water takes its revenge. As was predicted, I'm sorry. My insides are being torn apart.

To make things worse, the running water shut off before we went to bed. Not unusual, I'm told. By morning the streets of Saigon are a breath of fresh air compared with our room—indeed, the entire upstairs of the villa. And my roommate doesn't appreciate my having kept her up all night.

The Saigon Revenge doesn't excuse you from duty in this country or they might have to call off the war. A Jeep and driver pick me up, and it's off to the placement center we go, roughly seventeen miles away with nary a bush to squat behind. The driver is no help, jouncing us through potholes as everyone in this country seems driven to do.

My fervent regret for having drunk that glass of water mixes with a rising curiosity about how strangely things run in this country. You would think that if a jet were attacked in broad daylight at Tan Son Nhut one day, it wouldn't be safe to drive through this sparsely populated area the next day without an armed escort. Yet my driver acts as though he hadn't a care in the world—except for missing a pothole or two.

When I enter the Long Binh Placement Center, all eyes in a roomful of men turn my way, but I'm too close to exploding to worry about modesty. Where, I beg, is the ladies' room?

The soldier behind the counter appears stunned by my question. "There *has* to be somewhere I can go," I say.

"There is no place for American women," he stammers, "but there is one for Vietnamese maids. . . . "

Bursting into the six-holer, I'm confronted by three women—each squatting over a hole in the Vietnamese style.

I claw desperately at the unfamiliar buttons of my new fatigues and fairly fall into a hole, sitting down in the American fashion. When I open my eyes in relief, the three unsmiling faces are still gaping at me. Haven't they ever seen an American woman? And who's odd here anyway? They don't even know how to sit right in an outhouse.

Never mind. At long last the painful cramps have been relieved. But not for long, and I dash back for seconds.

Back at our villa, the water pump is in commission, but the tiny window can't clear the air. However, rain pours through it during the late-afternoon storm—a daily occurrence because this is the monsoon season. After running to the first floor every time I want a glass of water, I finally drag up a four-gallon can of potable water—"potable" being a relative term. There must be enough iodine in it to prep patients for surgery. As of this day, I take to drinking beer like an old regular.

Having been stuffed in a duffel bag for a month, my nursing whites look as if they've already been through a war. My spirits, low after two nights with the trots, sink even lower. By the time I reach the hospital, my white shoes are covered with mud and my white nylons have been splattered by a passing Jeep. I report for my first day of duty looking like something the cat dragged in.

The medical ward is at the back of the hospital, about as far from the only women's latrine as it can be. The ward includes the second and third floors, connected by an outdoor staircase. The upstairs is for self-care patients, usually upper respiratory infections and fevers of unknown origin, where for the most part I make hourly rounds, pass pills, and give shots. This is familiar territory after Fort Dix and a cinch after Japan, where we carried twice the patient load with the same amount of staff. Plus most of the corpsmen here have rotated from the field for the last months of their tours or to heal from injuries that keep them out of the field but not out of work. They can do just about anything I can do. Sometimes more.

The downstairs patients are strangers to me. They have medical diseases I haven't seen since nursing school. Some, such as malaria, I've never seen at all. No matter how major or minor, if it's medical, it comes to us since our doctor, Ted, is the only medical doctor assigned to the hospital. He manages nonsurgical problems on other wards and the emergency room as well, twenty-four hours a day every day. So that he can sleep, he gives me a crash course in the basics: life-threatening cardiac rhythms; wheezing and decreased breath sounds. The ward is quiet now, but the day will come when he must leave me alone with critical patients. His anxiety imparts to me a mortal fear that when he does, something will go wrong. And he calls every hour on the hour all night long, to be certain it hasn't.

From the home front my mother writes that President Johnson might stop in Saigon during his Asian tour. News to me. I didn't even know he was coming to Asia. And, she says, the street bombing in Saigon was shown on TV. I didn't know there had been a bombing. She warns that VC are all around us and to stay out of the city.

Saigon proper is strictly off limits. MPs are instructed to arrest anyone without orders authorizing him to be there. But downtown is just begging me to visit, and all I have to do to get there is don civvies, walk out to main street, and hail one of the multitude of pedicabs. No one ever stops me. People must assume a woman is a civilian.

Word is that Saigon has top-notch restaurants with French cuisine and decent coffee, so I skip breakfast at the Redbull Inn. When

I step onto main street, there's a scramble of a half dozen pedicab drivers to reach me first. Then the haggling begins. Our superiors have admonished us not to pay more than a hundred piasters. The gooks will try to cheat us into paying more, but to do so would inflate the economy adversely.

I believe what they tell us. Besides, the idea of being cheated irks me. Aren't our soldiers helping these people defend their freedom and democracy? Where is their gratitude?

No, I shake my head, that's too much, whereupon another driver agrees to my price.

Under way I find the swaying rhythm of the old man's pedaling soothing, almost hypnotic. A faint coolness lingers from the night; the air is not yet heavy with noxious fumes as it will be by mid-morning, when the streets are clogged with traffic. Early-morning light brightens the green of the palm trees that line the way and bathes the old French villas in rosy tints. The pastel shades are gentle on the eye, the scars on stucco walls hardly noticeable.

The tempo quickens in the heart of the city, where sidewalks are being transformed into a shopping mall of street stands. Men and women, many wearing those black pajamas, hunch under baskets balanced on either end of a pole. Vendors open for business call to passersby, ready to bargain for everything from black-market goods to cheap souvenirs—baseball caps, T-shirts, lacquered chopsticks, and porcelain dishes. On the back of a rice bowl with a blue dragon design, I read in block letters: "Made in Hong Kong." No, thanks. I shake my head to the vendor hovering over me. But I'll take a pack of cigarettes.

A hundred piasters! That's a whole dollar, and they only cost ten cents at the PX! But I'm useless as a bargainer and want a cigarette, so a dollar pack it is.

There's an open café, French-looking, just across the street. Traffic teems from the left rather than the right as it did in Japan, and none of it stops for pedestrians. I let a Lambretta and an old Renault taxi pass, hacking from the exhaust they spew into the air. Then an ancient-looking bicycle with husband, wife, and three children, wobbles across my path. School must be about to start; adolescent girls in white ao dais slip through the madness with books tucked under their arms.

The rich aroma of real coffee draws me up the café steps to an open-walled veranda with potted plants and tables draped in white linen. The street runs just beyond a waist-high wall and leaves a strange illusory impression to this city—the physical European influence, the underlying awareness of a war, and the overwhelming Asian reality of people going about their business.

A Vietnamese waiter smiles broadly and follows me to where I sit. He speaks French to me.

I return the smile and ask if he speaks English.

Yes, quite well, as it turns out. But his smile evaporates, and his manner is notably cooler. I wonder if I said something wrong.

Between the coffee and cigarettes, I can't sit still long. When I stand, my head starts spinning. I can't even walk through the tables without stumbling.

A few doors down a boy about twelve years old blocks my way and asks if I can spare a few Ps. Our superiors have told us that supporting beggars only supports begging. I shake my head no and push past him. But he won't take no for an answer, dancing around me with an outstretched hand as I walk down the block.

"No!" I finally shout. He turns back, but now I feel terrible. After all, what's a few piasters?

Close to noon I realize that I forgot to eat at the café. I'd even forgotten I was hungry. It must have been that superstrong coffee although caffeine has never affected me this way before. Yet I feel fine, not even wilted by the blistering heat as I meander wide-eyed through this exotic city.

I don't head back to base until late afternoon, when suddenly I feel lonely in the midst of pressing crowds, the singsong sound of Vietnamese is grating on my nerves, and the street's fumes turn my stomach. Very suddenly I'm exhausted. Even the cool air of the afternoon storm doesn't revive me.

After dinner at the Redbull Inn I light up another of those dollar-pack cigarettes. Whiffing the smoke, a jet jockey informs me that it's laced with opium.

How did they do that? It was a sealed pack. He smiles knowingly. Very carefully, he tells me, with a razor blade and a hot iron.

No wonder they were so expensive.

* * *

No American would call this life easy, but our lives are considerably eased by our Vietnamese maids, whom we call mamasans. They take care of our clothes as well as our rooms, and those assigned to nurses must wash, starch, and iron our whites. For this, they squat in front of two large basins, one for washing and one for rinsing. Then they spread towels on the floor for an ironing board and press our uniforms with irons filled with hot coals. In this weather, watching them is enough to make me wilt.

Captain Cruz and I share a maid, a four-foot-nine-inch old woman with wrinkled skin, graying hair, and teeth stained dark red from chewing betel nuts—said to give a mild high. She works hard, even shops for us. We figure she supports the black market, but we don't much care; the PX is in Cholon, four miles away, which is an hour's trip on the shuttle bus. None of us wants to spend our one day off getting there, much less ride the shuttle bus behind its barred windows meant to protect us from terrorist grenades.

But then travel here is never comforting. There's the deuce, a two-and-one-half-ton truck with steel plates for windows, except for the windshield. There's the ambulance, a ride so rough that by the time you get out your back feels scoliosed. And there's the Jeep, our usual mode of transportation, without top or doors to keep out the choking dust or splattering mud. All require careful maneuvering in a tight skirt and heels, a problem solved when I switch to cotton shifts and sandals.

Mondays are our days for malaria pills, sitting in big bottles on the breakfast tables. They always give me diarrhea, but I suppose that's better than malaria. I've lost ten pounds over this first month and will lose another fifteen over the coming year, my baggy fatigues getting baggier and baggier. But it hardly matters; a round-eye is lusted after in this land no matter how her clothes fit.

Three long weeks pass, a small panic rising inside me before Peter's first letter arrives. He's fine, was out in the field so didn't get my letter right away. He adds that the use of Jeeps is strictly regulated, so getting to Saigon is impossible. The twenty miles to Cu Chi might as well be two thousand.

There's a better chance I'll get to see Chris, my chopper pilot buddy from those last days in Japan, even though he's two hundred miles away in An Khe. He has written that choppers come to Saigon for supplies, and his name is on the list to make the trip.

CHAPTER FOUR

NOVEMBER 1966: Seeds of Distrust

THE first week of November we're restricted to quarters, mess, and place of duty owing to a rash of terrorist attacks in the city—the Vietcong contribution to South Vietnam's National Day. As a result, American forces are sweeping the outskirts to flush VC from their strongholds. With the action come increased casualties, though we don't see them on our ward.

When restrictions are lifted, I head downtown to be fitted for an ao dai with another first lieutenant nurse, a woman from Uruguay who cares no more than I do that downtown is off limits.

The Vietnamese dressmaker greets us in French with a gracious smile, as is often the case in high-class places. I ask if she speaks English, and as is always the case, the answer is a curt yes. My Hispanic companion, on the other hand, is treated warmly although she speaks no more French than I do.

I'm still irritated when we leave and go our separate ways.

Halfway down the block a Saigonese shoeshine boy asks if I want a shine. "On sandals?" I ask sarcastically. "No, thanks." And I try to move around him.

"Ps, Ps," he begs, blocking my path.

"No!" I say loudly. When he continues, I shout it. "*No!*"

His doleful eyes fill with undisguised anger. "*Yes!*" he yells back.

Suddenly he has a friend. One pushes at me, the other grabs at my purse. They're like birds of prey, pecking at me.

"Get out of my way, you dirty little bums!" When they refuse, I whirl around to go back. Laughing shrilly, they dart back in front of me and smear black shoe polish down my dress, my legs, my sandaled feet. Then they disappear into the crowd.

I'm trembling. When I look down at my ruined dress, I want to cry. I've got to go home, I think, retreat to the safety of fellow Americans.

From home my mother writes: ". . . Pres. Johnson is getting quite a greeting on his trip, altho' the ever present Vietniks are there. Our FBI Director Hoover has said they are members of the Young Communist League. I do think a way should be found to control them as well as the College Campus Reds. . . . "

We can feel the beginning of summertime. The humidity is higher, temperatures soar into the hundreds, and there's less rain— sometimes none for several days.

Six days a week I walk to and from work through streets that reek of sewage. By now local Vietnamese are familiar to me, and I assume they recognize me as well. Yet none ever looks me in the eye. Indeed, one old man makes a point of staring at the ground as he passes me on his rickety bicycle. And one old woman stops and turns her back to me until I've passed. No one has explained that for the Vietnamese not meeting someone's eyes is a sign of respect. Where I come from it's cause to distrust. In war distrust breeds fear, and fear fans anger and contempt.

Only one neighbor, a boy who might be ten years old, looks me in the eye. He's barefoot and ragged and so skinny his arms and legs look like sticks. A permanent fixture on his hip is his baby brother, who wears only a dirty shirt. Whenever we pass, the boy pleads for money. I've been told not to give in, or he'll never let me pass in peace. I do as I'm told, but I never do pass in peace.

I remember the fantasies I began having after that trip to Korea—my visions of scrounging up food, finagling clothes and other provisions for the most innocent victims of war, the children. I came with the hope of serving them in some way, not just our soldiers. Now I pray they will leave me alone.

Chopper is different, of course. He is a month-old Vietnamese baby on our ward whose tiny ribs gleam through the gaping wounds on his chest and back. I don't know why we call him Chopper; unlike most casualties, he didn't come by helicopter. Nuns brought him here from St. Elizabeth's, the Catholic orphanage our hospital supports. He was left on their doorstep in the middle of the night.

At first we didn't know what caused the wounds. Ulcers? A tropical fungus or microscopic worm? Medical textbooks piled up in the nursing station as Ted searched for an answer. It was the corpsman working with me tonight, a former field medic, who solved the riddle. Not ulcers but burns—napalm burns.

Napalm is an inflammable, gelatinous substance that sticks to the skin of its victim. Trying to wipe it off just spreads it around. After the flames go out, napalm holds the heat and continues burning deeper and deeper.

We were spared seeing Chopper on fire, but just imagining it makes me cringe. "How could the VC do this to their own people?" I ask, nodding for the corpsman to lift Chopper so I can rewrap the burns.

The corpsman squints. "The VC don't have napalm. We do."

To my dismayed look, he explains: "He must come from a VC village that had an air strike called against it. Whoever dropped the load never knew what they were hitting. They just drop the money and run."

There's a lot that goes on here that's hard to believe, raising some hard questions about the war. Many of these are asked by our head nurse, a captain named Carol, about twenty-seven, who has become a friend. She's got the only private room in our villa—a source of envy no matter that it's the size of a walk-in closet—where we can talk freely. And she has the only record player among us, introducing me to Bob Dylan's "Masters of War" and a liberal point of view, both unusual in our ranks.

Why, she asks, must we bomb South Vietnamese villages to save them from North Vietnam?

Because those South Vietnamese support the Vietcong.

Because they *are* the VC, she maintains. It's them we're fighting.

Only because they've been brainwashed, I counter. If they knew what a Communist regime would be like, they'd support us.

So why don't we let them find out and come back when they really want us?

They do want us. Their government asked for us.

This government doesn't represent the people here. This government is overwhelmingly French-appointed Catholics.

What does religion have to do with it?

Catholics are only twenty percent of the population in Vietnam and oppress everyone else to stay in power. What do you think those Buddhist monks who douse themselves with gasoline and burn themselves up in the streets are protesting about?

The theory is, I remind her, that the French put *educated* people in power, who are a lot better able to run a government.

She shakes her head, sighing. What kind of government supports bombing its own villages?

We're back to the beginning of our conversation. It's a riddle, the answer to the question a puzzle to me.

Miracle of miracles, a telephone is installed in our villa. Or what we call a telephone. It's really a radio hookup that works like a telephone—sort of. To call the Twenty-fifth Division headquarters in Cu Chi, where Peter is stationed, takes four operators and three hours. And Peter's not even there. It has taken three hours to leave my telephone number twenty miles away. What a way to run a war.

When Peter calls back, conversation is stilted by long pauses to allow transmissions to pass through the four operators. And he can't talk for long.

"When's your next day off?" he asks. "Over."

"In seven days. Will I be able to see you?"

Too long a wait. I forgot to say the password. "Over."

The long wait. Then: "I'm off for a few days now, but then I go back to the field. Doesn't look good until I start clearing. Over."

Clearing! The shuffle to get paper work processed when transferring to another base. "Can't I see you before that?" I can't hide my disappointment. "Over."

Long pause. "Afraid not. I've arranged to fly out of Tan Son Nhut the week before Christmas. Can I see you then? Over."

"I live here, remember? Over."

Pause. "I'll write. Don't take any chances I wouldn't take. Over."

I want to say how much I miss him but can't with four operators listening in. "I'll try. Be careful yourself. Over."

The long wait. "See you before Christmas. Out."

At work this afternoon the first storm we've had in several days hits. I'm sitting by the screen door to do my paper work—close enough to take advantage of the cool breezes but far enough away not to be sprayed—when an upstairs patient bursts through the door.

"Quick! Mack can't breathe! He says it's asthma!"

I bolt from my chair and follow him into the driving rain, up the outdoor stairs.

Mack is sitting on the edge of his bed, wheezing loudly through lips that are already blue. He needs oxygen, but there's none up here; we must get him downstairs. He's barely able to stand. The other patient and I half drag and half carry him through the downpour. Once downstairs, a corpsman helps the upstairs patient lift Mack onto a bed while I put on oxygen and then go for equipment to start an IV. The corpsman calls the emergency room.

Ted is there and comes quickly. He orders a shot of epineprine and takes over the IV so I can go for medication. Within minutes Mack's breathing is much easier and his lips are pink.

By then the storm has ended, but four of us are still drenched—Mack, the upstairs patient, Ted, and me. The patients change into dry pajamas. Ted and I are stuck with our starched uniforms glued to our bodies. "At least"—Ted smiles— "I'm cool."

A few days later Chris flies down from An Khe with his copilot to pay me a visit. The copilot is as dark as Chris is light, with mischievous dark eyes and brown curly hair much longer than regulation length. They're good buddies, have been through the thick and thin of battle together. In fact, he's introduced to me as Good Buddy, the only name Chris ever uses for him.

We spend the evening painting Saigon red, though I'm less than comfortable in the bars where Chris and Good Buddy's well-worn fatigues attract attention. When Saigon closes for curfew, we go to the Redbull Inn. From there, drunk as skunks, we pick our way through a maze of potholes to my villa. The street is inked out—no moon nor so much as a ray of light from any window at this late hour. It's my territory, so I'm in front, but I'm not doing a very good job of leading. I should've skipped that last drink at the club.

Chris stumbles and swears. As we help him back to his feet, our peals of laughter pierce the night. My turn to trip. "Shit!" More laughter.

Closer to home I know the potholes by heart. Picking up the pace, we step into the outer reaches of our villa's floodlights. From here it's a cinch.

Suddenly there's a sharp crack—a backfire, no doubt from main street—and my companions push me into the dirt.

"What the shit are you doing!" I sputter, trying to get up.

"Shh!" they hush me. Nor will they let me stand, insistently playing warriors on the streets of Saigon. My dress and nylons are ruined. Worse yet, my hair is lying in mud that smells like an outhouse. I stay quiet for a while, thinking they're edgy from being in the field too long. Finally they let me sit up.

"It was just a backfire," I say, looking down at my dress.

"If that was a backfire, I'll eat crow," Chris answers tersely.

It's time to move on but, I suddenly realize, the floodlights have been turned off. Tracing the wall, we silently approach the MP.

"Did you see where it came from?" Good Buddy demands.

"Yes, sir." The MP nods across the street toward a shack built of scrap lumber and corrugated tin. A Vietnamese family lives there, has planted a garden in the empty lot bordering the street. We peer into blackness.

"This happen very often?" Chris asks.

"It's unpredictable, sir. Sometimes a couple of times a week. Sometimes a few times a night. It's more a form of harassment than anything else, sir." Can that be true? Why didn't I know about it?

"So far they haven't hit anything but the villa wall, sir," continues the MP. He sounds ill at ease, standing stiffly at attention.

"Did you ever consider that a sniper might one day miss the wall and hit a person?" Good Buddy asks, his eyes narrowed.

The MP hesitates. "Yes, sir."

"Then why don't you do something!"

"Sir, the policy is not to do anything."

"*Why,* in God's name, *not?*" A pause. "Or don't MPs go after *enemy* soldiers?"

The dig shows on the MP's face. "Sir, would you like to discuss this with my commanding officers?"

"Damn straight we will," says Chris with a sharp nod.

This whole conversation strikes me as crazy—standing around and talking about getting shot at. "It's late, and I have to work tomorrow," I say, turning abruptly to pass through the gate.

Chris and Good Buddy follow me to the dimly flickering light in the stairwell to say good-bye.

"Are you okay?" Chris asks.

"Fine. Just a little shook up."

"If you think that shook you up, wait'll you get a gander at your hair," Good Buddy says, grinning.

"What about you? Is it safe for you to walk back to Tan Son Nhut?"

Chris chuckles. "Don't you worry now. Those yellow bellies don't dare touch us if they know what's good for them."

"Amen," Good Buddy agrees. "But I wouldn't mind leaving a reminder of what's good for them! Like with a couple of M-sixteens."

Conspiratorial grins pass between them.

Bravado? Maybe. Either way, they're unarmed. Long after getting ready for bed, I listen for distant backfires.

* * *

Lisa is a nurse in our villa, a captain with hair so short it would pass for a crew cut if it weren't so curly. Her mannerisms are mannish, leading to speculation within our ranks that she's homosexual. More out of fear than loathing, I've kept a safe distance between us.

A few days ago she stopped me to say her year is almost up and she's looking for someone to take over her work at St. Elizabeth's Orphanage. She asked if I'm interested.

I'm not sure. There was that old fantasy of helping the children, but Vietnamese street urchins have pretty much rid me of that, and I've been exhausted ever since I got in-country. Where, I asked, does she get the energy?

She laughed. "Being tired just gets to feel normal after you're here for a while."

Now I'm glad I've decided to check it out. We're chugging along in a deuce—Lisa, two corpsmen, and I—headed for the orphanage. This is more what I expected when I signed on for this tour of duty.

The outskirts of Saigon thin into Vietnamese countryside. The lush tropical greens seem a world away from pastel French architecture. It's quiet; the air is fresh and breezy. No incessant din of city traffic and none of the stink on main street. Even air traffic from Tan Son Nhut, a constant background noise to our hospital area, is so high and far away as to be hardly noticed.

Children besiege our troop carrier as we lurch to a stop. The Vietnamese nuns, wearing conical straw hats with black cotton habits, linger in the background. They're graceful, petite, and soft-spoken. Their English bears traces of a French accent.

When I climb down from the carrier, the children's stares clearly ask if it is possible for a woman to be so tall. The stares fix on my hair, refined to a frizz of unprecedented levels by tropical humidity. I can see they wonder if it's real.

Kneeling, I smile and motion for them to touch it. Tentative at first, they're soon running their fingers through it. My French twist can't hold up under the assault, so I take out the bobby pins. The children are fascinated by the color, by the way it stretches and springs back into a frizzy curl.

There is one girl, arms crossed protectively in front of her chest and fingers plucking nervously at her shoulders, who does not venture to touch me although she watches intently. She's about the size of a five-year-old American child, so I guess that she's eight or nine. When I catch her eye, she runs away.

Central to the layout of the orphanage is a small adobe church fashioned after churches in French villages, complete with steeple and bell for calling worshipers. To one side is an adobe dormitory, a single room with straw sleeping mats that cover every square inch of floor space. The capacity of the orphanage, thirty-seven girls, is apparently determined by how many mats can be squeezed into that room. Each girl has one set of clothes, a comb, and a pen or pencil. Any other belongings, such as an old button or a piece of newspaper, are prizes to be carefully tucked under a mat.

There's no running water, no electricity, no telephone, no motorized transportation, no nearby schools or medical facilities, and no way to keep flies out of the food. A well provides water; candles and lanterns provide light; bicycles carry nuns to ferry supplies; classes are taught in the church and dining area; medicine and bandages are dispensed from a first-aid kit.

I'm not here in my capacity as a nurse. Our project this day is to build bunk beds, but the children have no idea what they are until we place the sleeping mats on them. Then their delight erupts in ear-shattering squeals, and they clamber up and down the ladders, negotiating for uppers and lowers. When the Angelus peals forth from the steeple, all but one of the little girls quickly kneel and cross themselves to pray, then dash off for the noonday meal, chattering nonstop.

With her arms still crossed, still plucking at her shoulders, she looks like someone trying to keep warm—though it's surely a hundred degrees here. Her lips are fuller and her eyes rounder than the Vietnamese I've seen in Saigon, making me wonder if she's Amerasian.

Fearful she might once again run away, I sit at a slight distance. She stares at my hair, so I let it fall over my shoulder closest to her. To my surprise, she does not hesitate before moving closer to touch it. When she reaches for my hand, I squeeze hers. Suddenly she throws her arms around my neck. I wrap my arms around her, rocking back and forth. The loneliness and despair in her small body bring an ache to my heart. Tears brim my eyes.

Though her back is to the door, she senses the nun's presence before I see her. Pulling away, she runs toward the mess hall.

"Please don't be angry with her." I nod after the girl.

"I'm not angry. Only concerned that she eat." A slight bow. "As you can see, there is not enough love to go around, and Le Ly needs more than most."

"How old is she?"

"We can only guess, for she has not spoken since she came. We do not even know her real name."

"And her family?"

The nun's words come without show of emotion. "Her village was bombed and burned to the ground. One of your field medics found her curled against her dead mother with her dead baby brother in her lap."

I don't ask who bombed the village. I know the VC don't have bombs.

By late November the monsoon season is over. Dust tints the world in red, casts a pall over the green palm trees and the pastels of old French villas, sticks to sweaty skin and sinks into the fiber of sweaty clothes. At least everything doesn't rust or mildew overnight.

Things have settled into a routine. When I'm on days, I visit the Redbull Inn after work. Working evenings, I make day runs to the PX for cases of Tiger beer or Niagara starch, head downtown for such things as bras or nylons, or catch up on letter writing before work. When I work at night, I hit the swimming pool at the nearby officers' quarters in the morning to get as cool and clean as possible, then sleep as best I can in the sweltering heat of our room. Tuesday is the orphanage, unless I'm working days. Monday is still the day for our malaria pills, no matter what shift we're working.

Weekly my mother writes long, newsy letters about the house and pets, yard and birds, shopping trips and new clothes, television programs and weather, neighbors, Daddy's work, and family ill-nesses. Tucked in the middle are tidbits about the war, here and on the home front: "It seems the war is really speeding in all directions and I guess the people in this country will just have to get used to the idea that we are in there to stay for a while. It seems such a shame that we have to sacrifice so much to keep communism penned up—and I wonder if we can. It seems we have an awful lot of very devout Communists in this country with the protection of our Supreme Court—the colleges are so infested. . . . "

Thanksgiving falls on my day off. The desperate state of my one pair of sandals, mildewed and held together with surgical suturing thread, sends me into downtown Saigon.

Dust and fumes clog the air, already sticking to me in a thin, grimy layer—a passing convoy saw to that—and the noise level of main street is at its midmorning feverish pitch. Eager to get downtown and back, I've agreed to the outrageous price of two hundred piasters for a pedicab. No matter how damaging it may be to the economy, I'm in no mood for haggling.

The driver stops on an unfamiliar street, indicating I should step down.

I shake my head. I want the Hotel Continental.

He shakes his head to say he doesn't understand.

I try again. "No," I say. "I want Ho-tel Con-tin-en-tal."

He points and singsongs, insisting this is where I'm to get off.

Refusing, I repeat loudly as if he were hard-of-hearing: "Hotel Continental!"

He shrugs. "Four hundred P," he says.

Infuriated, I shout: "No! Two hundred P! You said two hun-dred P!"

He turns his back to me, refusing to budge. I'm determined to pay only the agreed-upon price and step out of the cab with two hundred piasters in hand. I'll find another pedicab to take me the rest of the way.

When I hold up the money, he shouts shrilly: "Four hundred P! Four hundred P!"

Fine. If he doesn't want the money, tough shit. Tucking the money back in my purse, I turn to leave.

Was I too angry to notice the circle of Vietnamese moving in on us? Shaking slightly, I move to pass through their line. They close ranks.

A small panic creeps into my throat. No one has to tell me this could be trouble deep. I swallow my pride, extract four hundred piasters from my wallet, and hand them up to the scrawny bastard.

When the count is right, he looks me square in the eye before smiling obsequiously. Pointing up the street, he speaks in clear English: "Hotel Continental."

The crowd parts to let me through.

I'm uncertain I can walk. Not until the Hotel Continental comes into sight, four blocks later, do my legs gather strength. No French coffee this morning. I need a drink.

I'm not the only American here, albeit the only round-eye woman. Four officers leap to their feet when they see me sit at the bar, and in a flash there are four Bloody Marys sitting in front of me. The men are wearing stiff khakis, no doubt fighting this war from behind desks—what we term desk jockeys, or Saigon warriors, or rear echelon mother fuckers (REMFs). I acquired a disdain for them from my warrior buddies in Japan, but right now I welcome their company.

"I never heard of such a thing!"

"Take me there! I'll kill the yellow-bellied gooks."

"You're lucky they didn't take you for every red cent."

"Best just to forget it" is the final word.

When I buy the sandals, I'm too drunk to figure out my size in centimeters or to take care they fit. It doesn't matter. They'll rot before I leave anyway.

Shortly after I return from downtown, Chris appears on the doorstep. He didn't tell me he was coming. Just seeing him lifts me up, as if I've found my long-lost brother, and a very handsome brother at that, one who makes my heart leap. Chris knows about Peter from when we were in Japan, but I realize guiltily, I wish he didn't.

He's taking me out for Thanksgiving dinner at a French restaurant and, in honor of the occasion, has switched to civvies. I pretend that we're tourists on vacation, that he takes care of me. I've never wanted to be taken care of before.

Thanksgiving, Saigonese style: We are seated near French doors opening onto a rooftop patio, watching night fall over the low-lying skyline, eerily silhouetted by sputtering flares.

Chris orders my meal, French onion soup and a steak dinner. Afterward we move to the fancy bar, sipping at *iced* drinks. We reminisce about the good old days in Japan—the officers' club, Retta and her VW bug, John Wayne movies dubbed in Japanese—and we laugh. Then we dream about Thanksgiving dinner back in the Real World.

How I've missed him, all the warrior buddies and our fun times. If only I could be closer to where they are—Pleiku or Qui Nhon.

"No!" he says vehemently. "I rest better knowing you're in Saigon. If those yellow bastards so much as harm a hair on your head, I'll go on a killing spree that'll land me in the brig!"

It's the side of Chris that I first saw in Japan, when I shared my fantasy about helping the Vietnamese children and he angrily warned me to stay away from them. I saw it again at my villa, when he was furious with the MPs for not going after the sniper. Every other time we've been together, he has been so good-natured and polite that these outbursts always take me by surprise.

He's still agitated, his lips pressed tightly together, shaking the ice in his glass. I want to say something, but I can't think of anything to say. What is there to say? Only that war changes warriors. Everyone knows that.

CHAPTER FIVE

DECEMBER 1966: War Zone Holidays

TAN Son Nhut is less than a mile away, but a mile goes a long way in this country. When Vietcong pounded the air base with mortars through much of last night, security at the hospital wasn't even tightened. On front wards, patients and staff lined the windows to watch the fireworks. On our ward we saw nothing and heard little more than muffled explosions.

Word of wounded in triage came to us through the grapevine. Most were from a direct hit to transient barracks—soldiers awaiting flights home. "Psychological warfare" is what our leaders call it. To my way of thinking, it's the real thing.

At breakfast in the Redbull Inn, Sheila Murphy, a captain nurse I know from trips to the orphanage, recounts her experience during the attack. She's a beautiful blue-eyed blonde with dazzling dimples, and I envy her self-assurance and status as an intensive care nurse. Now I listen enviously to her story.

She was pie-eyed at the Redbull Inn when the attack began but nevertheless thought she'd be needed to care for incoming wounded. Because only an open field separates the hospital from where mortars were falling, two drunken companions offered their protection.

Lights had been doused in the alleyway, and cracks in the pavement and their inebriated circumstances caused them to make their way unsteadily. No one was surprised when, just as they reached the gate on main street, one companion fell flat on his face.

Sheila and the other officer laughed so hard they could hardly breathe, she tells us with dimples flashing. When the fallen man didn't respond, Sheila thought he had hit his head and knocked himself unconscious. When they lifted him from the ground, they found he had been shot in the chest.

"So I worked on *him* in triage." She laughs.

We laugh with her.

What's happening to us?

Back at the villa, our water pump is working, but the shower drain has been plugged up for days. My roommate, Captain Cruz, steps out of our accumulated scum in disgust. Our villa was formally condemned last month, but new quarters are still under construction.

This will end *today,* proclaims Captain Cruz. She dials one number after another, looking for someone to *do* something, her anger intensifying with each call. Finally she threatens to make out a report if help isn't sent. A Vietnamese engineer appears. He shakes his head at the scum, shrugs his shoulders, and turns to leave.

Captain Cruz goes berserk, shrieking in Spanish as she chases the scrawny little man down the stairs. He cringes under her angry words, eyes lowered and jabbering disconsolately to himself as he disappears through the gate. Captain Cruz then stomps over to the hospital administrator in a purple rage.

Another Vietnamese engineer arrives, a box of tools in hand. Without so much as a glance at the glowering captain, he laboriously drills a hole through the shower stall's thick adobe wall. Gravity takes over from there our soapy scum now trickling down the outside wall into the courtyard below.

The mosquitoes love it.

AMERICAN DAUGHTER GONE TO WAR

* * *

Retta is now stationed in Qui Nhon, two hundred miles north of us on the coast. She has managed to get three days off and a chopper ride to join us for our hospital picnic—good food, plenty of booze, predictably sunny skies, and water-skiing on the Saigon River. Not bad for a war zone.

Other than lose the usual ten pounds over her first month in-country, Retta hasn't changed much. She's still exuberant and full of jokes. Just being with her has brought back the lighter moods of the good old days, a lightness that dampens as I drop into the murky Saigon River. I've never water-skied before, and my nervousness about giving it a try is fanned by those who have—not to mention my not being a great swimmer. But there's no turning back or I'll never live it down.

So far so good. The floatation belt really works.

"Pull up!" they shout.

No sooner am I up than I'm down, gasping for air and gulping water used as a toilet for those who live on the river's shore. The boat waits as I struggle back into the skis.

"Lean back on the rope! That's the ticket!"

I hang on for dear life, eyes focused on the skis and the water until the boat speeds up. When my skis hit the boat's backwash, I hit the water.

I'm bobbing up and down in the floatation belt, and the boat is bearing down on me at full speed. Has the driver gone crazy? Just as I think it can't possibly stop in time, it does. Hands stretch out to hoist me aboard. Urgent voices prod me to hurry.

Is there an alligator? Heart in my throat, I look back. All I see are the skis before the boat flies off.

"We forgot the skis!"

"Fuck the skis" is the tight-lipped answer.

Everyone's crouched below the gunwales, peering intently toward the jungle coastline.

"What's going on?"

"Goddamn VC are shooting at us. Crazy fools. Our choppers'll rip them to shreds for trying."

The picnic ends for me shortly afterward; I'm working the

evening shift. Retta returns to Qui Nhon tonight, so we say good-bye now with warm hugs.

After work at the Redbull Inn the picnic is the topic of conversation. Sheila, normally very cool, is chattering away in a high-pitched voice, something about American bodies floating down the Saigon River, bodies so bloated they were popping out of their fatigues. The MPs had called for grappling hooks to pull them ashore, then chased away picnickers in case the bodies were booby-trapped.

Days have become shorter with the end of the rainy season. It doesn't get light until seven in the morning, and it's dark by six. We've rigged up an electric cord from another villa to our room for light, but it takes twenty minutes for the generator to warm up enough to work—too long to be of any use when we dress for the day shift.

On a grander scale, a telephone dialing system is being installed. Now, when you pick up the phone, you're as likely to be on a line from another war zone as on one of ours or to get two connections, neither of which is the number you dialed. Such communications problems couldn't have come at a worse time. Heavy casualties are pouring in from an operation near the Cambodian border to slow enemy infiltration along the Ho Chi Minh Trail. The surgical wards are full. Lighter wounds now come our way.

Arranging to take two days off when I rotate from the evening to the night shift means I can stretch it into three days off. I'll pay the price when I go from nights to days and must work a double shift, but it's worth it. Chris is taking me to An Khe, stomping grounds of the First Cavalry in the Central Highlands.

After work I grab a bag packed with essentials and meet him at the Redbull Inn.

He smiles ruefully. "I sure hope that bag holds something besides more fatigues."

I pretend to flirt and smile coquettishly. "Don't you like my outfit?"

"Why, little woman, I'd love you in full battle gear if you kept smiling like that."

Suddenly I'm not sure that I'm pretending. I say nothing as I try to sort out my attraction for him and my sense of guilt for unfaithful feelings toward Peter.

"You hungry?" he asks, breaking the awkward pause.

I shake my head. "Too excited. This is my first chopper ride."

He grins. Like all chopper pilots, he loves his "bird," and my enthusiasm pleases him.

Why has Tan Son Nhut always seemed so far away? We're there in a jiff, my excitement mounting as we cross the blistering tarmac to the waiting slick, a gunship helicopter. Chris's Good Buddy copilot and a ship's gunner are standing by, scuffling to be the one to help me aboard. Laughing, I take a hand of each.

No seat belts. No seats. Just a wide plank that can hold a litter when the need arises. The engine sputters briefly, whines as it picks up speed, and then there's the familiar *whop-whop* of whirling blades. The gunner, not a day over twenty, settles with practiced ease into his perch by the door behind an M–60 machine gun.

Good Buddy turns to give me the thumbs-up. His brown curls are matted to his forehead with sweat.

Evidently they're not going to close the doors. I clutch the plank under me to keep from falling out.

The bird shudders just before lift-off. We surge into the air with a power that feels as if it were flowing through my veins. It makes me catch my breath.

Oh, God, don't turn so sharply!

How strange. I'm not even sliding toward the door. Looking up in surprise, I see Good Buddy grinning at me. I shouldn't worry. I won't fall out.

I inch closer to the door, and a cool wind dries the sweat on my face. How clean it smells! I inhale deeply and exhale the stink of Saigon streets. I peek over the door's edge. Rice paddies and meandering rivers wink back the morning sun. Though the roar of the engine and the whopping blades make conversation impossible, the world is tranquil.

Good Buddy hands over his headset. "This is your captain speaking," says Chris, and launches into the role of tour guide. "We are presently headed due north, give or take a few degrees, flying at an altitude of eight hundred feet, give or take a few feet. Our cruising speed is subject to change, but estimated time of arrival at lovely An Khe is on schedule, give or take a few minutes.

"To your right is the South China Sea, famed for sandy white beaches and tropical warm waters. To your left is the Mekong Delta, famed for elephant grass and rice paddies. Beyond is the Iron Triangle, famed for triple canopy jungles and hot spots for GI Joes and Victor Charlies. Shortly we will fly over the Central Highlands, famed for cool mountain breezes and fun-loving First Cavalrymen hosting a shindig this very night."

Out the door the China Sea is no longer in sight, and the shimmering rice paddies are transformed to the darker greens of forested mountains.

The chopper veers, climbing steeply. I back away from the open door, see the gunner peering intently at the ground. I was struck by how young he looked when we came aboard. Now I'm acutely aware of his singular purpose for being here.

He points to the cause of alarm. Sharp flashes, innocent from this height, pepper the green. Somebody's shooting at us in a surreal movie clip without sound effects.

Not until we land do I learn there were Americans on the ground calling for help, impossible with me aboard. I'm not to worry my "pretty little head," though; other gunships have been called to assist.

A huge First Cavalry insignia is painted on top of An Khe's landmark mountain. From the air it doesn't sport much else—a hodgepodge of Quonset huts, watchtowers, sandbag bunkers, unpainted cinder-block and wooden buildings, concertina wire strung everywhere, and weapons of war all over the place. Bare ground throws up dust clouds. It's drab and dreary after the tropical landscape.

Aground, An Khe offers one of the classiest officers' clubs in-country. Tables are laid in white linen with full sets of silverware, china dishes, glass glasses, and some of the best food this side of the Pacific. Most remarkable of all is a large glass picture window beyond which the long rays of a setting sun are just giving way to shadows.

Where in the world did they get such a window? No use asking, of course. I love the thought of some fat cat general in his Saigon villa, scratching his head at a gaping hole in the wall where there should be a window.

We dine on Texas-size steaks, then hunker down to some serious partying. Only try as I may, I can't last for long.

"You look tuckered out." Chris smiles.

"Right you are. Where can I catch some shut-eye?"

"In my bunk," he answers. "Me and my bunkmate talked it over. We'll do just fine in one of those sandbag jobbies."

"There's really no need. I'm so tired I could sleep in a bathtub."

He laughs. "If we had a bathtub, you'd have to wait all night to get to it!"

One last pit stop while I have a guard at hand. One pass by the bunker where he'll be if I need him. Then over to his hooch, and out of the clear blue sky he bends to kiss me. A long, hungry kiss that takes my breath away.

Grinning broadly at my stunned expression, he turns smartly on his boots and is gone.

How could I let him do that? Worse yet, how could I enjoy it so much? Does this mean I don't love Peter? But I'm too tired to ponder the matter for long. I fall asleep soon after hitting the pillow.

Breakfast is reminiscent of a stateside Sunday morning: hearty portions of bacon, eggs, biscuits, and strong coffee to nurse our hangovers. Then a lazy afternoon, idled over warm beers and straight bourbon. Neither of us mentions the kiss.

When the sun's rays grow long, it's time to leave. Stepping through the clubhouse door, I'm overwhelmed by a sickeningly sweet odor that permeates the base.

"They're spraying the forest," Chris says, "with Agent Orange. It makes trees lose their leaves, to deny cover to the enemy."

"Agent Orange?" I ask.

"So called," Good Buddy explains, "because the leaves turn orange before they fall."

Back in Saigon I'm back on the night shift. Most mornings I go swimming with Sandy, a Red Cross worker from our villa. Sandy is not quite stocky but far from delicate. She has a heart-shaped face with auburn hair and dark eyes set in skin so fair that even the tropical sun of Vietnam has made little impression.

The pool is Olympic size—once exclusively for members of a private French club, now exclusively for American armed forces. The first time we came here, we were the only women among hundreds of GIs. Cowed by the odds, I sweated it out on a lounging chair covered from head to foot with a beach towel. Sandy, all five feet two of her, braved the gawkers to go for a swim.

When we pointed out our predicament to the lifeguard, he granted us permission to swim before the pool opens. We do this as often as we can.

A sign blocking the nine-meter diving platform reads OFF LIM-ITS, owing to a GI's being shot down by a sniper from across the street. The day the sign went up, Sandy and I exchanged nervous glances. There's a high adobe wall around the pool, typical of French architecture here, but maybe we should go back to swimming at the officer quarters' pool.

But the officers' pool is always open to the men who live there. It would be back to embarrassment and self-consciousness. So we've stuck with the Olympian pool before the sun blisters the sky.

This morning there's a new mortar hole in the sidewalk outside the adobe wall. I snap a picture of children playing in it and go swimming as usual.

After work the next morning, I forsake the pool for Christmas shopping at the central marketplace, a huge circular building with everything from fresh fruits and vegetables to brass tables and carved mahogany room dividers. A stateside fire department would go berserk over its rickety stands, aisles teeming with shoppers, and no sprinkler system. Not to mention the sanitation department. I wonder what it would make of naked babies sitting atop piles of fresh fruits and vegetables and of the flies everywhere.

These things don't bother me. What does is seldom seeing an American, man or woman, and figuring there must be a reason. The lighting is poor, so I shop near the huge open entrances, darting from one blaze of sunlight to another. Silly, I know. Broad daylight carries no guarantees; the safest thing is not to come. But the exotic wares and the singsong of Vietnamese, somehow melodic when out of the street stampede, keep drawing me back.

When I'm too exhausted to shop, I hop a pedicab back to the hospital and I hit the mailroom. Nothing from Peter, but there is the weekly letter from my mother. She writes:

I don't know, but it seems the U.S. is really digging in for a rather drawn out expensive war.

I do think we have to be there, if not for this generation, for the next. I do think Red China would move out over the East & then it would be the Western world next. When you figure how far Russia got . . . I think I'll be an ostrich and let things be day to day.

Winnie, we want you to be happy and enjoy and live a normal life. We know that is what you want and that is what you are doing. . . .

When we have no critically ill and can turn out the lights, it feels cooler, but it's still hot. To take advantage of whatever breezes there might be, the corpsman and I are sitting near the screen door.

The midnight hour has come and gone; patients sleep on the darkened ward. All but Chopper, now nearly three months old, who sucks weakly on a bottle in my arms. His condition has worsened; the burns on his chest and back are infected and sapping him of strength even to fill his stomach. Ted searched in vain for a feeding tube small enough for an infant. Then he sent for one from the States. Until it arrives, all we can do is dribble food into Chopper every two hours.

The quiet night is suddenly broken by a deep rumbling, like a gigantic roll of distant thunder. This is followed by a tremor that shakes the building, followed by the tinkling of glass from a broken window in back of the ward.

The telephone rings a short time later: someone from administration to assure us we're not under attack. The Vietcong have just blown up the ammunition dump at Long Binh, seventeen miles away.

The corpsman nods sagely as I rock the baby. Not the first time or the last. The VC dig underground tunnels to the dump, he tells me. When they need arms or ammunition, they surface and take what they can carry. Our soldiers can sometimes see the VC removing munitions, but shooting at them risks an explosion, so they don't. When the VC have all the ammo they can handle, they blow the dump up. It doesn't work like clockwork, but the system is very dependable.

My starched white uniform is stuck to my midriff with sweat. Checking to see that no one is watching, I tug at my bra where it's chafing, press my arms tight against myself to blot the trickling under my arms, rub my legs together to stop the trickling down my thighs. Finally I tuck back the loose ends of my French twist. I must look a mess after working all night, but it's the best I can do.

Peter is watching me, eyebrows knit and light eyes intent, when I locate him at a back table. He's wearing khakis—a disappointment as I've never seen him in his warrior's fatigues. Now I never will. He flies back to the World tomorrow.

I can control my urge to rush to him but not my hot blush. I only hope it's not too obvious as I nod hello to others while making my way across the room. A smile lights his face when he stands and says how glad he is to see me. But his West Point reserve and my inhibitions prevail—no public display of affection.

"How was your trip?"

His smile widens. "Hot and dusty."

We laugh. What kind of trip did I expect him to have in this godforsaken country? The ice now broken, we sit down. His calf touches mine under the table. The nearness of our bodies makes my heart pound.

I ask how things are in Cu Chi, and he says pretty much the same, some days better than others. The frustrations of commanding tanks in mud or rice paddies hasn't changed since Japan, or of fighting an enemy that shows his face only at night, or of retaking an area over and over again. "If we're ever going to help these people"—he sighs—"we'll have to find another way to fight this war."

I describe my frustrations with the Vietnamese—with engineers who can't even unplug a bathtub drain, pedicab drivers and conniving street urchins who rip us off every chance they get, all the useless, ungrateful gooks who don't like us, just our money.

"Sometimes"—Peter frowns—"I worry that you're turning into one of those hippies."

I first heard that word in Japan, where I was teased about my long hair, sandals, and guitar. Yet, from all I'm told, hippies are shiftless bums who don't bathe, who spend their welfare money on drugs, and go to antiwar demonstrations for something to do, while I work hard, bathe every day that our water pump is working, and didn't even like marijuana the one time I tried it. I just can't help how I've come to feel about the people here.

The waitress slams our breakfasts onto the table: a slice of pressed ham, scrambled instant eggs, and untoasted bread.

"Watch out for the bread," I warn. "It's been known to sprout bugs."

For all the world, Peter looks like a little boy who has been given a carrot after being promised a piece of candy. "They wouldn't *dare* feed this to the troops," he snarls, more to the food than to me. "They'd get killed!"

After breakfast we stop by my villa, where I make a quick change. All that's left of my civilian wardrobe are loose shifts, one pair of too-big sandals, and one pair of pumps mildewing in my closet. Makeup is a thing of the past, doesn't last ten minutes with sweat dripping off my nose. My hair, too frizzy to control in this humidity, is in a tight twist on top of my head.

We retrace our steps to main street, weaving through the crowds of Vietnamese civilians and American soldiers. "You sure draw a lot of attention," he says wryly.

"Sometimes I feel like a piece of meat at the market."

A side glance. "I must confess to having those feelings for you myself."

I feel myself blushing. "Somehow I don't mind it from you."

Looking me in the eye, Peter says, "The problem seems to be doing something about it."

We're now in the stampede of main street. A convoy is gaining on us, adding to the noise, dust, and fumes. "Let's check out

Claymore Tower." Answering his questioning look, I add, "That's what we call our new quarters because the VC keep planting claymore mines there."

The convoy closes in, cheering and whistling as it passes. Clinging to Peter's hand, I wave to the men who gawk from the backs of trucks.

"I've noticed a distinct inability to blend in with the crowd when I'm with you," Peter says with that same wry tone.

"How many times I've wished I could!"

He looks incredulous. "You're kidding! I should think you'd lap it up. Think how many women would love to be in your shoes."

"That's because they don't know what it's like!"

Cocking his head as if trying to figure me out, Peter says nothing more as we walk. Nor do I. I'm trying to think of some excuse to get us into Claymore Tower since it's still under construction and off limits to all personnel. As it turns out, the MP salutes Peter's khakis without asking anything, probably thinks he's a Saigon warrior.

Voices on the first floor send us rushing up the stairs, stifling laughter until I'm short of breath. Darting past stairwell doors, we hear no one after the first floor. Aren't they even working on this place?

Seven flights up, we step through a tiny door to the roof. Street sounds are muffled, dust and fumes are filtered, and there's a slight breeze that went unnoticed below.

Peter lets out a gladiator's whoop. "It's perfect!"

The roof is made of terra-cotta tiles, which strike me as extravagant. The view from this third-tallest building in Saigon is unhindered. We can see the tents and air traffic at Tan Son Nhut and, in the open field between our compounds, an old French fort that seems too small to have ever been much more than a way station.

Peter discovers a small shed near the roof's door, a shed that locks from the inside. Even with air vents, it's a veritable sweat-box, but it's worth having a place to be alone.

We undress, hungry for each other, but our nudity embarrasses me. Lying down, we don't see, only feel. We can forget where we are and what tomorrow means. No matter what anyone thinks, even me, I want this time together.

A knock at the door startles us from our cocoon. We bolt up, start pulling on our clothes.

There is a more insistent knock, and a Vietnamese child's voice demands that we open the door.

I grab Peter's hand, whispering, "Wait. After he leaves!"

The voice outside threatens to go for help. When there's no answer, footsteps retreat back down the steps.

Peter unbolts the door, and I dart for the steps. He shakes his head. "This way."

So it is that when an American sergeant appears, we're nestled in a lawn chair unaccountably on the other side of the roof.

"Have you seen anyone else up here?" he asks.

We shake our heads.

"Heard anyone else?"

We haven't. When he's gone, we laugh long and hard. For this brief time all is right with the world.

Now is our time for soft kisses, tender caresses and lovers' words, and sleep. We awake when a helicopter passes low overhead, pilot and crew giving us the thumbs-up.

"We'd better go back," Peter says. Still, we sit a long time in the lengthening rays of the sun. If only this time would never end.

The next morning Peter refuses to eat another breakfast at the Redbull Inn. We opt for the rear echelon mother fuckers' headquarters for Saigon warriors. As expected, it's falling over with brass. Refined by Vietnam standards, the service isn't much faster, but the food is decent. I wonder if they rate an American cook.

A REMF major invites himself to join us, saying he knows me from somewhere but can't remember where.

I'm about to tell the major to take a hike when Peter, forever the West Pointer, saves him. Not only does he recognize the major, but he remembers when and where they met.

"You have a good memory," returns the REMF, "because I don't remember you." Then he conspicuously directs his attention to me, ignoring Peter altogether. Peter would be mortified if I told a REMF major to fuck off, so I keep my mouth shut. But why, oh, why do we have put up with this bullshit in our last hours together?

When it's time for Peter to head back toward Tan Son Nhut to catch his Freedom Bird, I know I should be happy he's getting out of this hellhole. But I can't get past the feeling that it's me he's leaving, not Vietnam. And I can't overcome my fear that back in the Land of Round-eyes, he'll forget about me before my remaining nine months are up.

Once again we kiss and hug good-bye. Once again I watch his figure grow smaller until it's out of sight. Once again he never looks back. But this time I don't have to will my tears to stop. They aren't there.

I don't know why. They just aren't.

Christmastime in a war zone wouldn't be complete without the Bob Hope show—the only possible reason for wearing sticky starched whites when off duty.

It takes place in a huge field at Tan Son Nhut Air Base, where Army engineers have erected a stage. By show time the field is filled with troopers. Fortunately our patients and their escorts rate front-row seats and folding chairs.

In case any of the thousands of men behind us has forgotten what a little skin looks like, they get an eyeful now. The show is decidedly tailored to the horny GI. I take a lot of pictures of famous people—Phyllis Diller, Anita Bryant, Joey Heatherton—and a lot of not-so-famous people. I'm grateful to have the camera to hide behind. The moans and groans brought on by half-nude women parading in front of sex-starved troops is mortifying.

General Westmoreland, the last performer, delivers a pep talk and receives a standing ovation. To close the show, Phantom jets thunder low overhead to our resounding cheers. Their second flyby is in the missing man formation. The thousands of us stand silently to honor their fallen comrades.

When I was a child, standing in a crowd to sing our national anthem as we saluted our flag always aroused an immense pride in my country. Those times never approached the surge of patriotism I feel this moment.

Christmas morning orphans from St. Elizabeth's sing for patients in the triage area. It's hard not to laugh at them, spiffed up in brand-new camouflaged Army green skirts, which they're wearing backward—the shoulder straps crossing in front.

In the audience our chief nurse major holds a Vietnamese child in her arms, a three-year-old girl whose legs are wrapped in burn dressings—another napalm victim. Close behind hovers a protective black sergeant, the bond between himself and the child obvious to the most casual observer. It's rumored that he plans to adopt her and take her back to the States.

I couldn't do that, I know. But what *should* I do about Le Ly? From the stage her eyes are riveted on me, and I can't hold her gaze. What will happen to her? What will happen to all of them? Most are attached to one among us, but assuredly, most will not be adopted.

Adorable and smiling, their faces flushed with excitement, they close the show with "Silent Night, Holy Night"—in English.

My heart aches as they clamber from the stage to enthusiastic applause. Le Ly races over to throw her arms around my neck. Part of me wants to hold her so close she can't breathe. Another part of me holds her away. She casts down her eyes in disappointment.

I hug her quickly to make amends, then take her hand when we climb aboard a troop carrier bound for the zoo.

The zoo holds the charms of a tropical park. Towering trees with flaming red blossoms are the backdrop for lush shades of green. Palm trees and bushes dot wide stretches of lawns, now turning yellow without the monsoon rains to feed them. Stone animals guard stone steps in front of stone buildings, reminiscent of a better past. Now the buildings are unused, and the gardens untended. Only a few zoo animals are left, and visitors are few and far between. Today there are a half dozen lanky boys with nets on long sticks, scampering up tree trunks in quest of crickets to sell, several scrawny old men in black pajamas sleeping on the grass under the palm trees, and us.

Christmas night I lie staring at the lights I bought at the central marketplace—miniature silken lanterns delicately painted with smiling figures in flowing ao dais and elegant temples and peaceful countrysides. Not the Vietnam I know.

My thoughts turn to my family, to Christmases past. I yearn for snow and solitude, for peace and quiet, for home and homeland. For warm tidings of peace on earth and goodwill toward men.

At the end of a long letter describing Christmas dinner and Christmas presents, my mother writes:

> Well, things seem to be really *hot* in Vietnam. I guess things are at the point where a decision will have to be made as to whether to escalate or become static—and now that Thailand has become so involved I imagine it is going to be a long drawn out affair and will continue to spread. It's easy to understand some people's point of view—that we should try for a win or get out. And of course the Viet people don't help with their attitude but when you realize what they know is war, confusion, etc. It's a real confusing puzzle. I do think the U.S. is handling it beautifully but then I could be wrong. . . .

CHAPTER SIX

JANUARY 1967:
Hard Roads to Travel

Returning from work one afternoon, I'm surprised to find the MP Kiosk transformed into a barricade of sandbag walls and sandbag roof. An unfamiliar MP holds an M-16 rifle that pokes through a slit between bags. Conspicuously absent are the pesky urchins who always hound the Pied Piper.

"Man! What a sweatbox! Who made you put that thing up?"

"Snipers," comes the grim response.

They got the Pied Piper this morning. Of all the MPs, it seems most unfair for it to have been the one who loved the children. The one who always had a warm smile for everyone. The one with skin so smooth it always made me wonder if he had started to shave.

Snipers are now taken seriously. Ambulances are dispatched to transport us to work, and we're told we should have an MP escort us home when we get off duty.

Yeah, sure. What about our coming home from the Redbull Inn at all hours of day and night? Anyway, snipers have no interest in nonwarriors. Why bother?

Warriors at the club are not so contemptuous of the rules, but they can't change my conviction. Nor can they do anything about too few MPs to run us around at all hours. The solution, declares an infantry officer, is to transfer to an American compound.

"This *is* an American compound!" I laugh.

This week our ward is quiet, allowing the long walk and longer wait for lunch at the Redbull Inn. Passing one of the hospital courtyards, once planted with grass but now mostly patches of dirt, hospital workers have gathered to watch a platoon of Vietnamese men attempt to transfer a block of ice from a deuce truck to the hospital's chest freezer. The block is taller than the men moving it and, it's easy to see, way too big for the freezer. I wonder if they'll saw it into pieces.

Anything is possible. For days a small army of Vietnamese men have been squatting in front of our villa, chiseling hardened bags of cement to fill potholes.

A burly sergeant drenched in sweat is barking orders in drill sergeant fashion at the dozen Vietnamese who carry the ice—barehanded. From the triage area, across the tiled walkway and over the patch of dirt, they go. Halfway to the other end of the courtyard it hits the ground.

The dripping sergeant towers over his crew with hands planted firmly on his hips, swearing so hard his face turns purple. His crew runs excitedly around the block of ice, chattering in singsong. Suddenly the crew disappears.

"Goddamn!" bellows the sergeant, throwing his hat on the ground where it soaks up dirt like a sponge. "Fucking A!" He shakes his fist at the huge block of precious ice streaming in the tropical noonday sun. His glare at us says we should skedaddle and we're about to when the crew returns.

The audience chuckles. They're carrying buckets of *hot* soapy water and long-handled brushes. When they start scrubbing the ice, the dripping sergeant's eyes practically bulge from his head.

"What the fuck are you doing!" They scrub harder.

"You goddamned fucking stupid little yellow-bellied bastard gooks!" They scrub faster.

"There seems to be," someone in the crowd observes, "a breakdown in communications here."

AMERICAN DAUGHTER GONE TO WAR

One of us fetches a Vietnamese secretary to straighten out the mess. She barks at the little men. They lower their heads. "Dumb gooks," she spits, clicking past us in spiked heels.

My mother must have made a New Year's resolution to post a novel every week. Tucked into page after page of painstaking detail about what's going on with the family and neighbors, she writes:

> I'm very glad you are enjoying yourself. Nursing can be a very demanding job and if you don't get out and away from it, I do think you could become a very sour old maid at a young age. I don't want you to get ill but I think you are pretty healthy and with such recreation as swimming— it's wonderful.
> ... Seems as tho' the Doves are doing a double take over what Cardinal Spellman and Billy Graham said, but I'm sure it won't affect the student demonstrators (college). They are getting worse than students in South America and if something isn't done their right to "Free Speech" will be watered down in some fashion. Billy Graham came back and told the U.S. that he was sure that China is making every effort to take over the world—and of course Spellman emphatically stuck with his statement that 'we had to win the war.' That really was a shock to the Catholic world because the Pope has been trying to get this country to 'stop bombing, only fight when they have to.' ...

After work I write back that I'm sorry about all the demonstrators, but I've about decided that our empire must fall as all great empires fall. "Too bad," I add. "I thought we had the answer too, but the world just isn't enough like us."

I'm writing from a desk in Claymore Tower. After taking two months to decide it's safe enough to live in, our leaders have moved us to our new quarters. As far as I'm concerned, the Vietnamese definitely got the better end of this deal. We leased the land and paid their government to construct the building. Now we rent it from them. The building had no electricity, so we put in the generator and wiring. The running water was inadequate, so we installed a larger pump. There are no fire escapes, so we're adding them. Last but not least, there is no elevator. There is an elevator shaft, but it's narrower at the top than the bottom, so there can't ever be an elevator.

Women live on the seventh floor, a long climb in any case and a real chore when carrying up four-gallon cans of drinking water that there's no way to cool because the building's only water cooler and refrigerator are on the first floor. When we asked to be moved to the unoccupied first floor, our leaders denied the request, saying we're safer where we are.

With my new room comes a new roommate—Sandy, the Red Cross worker—and a great deal more space. But the bathroom is an accident waiting to happen, especially on midnight runs. To reach the throne, one steps up three inches at the door, down three inches through the "tub," and up seven inches onto a platform. However, it does have a pull chain.

Running water (not to be confused with drinking water) comes from a reservoir on the roof. The water pressure is determined by gravity, which is fine for the first floor, but up here we hope for a forceful dribble. The water pump that fills the reservoir lacks a shutoff valve, so on quiet days, when not enough people take baths, water pours over the roof.

Befitting fourteen-foot ceilings, the windows are tall enough to stand in. They offer views of the stampede on main street, the open field with old French fort, and beyond, the unending air show of Tan Son Nhut. After dark there is the added attraction of flares wavering over the open field and, on special occasions, a fire fight.

Below our windows resides our generator, which delivers electricity at the flick of a switch, save from eight to ten in the morning and two to four in the afternoon, when it rests. When it's not resting, it's so loud that we have to shout to be heard.

To escape the generator, there's the roof. Mostly I'm the only one who goes there. I can sing with my guitar or spin around and yell. Or just sit for as long as I like without even having to think. I wonder why more people don't go up there for the same reason.

* * *

AMERICAN DAUGHTER GONE TO WAR

Tuesday, after the night shift, I climb the six flights to our room to don fatigues, then go back down to grab a deuce headed for the orphanage. Our project for the day is to convert an empty bombshell into a water tank. We don't ask where an empty bombshell came from. Nor do we ask about the dandy little generator to run the unexplained water pump to carry water to the empty bombshell.

The job goes smoothly; the water tank is soon in operation. "Not bad for government work." We nod with satisfaction. Leaving the girls to take their first showers, we accept tea with the nuns.

Their stories are fascinating. They tell about walking here from North Vietnam with twenty children, none older than twelve. We learn that there are only forty nuns left in the North since converts are not allowed and that the people must pay taxes to attend church and the church is taxed to stay open. They say they never heard of communism before coming here.

Before we leave, I retire to the rickety steps that will be next week's project, to scribble notes on what we'll need. Le Ly sits next to me, watching mutely. I draw Mickey Mouse, mastered long ago in grammar school. Her eyes widen.

I pass over the pencil and pad. She carefully copies the drawing. It's not bad!

I draw Bugs Bunny. She draws Bugs Bunny. I draw a face. She draws a face, freckled with frizzy hair just like mine.

I'm "hers" now. She wards off any of the other girls who seek my company. I have a fantasy that through our friendship she will speak again.

Standing with a sigh, I nod for Le Ly to keep the pencil and pad of paper. If they are to be found in this land, I'll bring water paints on the next trip.

When I bend to hug her good-bye, I think how tired I am, how I'm always tired.

It is the quietest hour, when those in bed are in their deepest sleep and those awake are sleepiest. No artillery, no helicopters, only jets to crack the still night air. I sit next to the screen door, listening to the geckos croak in broken harmony with a drone of crickets.

Half dreams, half memories crowd my mind. Hot and humid summer evenings halfway around the world, my family and my child self on the front porch; lightning bugs twinkling in twilight, the sweet smell of dewy grass, and birds singing.

The screen door opens with a creak, like our old screen door. With a high sign to say all is well upstairs, the corpsman passes toward the back of the ward.

The small bundle I cradle in my arms whimpers as I shift my position, a sound more like the mewing of a kitten than the cry of a baby. There is no way to hold Chopper without contacting the napalm wounds, but his whimpers grow louder when I lay him in the box that serves as his crib.

We never considered he would die. But then the wounds became infected and grew larger, and he got weaker. When the specially ordered feeding tube arrived from the States, we thought better nutrition would reverse his decline. It did not. Every day Chopper's road to travel has grown harder. First he lost the strength to lash out at pain when we changed his dressings, then to cry at all. But we cannot accept that he might not be saved, through either the miracles of modern medicine or the divine intervention of a just God. As long as he lives, we will not give up. Not even to free him of his torture, to let him die in peace.

Eventually Chopper grows too weak to breathe. A corpsman wraps him in a white sheet and places the small bundle on top of black body bags designated for the morgue that day. There is no family to claim him. No funeral rites. No name for a gravestone, should he have one.

Daytime sleep never comes easy in this land, but today I have more trouble than usual, not dragging myself out of bed until early evening. Popping a can of warm beer and lighting a cigarette, I scan a letter from my mother. "The war over there is going great guns. We really get good news coverage—all the TV channels have newsmen out there and they really go all over. . . .

". . . the soldiers all seem to be so happy. Actually they seem to be happier than people on the streets over here. . . ."

Tossing the letter aside, I pour myself a stiff Hennessy straight; I still have three hours before work, plenty of time to sober up. I haven't heard from Peter in two weeks. I'm worried he has a new girl friend, but I try not to think about that.

Saying something about practicing my guitar to Sandy, I climb up to the Starlit Roof, where on my guitar I pick out "I Never Will Marry," a moody ballad that strikes a chord inside me. Why do I feel so lonely yet crave a place to be alone? Why do I seek the company of men when I hate their gaping at me? Why, since I don't want romance, do I want someone to hold me in his arms? And why do I drink so much booze when there's nothing particularly wrong in my life?

I polish off the glass of Hennessy and pack of cigarettes, my attention now turned to the jet air traffic at Tan Son Nhut: F-4 Phantoms, straining at their harnesses before streaking the night sky with long flumes of afterburners; B-52 bombers, heavily laden and lumbering along the runway before their long, slow climbs; and 707 Freedom Birds, banking sharply as they rise and set course for the east, homeward bound from the Green Hell.

My haven is assaulted by a burst of gunfire in the open field across main street. Shadowy figures dart under flares, disappear when the flares sputter and fall, then reappear when another burst of fire pierces the night. It's impossible to tell who's who, much less who wins.

The field is dark and quiet when the eleventh hour approaches and I walk to work.

It is Sergeant Crenshaw's third night of forced wakefulness. He's awaiting evacuation to Camp Zama, where he can be placed on a special ward in which the air is filtered and cooled. It was intended for GIs who developed asthma from smog in Japan. Clouds of dust and mists of chemical defoliants cause the same debilitating effects.

Clutching a pillow, fighting for every breath, the sergeant won't be able to go on this way much longer. On his bedside stand is a tracheostomy set should he need to be intubated and put on a respirator—something we've avoided because there is a shortage of respirators and we worry he might never get off the machine. If he falls asleep without a respirator, there is danger he will never wake up. So he's poked and prodded, slapped when need be to keep him awake—and breathing.

Had we known his evacuation would take so long, we might have done it differently. But we couldn't predict Operation Cedar Falls, an offensive to flush Vietcong from the nearby Thanhdien Forest and Iron Triangle, launching pads for terrorist attacks on Saigon. With the offensive came a pickup in casualties—a push. ICU is now using all the respirators and has priority for available evacuation slots.

Next to Sergeant Crenshaw is a colonel who has had a heart attack. He's attached to one of the two cardiac monitors in the hospital, a concession to Ted, who won it by insisting that treating a heart attack without monitoring the heart is tantamount to malpractice. The colonel's morphine-induced sleep is in sharp contrast with the sergeant's forced wakefulness.

Both require oxygen. Since there is a shortage of pressure gauges for oxygen tanks, we've rigged up a Y tube to deliver the life-sustaining gas to both from the same tank. Only this means the tanks don't last very long, and our corpsman is off the ward right now, picking up a refill from the main storage area. Ted is gone as well, helping out with mass casualties in the emergency room. Being alone makes me nervous.

On top of everything else, there's a sergeant upstairs with severe upper left quadrant pain. I suspect pancreatitis, have given him morphine. He needs help to walk down here, but I dare not leave my other patients.

When the screen door opens, I expect to see our corpsman with the refill tank. Instead, an enlisted specialist stands there, looking like a kid straight off the farm.

"They need you in ICU," he blurts. "They need help bad."

"What about this ward?" I demand, feeling protective of my patients and angry that I'm ordered to leave.

"Go ahead, Lieutenant," our corpsman breaks in, backing through the screen door with the refill tank in tow. "I'll wake up Jerguson." He's referring to a field medic, admitted to the upstairs ward for a fever of unknown origin.

94

It's strange to be leaving my ward at this time of night, when the main walkway is empty and dimly lit. My stomach tightens at the sight of an ambulance unloading in the triage area, everyone moving swiftly to check wounds. Turning the corner for intensive care, I follow a gurney carrying a head injury. It turns off, pushed through silver swinging doors into the pre-op/post-op area. Twenty more feet, and I swing open a second set of silver doors.

Bright overhead lights thrust the ward into sharp focus. There must be a hundred IV bottles suspended in the air, and I'm struck by how noisy it is: the hum of continuous suction machines and oxygen tanks hissing, respirators whooshing and someone coughing through his tracheostomy tube, a hopper flushing in the utility room, and cries for help. As many beds as possible have been crammed into the room—four on each side, two rows of four placed back to back down the middle, and two on the far end. Directly in front of me, closest to the nursing station, a Stryker frame for a paralyzed patient occupies one of the spaces. And every bed is filled.

The patient to my right, closest to the doorway, is staring at me. I try to smile but cannot look him in the eye. Both his legs are missing below mid-thigh, the stumps wrapped in bulky layers of Kerlix dressings. Thick tubes drain blood from his chest into a suction machine on the floor. The same machine also receives chest tubes from a patient in the next bed.

A sudden buzz jerks my attention to a corpsman, who has flicked on a machine to suction phlegm from a tracheostomy tube. I don't move, watching until he has finished and rolls the machine to a patient whose head is swathed in gauze.

"Hey, Watson! Hang more blood on the guy in bed twelve. And while you're at it, make sure he's got a blood pressure," comes an order from the other side of the room.

I can't see her, but I recognize Sheila's voice. When she stands, a chest tube bottle full of blood in hand, she sees me frozen by the silver swinging doors.

"What do you want?"

"I was told you need help," I stammer.

"Over there." She waves toward the pre-op/post-op on the other side of the nursing station, not a trace of a dimple in sight.

The Stryker frame soldier is staring at the ceiling with the same empty expression as the one with missing legs. His body is so swollen that his skin is shiny. And he is motionless on the frame, no doubt a quadriplegic.

When he coughs through his trach tube, I look at him in alarm. His stare falls on me briefly, then returns to the ceiling.

Next to his frame, a chest tube bottle is taped to the floor. I alter course to avoid kicking it, then notice a lot more bottles taped to the floor—big bottles for chest drainage, recycled IV bottles for urine, and plasma bottles for bile.

A patient against the far wall is waving at me to come over. I'm scared of him, of this place. I pretend not to see his wave and pass through the empty nursing station.

Four beds line the near wall, and three more loom in the center of the room—all filled. More wounded lie on gurneys with more bottles hung in the air and taped to the floor. But I'm only vaguely aware of these things. My eyes are riveted on the casualty closest to me.

He is part of a body, ragged edges of torn tissues where there once were legs. Part of a body, ripped and torn, bleeding from hundreds of razor-sharp pieces of shrapnel that tore through his face and chest. Part of somebody, dark and mottled from blood and mud and not enough oxygen. Somebody who was a whole person just an hour ago.

It's as if I'm floating and everything is in slow motion. Sounds seem shut out from this place, as though all of time stands still here.

"Are you the nurse they sent to help?" The question comes from far away, takes a long time to reach me.

I nod numbly, looking up at the doctor staring at me from the other side of the bed. A nervous twitch bats his right eye.

I'm not sure I have a voice. "I've never worked in ICU."

"You *can* take a blood pressure?"

The snide remark makes me bristle, brings me back. Who does he think he is? I place my stethoscope in my ears and pump up the cuff. There's no blood pressure. I try again, holding down panic. Still nothing. I look up in alarm, shaking my head.

"Aramine drip!" he snaps.

I find the medicine cabinet, but I can't find Aramine. A clinical specialist walks in, asking what I need. All I see is his name tag printed in big block letters. It reads "Hooper."

Hooper says he'll mix the drip for me. I'm grateful because I'm not certain how to do it myself.

The doctor is pumping in two units of blood simultaneously. The more he pumps into the soldier's veins, the more oozes out from all the holes.

Not knowing what else to do, I bend to take another blood pressure. Sixty systolic. Not good, but better than nothing. I say the number.

The doctor nods. "Ambu."

I look at the soldier uncertainly. An ambu bag is used to breathe for someone, but he's already on a respirator attached to a tracheostomy tube. Like everywhere else, blood is pouring from the site.

"Here, pump the blood."

He doesn't sound sarcastic this time, but it would be deserved. What's the matter with me? Am I afraid of a little blood?

He orders four more units of blood from a corpsman, begins squeezing oxygen through the ambu bag.

Specialist Hooper is hanging the Aramine. I watch carefully so I can do it next time. He sets it at a fast drip and leaves to get something for the ICU side.

I stop pumping long enough to get another blood pressure on the patient. Ninety over sixty. When I say the numbers, I feel a rush of hope pass between the doctor and me.

The corpsman comes back with the blood, hangs two of the bottles, and returns to other patients. I stop pumping long enough to replace fluids on a third IV and take another blood pressure. It's still ninety over sixty.

The doctor speeds up the Aramine; I resume pumping. My hands and forearms ache, but I must not slow down. Then, with horror, I notice the soldier's arm is swelling. His IV has slipped out of the vein!

The doctor calls for a cutdown tray. I take another blood pressure. Sixty over forty. I try to keep my voice steady.

The drip is wide open. The faster I pump the blood, the faster it pours out of the soldier.

Inside, I'm crying, No! You can't die! This is an American hospital! The ICU! We're here! Please don't die! But I no longer hear a blood pressure. The doctor listens to the bloody chest and hears nothing.

He pumps on the soldier's chest, shouts for the crash cart and bicarb. The corpsman takes over squeezing the ambu bag with one hand, working a blood pump with the other.

My hands tremble as I draw up the 50 cc and plunge it into the IV tubing. "Bicarb given."

"Calcium."

"Calcium given."

The doctor listens to the chest again. He hears nothing. Blood squishes with each compression of the chest. I draw up epinephrine with a cardiac needle, wince as the doctor thrusts it into the soldier's heart.

He listens for a heartbeat. Repeats the procedure. Shakes his head.

The corpsman stops squeezing the ambu bag, clamps off the blood tubing. Don't give up! screams through my head. But I know there is nothing more to do.

Part of me is exhausted beyond feeling. Another part wants to cry. I begin doing what I've been taught to do. I take out the IV needles, despairing of the blood oozing from everywhere no matter how tight the dressings. In time I will know to tie off IV tubes. I remove the silver tube from his throat, cover the gaping hole with a dressing. His eyes won't close. I wrap Kerlix over them.

The corpsman finds me in the utility room, looking for a washbasin. He stares at me in astonishment.

"Forget it, Lieutenant. We're too busy to spend any more time on that guy. They'll hose him down at graves."

The distorted, discolored form is lifted onto a gurney. Dog tags, the ticket for his last ride home, dangle from the dead soldier's neck. He's rolled out the door, and another wounded man is rolled into his place.

Time now returns. I must go back to my ward.

"Thanks for your help," the doctor says, walking beside me.

I smile weakly, saying nothing.

"Where do you work?" as we pass through the swinging doors. I'm struck by how quiet it is on this side.

"Ward Eight." I'm really not in the mood for small talk.

"Why don't you come work here?"

I dart him a sharp glance. He looks serious.

"What was his name?" is how I respond.

He searches my face with squinted eyes. "Jimmy. He jumped from a helicopter and landed on a claymore mine."

Jimmy. I wonder what his mother and father are doing right this minute. Eating? Watching TV? Is it true that loved ones have a sense about such things? Or are they laughing with friends this very minute?

The doctor is holding out his hand. "Alex."

"Winnie," I say as we shake. The formality strikes me as odd. He hangs on until I tug my hand away.

"Your mama-san's not going to like that." He nods at my uniform.

Looking down, I see I'm spattered with Jimmy's blood. The part of me that wants to cry is sneaking back up. I push it down. The night's work isn't over yet.

Behind me the screen door shuts softly just as it has done so many times before. I think how cool the ward feels. No, not cool. Just dark and quiet. I hear the sergeant's labored respirations and am faintly surprised. Shouldn't he have left by now? Checking my watch, I'm surprised to see I've been gone for less than two hours.

The corpsmen say nothing, seem not to notice Jimmy's blood. I slip on a hospital pajama top over my uniform, then hold up a flashlight to say I'm going to make rounds. They nod. They understand my need not to speak.

Upstairs everything is so peaceful. When a patient startles at my approach, I instinctively direct the flashlight to myself so he can orient himself. A few others stir as I pass, and I feel comforted by how familiar they are, by how familiar such rounds are after so many at Fort Dix, Camp Zama, and here.

Still not wanting to speak to anyone, I sit on the outside steps before going downstairs. Nearby, helicopters chop at the tepid air. Far away are the rumble of artillery and closer, all around, crickets chirping and geckos croaking. The ICU is ages away from here.

I can't dawdle all night. I'm two hours behind in my work. Stepping through the screen door, I stop short at the empty place where Chopper's crib used to stand. Somehow, by some trick of the mind, I had expected him to still be with us.

There's a cup of coffee waiting for me at the nursing station. I watch the cardiac monitor absentmindedly, as the corpsmen fill me in on what happened while I was gone. They hadn't bothered to awaken the patient from upstairs after all. Sergeant Crenshaw will be picked up on schedule, and the heart attack colonel is to be kept sedated. Everything is oddly the same.

On this day I request a transfer to ICU, and it is immediately granted. My old dream, to become a combat nurse, is about to come true.

CHAPTER SEVEN

FEBRUARY 1967: Intensive Care and Recovery Room

Nursing report on Ward 4–5 is held in the utility room, the only place inside where we can smoke. It's a tiny room with shelves for supplies on one wall and a counter with sink against the other. This morning the head nurse, Janet, the clinical specialist, Hooper, six corpsmen, and two staff nurses—Sheila and I—are sprawled over the sink, counter, footstools, and floor. I've landed the hopper, as undistinguished as it is uncomfortable and subject to temporary removal should a bedpan need flushing.

My arrival occasions a few nods but not much more, and the report tells me why. The ward is what they term "busy." Busy, I will learn, means trouble finding time to go to the bathroom. Many casualties are left over from Operation Cedar Falls, which ended a week ago. More are arriving from two new offensives along the Cambodian border: Operation Gadsden to stem enemy infiltration from the Ho Chi Minh Trail, and Operation Big Spring to flush Vietcong from their strongholds.

The ICU side is full—eighteen patients including two Stryker frames. Most have been admitted during the past week, and none is deemed stable enough for evacuation, but should push come to shove, two can be considered. Shove, I gather, means a push too big to handle, a kind of second-round triage, where a casualty with a reasonable chance of surviving the trip to Japan is shoved out by one who has none.

There's no time or staff to orient me, so I'm to take charge of the recovery room side. If I have any questions, Janet says, just come to her.

We're filing out of the utility room in a cloud of smoke when someone yells for the crash cart, and everyone bolts into action. From the doorway leading to ICU, I watch the staff resuscitating the patient closest to the nursing station. One corpsman pumps the heart from outside the chest, another pumps oxygen into the lungs, and a nurse pumps drugs into an IV.

"For God's sake, Lieutenant, call for a doctor!" yells a corpsman in my direction.

I leap to the phone. "Cardiac arrest. Ward Eight," I alert the emergency room and hang up. Unable to think of what else to do, I once again stand in the doorway.

"Maybe you should see to your patients," Sheila snaps.

Blushing, I turn for the recovery room just as two doctors burst through the silver swinging doors. One is cursing about being misdirected to Ward 8.

My face turns beet red. Less than two minutes after report on my first day, and I blew it. Pushing down my disgrace and rising panic, I go to work.

Three overflows—what we call surplus ICU patients in recovery room—line the wall to my right, bearing chest tubes, Foley catheters to drain urine, IV bottles, blood products, manifold dressings. Where there are no dressings, there is dried mud and blood. Four routine postops lie to the left, beyond a space for emergencies. The far wall is empty except for yellow curtain screens pushed into a corner.

My internal alarm is on full alert. Methodically I locate supplies I might need in a hurry: dressing cart—check; crash cart—check; emergency tracheostomy, cutdown, and thoracostomy trays—

check. IV solutions. Extra oxygen tanks. A portable suction machine for pulmonary secretions that is rolled from patient to patient as the need arises. At each overflow's bedside, a red rubber suction catheter soaks in a bottle of Wescodyne solution. The solution and the catheter, I learn, are changed once every twenty-four hours by the night shift.

The one corpsman assigned with me on the recovery room side is Mott, who looks about twenty. He's slim—my height and build—and carries himself with a confidence that says he knows his stuff. I sure hope so, or we're in trouble. From his scowl I'd say he figures we're in trouble no matter how good he is.

Mott is eyeing me as he cares for the routine post-ops. My checklist completed, I bend to take a blood pressure on the closest overflow. Normal. So are the other overflows. I dare to nod at my corpsman. He nods back. Good.

Now what? I find a basin and begin washing the blood and dirt off the face of an overflow when Mott informs me that one of the routines is ready to be signed out.

Drying my hands, I check the patient. Awake. Vital signs stable. Dressings dry and intact. Morphine given two hours ago. I smile at him. He's been staring at me since I entered the ward. I know the look. He hasn't seen a round-eye in months, thinks I'm beautiful, and will I marry him? Or something like that.

Sure, he can go. I sign him out, and Mott pushes him through the silver swinging doors.

There should be someone else to push him back, I think. What if something happens while Mott's gone? Easy, Smith. Just take blood pressures, check out IVs and dressings while you're at it. Everything's in order. I return to the bath, but the water's cold and muddy. I'm changing it when Mott returns; he winces when he sees what I'm doing. No one has to tell me I'm making him nervous.

Mott begins measuring an overflow's urine to be certain his output is adequate. I blush. How could I forget? I start doing the same. We measure urine in the utility room, then retape the bottle to the floor to collect the next hour's worth. Meanwhile, the bath water turns cold again. I move to change it but now notice that the chest tube bottle on Overflow No. 1 is full. That's a lot of blood. I call the doctor, who tells me to empty the bottle and see how fast it refills. Mott shows me how, clamping the chest tube, unscrewing the drainage bottle and emptying it in the utility room sink, then replacing the bottle and unclamping the chest tube.

He must think I'm pretty dumb not to be able to figure that out.

The cutdown dressing on Overflow No. 3 is bloody, so I change it. I recheck the chest tube bottle on Overflow No. 1, which doesn't seem too bad. I start to call the doctor to report back when Mott asks me to sign out another routine. I'm suddenly aware that I haven't even looked at those patients. Mott has done everything for them.

I start to sign out the second patient but notice his leg cast is too tight. Something I know about! I call another doctor to inform him before transferring the patient. The doctor thanks me for letting him know, and it bolsters my confidence. I sign the soldier out, and Mott rolls him out the door.

It's dawning on me that there is no time to give baths, so I throw away the water. Mott will be very relieved.

Time to check blood pressures. First the overflows, then the remaining routines. When I touch the first patient, he opens his eyes wide in astonishment and then bolts into a sitting position, looking around in panic. "Where am I! Am I dreaming or something?"

"You're in recovery room at Third Field Hospital. Your operation is over."

"Operation!" he cries in alarm. "What kind of operation!"

I'll get used to the question. Many wounded "didn't see it coming," have no idea what their injuries might be when they hear they were hit. I pick up his clipboard to find out what procedure was performed, but he can't wait for me to read it. He jerks off his sheet, blushes at his nudity, and then groans.

"It's my leg! What did they do to my leg!"

His clipboard reads T&T GSW RLE, the standard abbreviations for a "through-and-through gunshot wound to the right lower extremity."

"Looks like a bullet went through it. All they did was clean it up for you. It should be okay."

104

He's ready for the ward, so I sign him out. His eyes follow my every movement as I bend to take blood pressures on the other routines. I sure wish he'd stop.

Mott comes back, and I indicate the man I've signed out. He nods approvingly, rolls the gurney out the door. The blood pressure on the last routine is too low. I speed up his IV. We're too busy to keep up with the vital sign sheets on routines, so there's no way of knowing what it was for Mott. I wish he'd get back. I feel helpless when I'm left alone.

The head dressing on Overflow No. 2 is bloody. I find Kerlix dressing, label the tape "Reinforced 0830." When I write the time, I know it's going to be a long day. I've been here for only one hour.

Overflow No. 1 coughs through his trach. The gurgling makes me nervous. I roll the suction machine to his bed, plug it in, reach for the catheter on the bedside stand, suck up the mucus, hold back a gag when I pull the slimy catheter out. Sputum is the secretion I hate most.

"Hey, Lieutenant?" Startled, I kick the chest tube bottle. Gasping, I look down to see what damage I've done. None, thanks to the four-inch-wide adhesive tape. I turn toward Mott, standing by the last routine. He looks worried.

"Did you get a pressure on this guy?"

I nod. "It was low, so I sped up—" Oh, my God, the IV is empty! Dropping the suction catheter, I run for another bottle. "What is it now?"

"Sixty over nothing."

My heart lurches. I'm killing a patient on my first day! Mott picks up the sheet as I hang the IV. The thigh dressing is saturated, and there's a puddle of blood beneath it.

Oh, God! Why didn't I check for bleeding? Mott is cutting away the dressing as I run to phone the doctor. Over my shoulder I call back, "Put on a tourniquet."

Janet is sitting in the nursing station, pays no attention as I call for a doctor in the emergency room. I swallow my irritation. She's the captain.

It's Alex, the doctor who worked so hard to save Jimmy's life, who responds. A nervous twitch still bats his right eye, but I'm

calmed by his presence. He knows what he's doing and he knows
I know nothing. Mott announces the blood pressure is up to eighty
over sixty. The IV I just hung is already half empty, so I run for
another.

"Better hang blood, too," the doctor calls after me. Mott goes
for the blood. I go for the dressing cart. The doctor is removing
packings, exposing the wound to find the bleeder. The incision
runs the entire inside length of the thigh. Shouldn't this be done
in the operating room?

Mott is back with the blood, so I hang it. This patient is well
covered, so I return to the other patients. Overflow No. 1 is
coughing again. I suction him and then check his chest tube
bottle—still no heavy bleeding. Blood pressures are all fine. I check
under sheets and measure urine outputs. I'm standing at the foot
of a bed trying to remember if I've forgotten anything.

"You need help, Lieutenant?" It's Mott, sounding concerned.

I smile weakly. "Just checking to see what I've forgotten."

He nods with a slight smile. I do not yet know that I wouldn't
be the first nurse to "lose it" on this ward, that even though the
ICU is so busy, they have given me Mott, the "best we have,"
to keep a watchful eye on me. I do know I couldn't survive this
morning without him, much less the whole shift.

After suturing the bleeder on the thigh wound, Alex comes
over. "You work here now?"

He's standing a little too close. I step away, pretending to check
something, before answering. "At least for today. I'm not sure
they'll let me back tomorrow."

He laughs, then frowns. "Where's the head nurse?"

"In the nursing station."

"Why isn't she out here helping you?"

"I guess she's busy. Or maybe she doesn't realize how green I
really am."

"Janet doesn't know what the hell's going on out here, and she's
either too lazy or too scared to find out," he almost hisses, his
right eye twitching furiously as he glares toward the nursing station. Then he shrugs as though to shake off the thought of her
and returns his attention to me. "Listen. I have to get back to the

ER right now, but I'd like to see you. How about eating together tonight?"

I know a play when I hear one. I also know a married man when I see one, ring or no ring. Still, he's the first person on this ward to offer friendship. I tell myself that I'll keep our relationship on a platonic level and accept. Guiltily I realize Peter wouldn't approve. But Peter is on the other side of an ocean.

No sooner has Alex walked away than I jerk to attention. I haven't given any medications! It's almost 1100 hours. How can it be so late? A routine on a gurney emerges through the silver doors. Mott is way ahead of me, nodding that he can handle it. I shoot a high sign and head for the medicine cabinet.

The thigh wound stabilizes after the unit of blood. Now awake and talking, the soldier is considered ready to be signed out to the ward. It seems too soon, but another routine is rolling in, and I sense more will soon follow. Mott moves quickly from one routine to the next and soon rolls the thigh wound out the door.

I go back to the overflows: take blood pressures, measure urines, suction trachs, look at dressings under sheets and at pupils on the head injury. At each bed I go through a mental list, a newly forming habit that will stick with me until I automatically see anything wrong without having to check if everything is right. For now I have no rhythm; my movements are uncoordinated and slow.

"Lieutenant?" Mott is nodding toward an empty IV bottle. Damn! I run for another, check the rate in the cardex, mark, and hang it. Chart the bottle completed and the bottle hung. Then check other IVs, make a mental note of those needing new bottles soon, and switch one from a unit of blood that is completed to saline solution.

Fuck. Three hours, and we haven't turned a single overflow. As I attempt to prop the first up on his side, Mott notices and comes to help. He's teaching me about teamwork, mandatory in this place where our duties mix and mingle. The constant need for blood pressures, pain medicines, IVs, suctioning, new admissions, and sign-outs brings the noon hour before we can turn them all.

Medications are due again. I survived the morning, but I'm uncertain I'll survive the shift. Another new patient is banging through the doors as I return with a tray of syringes and "piggybacks," small bags of fluid for IV antibiotics. I start to help Mott, but he waves me away. He'll let me know if he can't handle it.

The pace on the ward waxes and wanes, but I'm always too far behind to slow down. Every time I think I've caught up, some new problem arises or I remember something I've forgotten. Thank goodness for Mott, who keeps calamity at bay. Not until ICU is ready for two of the overflows is there any break, and by then it's three in the afternoon—time for report. One more mad dash to gather numbers before stepping into the utility room.

It's bad enough that I'm late, but I'm also besieged with stage fright for the first time since Fort Dix. My performance is worthy of a rank second lieutenant, but at least it's over. I sorely wish I could leave, but there's all the charting I didn't have time for earlier. It's close to six o'clock before I'm finished.

I cannot face the steps of Claymore Tower more than once tonight, not even to change my uniform, smudged with mud and spattered with blood. Half starved and dog-tired, I head straight for the Redbull Inn.

Alex waves his hand as I enter. I had completely forgotten we were to meet. Now I just want to be alone. To make matters worse, he's sitting at a tableful of doctors and nurses, one of whom is Sheila. I join them with a stiff rum and Coke in hand.

"Where've you been?" Alex opens with a wry smile and twitch of the right eye.

I shoot him a dirty look.

"I just got here myself. I was busy operating all day."

I order the special of the day, the one thing special about it being that it comes faster. When it comes, I dispense with it in big gulps, then pointedly say good-bye to Alex and adjourn to the bar for a rum and Coke.

I still want to be alone, but my first drink has barely arrived when a lonely soldier sits down to keep me company. Compliments of the lonely soldier, I drink many rum and Cokes in rapid-fire order. He keeps up with his brand of alcohol, an elixir to help us forget where we are and why, to help us remember where we came from. That place where cars have doors, and showers have hot water that gushes rather than trickles. Where people wash off a little grime, not layers of dirt and sweat and blood.

Back to the tower and up the six flights of stairs. I take a squat bath in our three-inch-deep tub and put on my baby doll pajamas. I pick up my mother's latest letter—about the weather, the menu for dinner, things bought at the flea market, and what she's sewing. Then: "The people here are really awfully sad about the three astronauts. Such a tragedy and one that seemed to be so needless, but then Gus Grissom had said we should be prepared for these things but it should never interfere with the program. White, of course, we can't forget because he was the first to walk in Space and Chaffee so young and before he even had a chance to get the experience of a flight behind him. . . . "

So young? He couldn't have been all that young if he was an astronaut! And what about the guys dying over here? Lying back on my musty sheets, I tell myself not to think about it. Nor about tomorrow, save that tomorrow will come no matter what.

Better for me I don't know how, this night, the corpsmen are placing bets on how long I'll last on ICU. The longest anyone gives me is two weeks.

Exiting from report amid the cloud of smoke, everyone goes about his or her business with a calm efficiency I envy. Mott is already at work; only Hooper and I are still in the nursing station. I have a question, and it seems a good time to ask.

"Say, Hooper?"

"Shoot."

"What's a condom cath?"

He knits his brow and clears his throat, squinting at the vial in his hand as though he needed glasses. He hems and haws a few times, then shrugs his shoulders helplessly.

I feel a hot blush creeping up my neck into my face.

Then he perks up. "It's a poor man's Texas catheter," he says. My blank look and beet-red face tell him I don't understand.

109

"For incontinent patients," he hints.

I still don't get it, and it's easy to see he can hardly believe my ignorance.

"We cut a hole in the end of a condom, tape a drainage tube in the hole, and then tape it to an incontinent patient," he says, as if he were speaking to a child.

Still blank.

"You *do* know what a condom is?"

One of the other corpsmen enters at this moment and stands by with an air of amused expectancy.

I shake my head.

"How old are you, Lieutenant?" demands Hooper.

"Twenty-two," I snap. "What's that got to do with it?" The lieutenant in me is rising to my defense.

"Nothing," Hooper replies. "I just thought kids grew up faster these days."

Mott now enters the nursing station.

"Just tell me what a condom is, so we can all get back to work!" My command voice surprises everyone, me most of all.

"Follow me," says Hooper, loping on his long legs into the ICU. He stops at a head injury and lifts a towel draped across the groin, nodding toward a condom taped to the penis. It drains urine into an IV bottle.

The corpsmen all are busy caring for patients when I turn back, but I know they're having a good laugh. No doubt it will make for more laughs at the enlisted men's club tonight.

My third day I suffer the miserable effect of Monday's malaria pill and am fighting cramps all morning. The recovery room holds four overflows, six routines, and an expectant, a casualty waiting to die. My greatest concern is a respirator on Overflow No. 1. I've never worked with one before, and every whooshing breath it delivers makes me nervous. I put off facing the machine and start my rounds on the far end of overflow row.

Overflow No. 4 has a temperature of 105 degrees. I leave a message for the surgeon in the emergency room and give the patient an aspirin suppository, then methodically check the other men and tend to needs along the way. Hang and chart new IVs, check dressings, call the neurosurgeon about a fixed and dilated pupil, suction trachs, empty a chest tube bottle, measure urines. By the time I reach Overflow No. 1, a surgeon has come to see about Overflow No. 4's temperature, so he explains the respirator to me.

In time I will learn to breathe with a patient and manipulate the machine until the patient's respirations "feel right." In more time I will reflexively respond to a respirator that doesn't sound quite right amid the constant background noise.

The doctor is still showing me how the dials work when one of the routines starts retching undigested food. Mott dashes to flip him on his side as I go for the suction machine.

In war soldiers don't pick and choose a time for surgery—empty stomachs are the exception rather than the rule—but at least grunts don't get big meals. The one good thing about C rations is that they don't fill a grown man's stomach.

Counting patients, I come up with one missing—the expectant mentioned in report.

Mott asks if I've lost something, and I explain. He nods toward the far side of the room, toward the yellow curtain folding screens.

There is an unnatural stillness behind the curtains, an empty silence that pounds in my ears. Before me is a body caked in muddy fatigues. Rivulets of blood from a soaked head dressing have puddled around the soldier's head and shoulders. I can smell his blood, sweet and metallic, much stronger here than on the ward. The body isn't breathing.

Inside me is a frantic cry to do something. But there's nothing I can do. A light touch of his hand tells me there will be no pulse.

I look into his face, see neither pain nor peace. The evacuation tag tied to his toe tells me his name. Robert. And his age. Twenty-two.

I take a deep breath and slip to the other side of the screen, reenter the world of bright lights and busy noise.

"He bought his ticket?"

I whirl to find Mott staring at me with no discernible expression, his face just looking young and tan like everyone else's. Yes, this casualty's ticket is paid in full. His Freedom Bird is waiting to take him home.

Time passes. Mott transfers leftover routines to the ward, and new routines transfer in from the OR. The ICU evacuates two patients to Japan and takes two of the overflows from recovery. By lunchtime, inexplicably, new routines stop arriving.

Mott asks permission to eat in the cafeteria.

Permission granted, but I beg that he not be long.

He asks if he can get something for me although it's illegal. Officers aren't allowed to eat at hospital expense because we receive a cost of living allowance. This is fine for big brass types, who have sedans to take them to gourmet Saigon restaurants, but a starvation maneuver for small brass hospital types when it's too busy for a trek to the Redbull Inn. Yes, I nod gratefully.

He hasn't been gone five minutes when the silver swinging doors bang open. Shit! I should've known better than to let him go. I grab a blood pressure machine and am halfway to the gurney when I see it's a little girl—a pre-op as the blood, dirt, and field dressings attest. Terror fills her face. For an instant it's the face of Le Ly.

"Why are you bringing her here?" I snap. A small panic, a looming despair of being overwhelmed, knots my stomach. Please, Mott, come back.

"The ORs are full," the corpsman says, leaving me to wonder how many operating rooms there are. I tell myself to calm down. Her blood pressure is good, a full IV bottle is running well, the dressings on thighs and abdomen are without heavy bleeding. There's no shrapnel, so it must be gunshot wounds.

Her dress has been torn away, and she's clutching at a few shreds of material. Dashing for a towel to cover her, I wonder how she got here and where her family might be. She's not crying, probably too scared, and I know no Vietnamese to reassure her.

Her long black hair is matted on her forehead, so I reach to smooth it back. She averts her head and pushes my hand away, which causes her to grimace and draw up her legs in pain. There are no papers with her, not even an evacuation tag, so I can't know if she has already gotten morphine. I doubt it but have no idea how much to give a child her size. I reach for her hand to comfort her, but she pulls it away.

The swinging doors burst open again, a sound I'm learning to dread. It's a post-op with an anesthesiologist pumping oxygen

112

into his lungs through an endotracheal tube.

"Get a bed. We need to sit this guy up. He's got emphysema," says the anesthesiologist. "It was a real flail in the OR," he adds, meaning things did not run smoothly. "Had to give him a lot of fluid to resuscitate him. He's got no business in a war zone. Pull out these foot IVs right away. Then do a CVP. And don't extubate him before I return. Restrain him so he doesn't pull the tube out when he wakes up. I'll be back as soon as we've finished the next case." And he's out the door.

Frantically trying to remember the string of orders, I hear the head injury coughing through his trach. Restraints. The last thing he said is the first thing I remember. Running for Kerlix, pads, and adhesive tape to tie down his wrists, I smile at the little girl, who watches with terrified eyes. That head injury won't stop coughing, the mucus he can't quite get up rolling back down his trach to make him cough again. Between fits of coughing, he gasps for air. It can't be good for his head. I'd better suction him.

My hands are trembling as I reach for the suction catheter and flip a switch to turn on the machine. The doors swing open. I look up from the thick green sputum. Mott! I'm so glad to see you!

He holds up the lunch bag before tossing it into the utility room. My stomach growls at the nearness of food.

He takes a blood pressure on the sergeant with emphysema before rounding on the routines. Just his being here gives me confidence that we can handle it.

"This guy's ready to sign out, Lieutenant."

I nod, then point toward a patient farther down the line. "And that guy's already signed out."

"Yes, ma'am!"

"Don't call me ma'am. It makes me feel old."

"Yes, Lieutenant!" He stands at mock attention and clicks his heels. "I'll get him out right away."

"Oh, no!"

He looks at me questioningly.

"It's just that I never thought you'd come back and now you're leaving again!"

"Missed me, did you?"

113

To my smiling admission, he pushes the gurney through the silver swinging doors.

What else did that anesthesiologist say? Oh, yes, take out the foot IVs. Both bottles are dry! I forgot to slow them down! Heart pounding, I reset the arm and neck IVs to the slowest drips possible. Blood pressure fine. Still asleep. Dressings dry. Take out the foot IVs before somebody hangs more fluids.

But I'm too late. The emphysema patient is coughing up thin, pink, bubbly secretions. I've heard of them although I've never seen them before—pulmonary edema from being overloaded with fluids. What do I do now? Get hold of yourself. You're no good to anyone if you fall apart. I dash over to ICU and ask the other nurse for help.

"You don't know how to do a CVP?" she cries incredulously when I explain what has happened.

Shamed by my ignorance, I shake my head. She runs back with me and teaches me now, reading a thin plastic cylinder that registers his central venous pressure.

"Thirty-three!" she cries in alarm. The number means nothing to me, but her reaction must mean it's very bad. I'm on the verge of tears. If he dies, it's my fault. "We'll have to get him on a respirator. We have a head with fixed and dilated pupils we can put behind the curtains. Let's get this guy over to the ICU!"

She sees to it, the exchange accomplished within twenty minutes. I've sentenced a head injury to sure death, and possibly a sergeant with emphysema.

Mott is ready to transfer the next patient, but I tell him to hold up. I toss down a second ounce of Kaopectate before dashing out the door to relieve my cramps. He stands aside as I bang out the silver doors.

It's barely two in the afternoon. Best not to think about it. Just check vital signs, change dressings, hang IVs, give medicines, suction, and turn. Measure urine, stomach, and chest tube outputs. Try to comfort the little girl.

Her temperature is up to 106 degrees; a feverish glaze has replaced the fear in her eyes. Even alcohol on cuts and abrasions brings barely a whimper. I fight back tears as I consider changing her blood-stained field dressings. I might find the cause of her

114

temperature, but it could start fresh bleeding. I think of Chopper, his tiny shrouded form atop black body bags. Push it out of my mind. Change her towels, already warm from her burning skin.

Mott returns. "What are you bothering with her for!"

"Her temp's one hundred and six."

"Let her die! She was probably tossing a grenade at our guys when she got shot!"

"My God, Mott, she's just a little girl."

"She's a gook! Bust your ass to save her life, and she's likely to return the favor by blowing up another one of our guys!"

I think of the shoeshine boys in Saigon, how I hate them. Maybe he's right. I don't know. I'm too tired to think about it right now, too confused to argue.

"Whoever she is, she's our patient."

"Let me tell you something," Mott warns. "This place'll fall apart if you spend your time baby-sitting."

I know he's right. I'm an Army nurse, and my first duty is to our casualties.

The silver doors bang open to admit a stunted form—a double amputee. Rolling his gurney alongside the little girl, we start the routine check of IVs and blood pressures. I sure hope he doesn't wake up before I leave. I don't want to be here when he looks down and sees his legs gone.

Before we get the amputee squared away, the doors bang open again. Multiple gunshot wounds of the abdomen with a splenectomy, repair of a liver laceration, and colostomy—a common combination of procedures in modern-day warfare. He needs a suction machine, but there is none, so Mott ties a rubber glove to the nasogastric tube. We must empty his stomach with a syringe every hour. If we forget, he may vomit before he's awake enough to keep it out of his lungs.

The ICU nurse's approach reminds me that I should check on the expectant head injury behind the screen. She informs me that another patient has died, opening a space on their side. Impossible as it seems, they must be having an even worse day on ICU. We send over our other head injury. It'll be a big relief not to have to suction him.

Time passes quickly, but the day drags on forever. Suddenly

it's time to give report, and I rush to gather the numbers. Once again I must stay well into the next shift to finish my charting.

The weekly newsletter from my mother is waiting in the mail-room. Weaving through the stampede on main street, I read:

> Last week I finally got my suits made and they are really quite pretty. The brown tweed is a dressmaker suit and the green & white plaid is a raglan sleeve which I like very much for casual wear. Also made two very nice wash & wear. Now I'm going to make shifts for the summer—for some reason I didn't make anything for myself last summer and really didn't have anything to wear—literally. I also bought a couple pieces of the wash & wear dacron crepe to make into a couple dressy dresses. . . .

Skip this shit. Skip the shitty food at Redbull Inn. Settle for a stiff rum and Coke. Then another and another. Until I've had enough to sleep.

The sergeant with emphysema dies after three days. I'm morosely drinking at the Redbull Inn's patio bar when Alex joins me.

"It's not your fault," he protests, running a hand through his thinning hair. "Things like that happen. That's when the head nurse is supposed to help." He nods to the bartender for another round. "You're just feeling sorry for yourself."

I stare mutely at my drink. How nice it would be to have a few ice cubes to clink around. They have ice at the club, but it never lasts long enough to cool the drink, much less clink around.

"That sergeant had no business being over here," Alex says, right eye twitching. "If he hadn't had emphysema, he wouldn't have died. That's the Army's fault, not yours. And what killed him were bullets, not a couple of liters of IV fluids. You can't blame yourself for every GI that dies under your care."

"They'd be better off with a more experienced nurse."

"Who do you think that might be? That Cruz woman? Or maybe that dingbat on Ward One?" He motions for another round of drinks. "And what kind of experience do you think any of us has had? There's nothing in the States to prepare anyone for these kinds of wounds, much less these conditions."

The pep talk works. I stick it out.

My second week, on nights, the Vietnamese girl dies. No one knows what killed her exactly, but Alex says unequivocally that my repositioning her stomach tube could not have done it. I'm not convinced.

I see quite a bit of Alex. This occasions a lot of gossip—another nurse sleeping with a married doctor. It's not true, but I don't bother to deny it. I no longer care what people think, and it keeps me from having to fight off other men. Besides, even though I worry that Peter has found another girl friend, I want to see him again when I return stateside—with a clear conscience.

Summer wears on. The days are so miserably hot and sticky that it's impossible to do much more than snatch sleep for minutes at a time. Yet I'm always so worn out that I can't work up the energy to go swimming and cool off, never mind trek out to the orphanage. Sheila delivers the supplies my mother sends for the orphans. Even though she works in ICU as well, she has taken charge of the orphanage work. I don't how she does it.

The eve of Tet my hideaway Starlit Roof is invaded by just about everyone not working. We line the railing or sit on the terracotta tiles, sipping drinks and puffing cigarettes until the midnight hour. When it strikes, the city erupts into a nonstop hourlong "fireworks" display. Rifles and machine guns pop and crack everywhere. Tracers, bullets visible in the night, streak in every direction. Flares light up the hospital, main street, the open field with the old French fort, Tan Son Nhut Air Base, and the Saigon skyline.

The happy celebration ends sharply at 0700 hours, along with the holiday cease-fire, and battalions of American forces begin moving against villages within fifteen miles of Saigon.

The night of Tet is my first shift on the ICU side. Butterflies in my stomach are hard at work; even Sheila noticed and made a joke about my "flitting from bed to bed" before she left. I'm working with four corpsmen, each assigned four or five of our eighteen patients. One patient had a cardiac arrest shortly after report. He's still unstable, requires multiple IVs and an Isuprel drip to keep him going, and would rate his own nurse if we were stateside. Here we don't even have equipment to regulate the drip or monitor his heartbeat.

By one in the morning things have quieted. I've just hung IV antibiotics that were due at midnight and, to save time, those due at two o'clock as well. Along the way I've restarted infiltrated IVs but have run into trouble with a soldier whose only arm is so swollen that I can't feel a vein. Nor can I see one; his coal black skin hides any trace of blue lines. We have a cutdown tray for surgical insertion of an IV, but that requires a doctor, and we won't have one of those until things slow down in the emergency and operating rooms. And that might be too late to save this soldier's kidneys; it's already been two hours since he put out any urine. One of the corpsmen shows me how to find a vein in the ankle when none can be found in an arm.

I'm taping the precious catheter into place when a patient calls softly from the next bed. "Lieutenant?"

I glance at the bandaged face, turned blindly my way.

"What color are your eyes?"

When I went for my driver's license, deciding what color to put down had seemed a momentous decision. Now I can't recall what I chose.

"Blue-gray-green. It depends," I answer, finishing my taping and turning back to him.

The head straightens. "I've heard the guys talking. They say you're real pretty."

Before Japan the compliment would have made me blush. Now I laugh ruefully. "All round-eyes are pretty in this country."

"They say you've got strawberry blond hair down to your waist."

"That doesn't make me pretty."

"No, but you've got a beautiful voice. When you can't see, voices are important."

His desperate need for reassurance weaves through his words, and I wish for the hundredth time we had someone to provide that. A squeeze of his hand might help, but they're both wrapped in burn dressings.

118

"Thanks," I respond after a pause. "I'm sorry I can't stay to talk. I have to restart another IV."

I feel cruel, leaving him alone in his darkness, but must go back to searching for a vein. This is another swollen arm, but at least it's white—or as white as it ever is with deep suntans and ground-in dirt from battle—so I can see the whisper of blue.

A corpsman calls from across the ward. "Lieutenant?" His voice sounds shaky, worrisome as he's an old-timer on this ward.

I look up briefly to show I'm listening, then back to the arm. "It's the guy in bed fourteen." He pauses for my careful thrust of the needle. "It looks like his guts are spilling out."

The needle spurts blood. Snapping off the tourniquet, I attach the waiting IV bottle and tape it down, offering myself a silent congratulation.

Bed fourteen holds a huge black sergeant who looks as if a Mack truck couldn't run him down but who succumbed to a fist-size grenade. The corpsman is right. When I pull off the dressing, already loosened by the swelling mass, the sergeant's bloated guts spill out, awash in gray, putrid-smelling pus.

"Call the ER," I gasp, averting my head to catch a breath. "Tell them we need a doctor ASAP." ASAP—as soon as possible—will bring a doctor when there is no casualty in danger of losing life or limb. In a real emergency we ask for one STAT.

I pull over the dressing cart to clean and cover the shiny mass of intestines. I hope it will keep down the sickly sweet smell as well. As I work, I remember that part of my mother's last letter saying that soldiers in the newsreels look so happy.

This night marks the end of my first two weeks on the ward. All bets on how long I would last are now lost. My perception of hard work, of exhaustion, of tragedy is forever changed. They have become facts of life, the standard by which we live and work, and I wouldn't have it any other way. I'm where I want to be—as close to a combat nurse as I can be, although I wear starched whites and work in an old French school.

After my shift I find a notice in the mailroom. The presence of "our" nurses is requested at a party at a big brass villa. We can read between the lines, know this is a command rather than a request. Most of us detest the lecherous old men who expect us

119

to kowtow to their field-grade braid. Even their lavish air-conditioned villas and savory meals are not worth the insinuating brushes to our breasts and pats to our bottoms, their whispered hints that it would be well worth our time to get away from the crowd. The higher the rank of the leering smile, the more agreeable we're expected to be.

These ongoing, tacitly approved efforts to get us into bed really irk me—especially since any woman who "gets in trouble" is treated like a slut and threatened with a dishonorable discharge. Fortunately I'm no career officer. I pretend not to notice disapproving frowns over my refusal to perform, just as I ignore disapproving frowns for not cutting my hair.

What can they do to me? Send me to Vietnam?

The next week, on the day shift, I change my first colostomy bag since nursing school. Those more practiced than I am can do it in a few minutes, but I must work slowly to be sure there are no wrinkles where I glue the edges to the skin. Wrinkles mean leakage of stool onto the surgical incision, and that means infection.

This soldier was always singularly quiet while the bags were changed, his face chiseled in stone while his eyes focused on the stool draining from his abdomen. He never mentioned how he felt. Nor did anyone ask.

Last week he was stable enough to be sent to a surgical ward. There he struggled to the ward's roof, tore his intestines from the colostomy site, wrapped them around his neck, and jumped. Since the building is one story, he succeeded only in breaking a leg. But the intestinal damage is serious.

Now, half delirious from fever, he alternately screams that he's going to kill us for what we're doing to him or sobs pitifully for us to let him die; demands that we untie his hands or begs us to let him go. There is no psychiatrist to talk with him, no family to reassure him, no buddy to encourage him. Our solution is to keep him drugged.

On the day he's evacuated, I'm working in the recovery room. Across the nursing station, I watch the ambulance corpsmen sandwich him between two litters and tie his wrists over the top. Through the drugs he screams and sobs that he is not an animal, that we have no right to treat him this way. He's carried on a litter across triage, to the waiting ambulance. His cries carry through the silver swinging doors. We fall silent in the face of his terror and misery. His tortured pleas haunt us long after they have faded into the distance.

I slip behind the yellow curtain, and the large room dwarfs to an eerie silence—a sensation that never fails to follow me here. I hesitate, watching for the expectant's breath. When it doesn't come, I step within reach of his wrist. Just as I extend my hand, he draws a long, deep breath—not unlike the sigh of someone soundly sleeping. My heart is pounding; the hair on the back of my neck rises as a chill passes through me. Silence. Then five rapid, deep, gasping breaths and once again silence. Cheyne-Stokes respirations—terminal respirations. I've only read about them.

The soldier's face is deeply tanned, not discolored like so many in death. The dirt of battle gives him the air of an athlete at rest after a workout. Sweat streaks outline helmet straps along his jaw. He could be a high school football player after a scrimage in the mud—except for the misshapen form under the sheet, flat where there should be arms and legs.

"Lieutenant?"

I haven't heard the corpsman's approach and draw a sharp breath as I turn to face him.

"Did he move or something?"

I shake my head.

"Are you okay? You look like you've just seen a ghost."

I smile through tight lips.

He glances toward the expectant. "He ready yet?"

"No, but it won't be long." I take a deep breath, take back my composure. No matter how much I hate that this soldier dies alone, there is nothing I can do for him.

I return to the world of sound and bright lights. It's been an hour since that head injury was admitted. He's still in a coma, decerebrate with his back arched stiffly, his hands curled and toes

121

pointed, but one pupil is now fixed and dilated. He should go straight to surgery, but the only neurosurgeon is already operating.

We've got Mannitol running at a fast clip in hopes of keeping down cerebral edema. It's all we can do.

An hour later the other pupil is blown. When I dig my knuckles into his sternum to test his response to deep pain, he doesn't flinch. The neurosurgeon is still operating, and a second bottle of Mannitol is to no avail. The handwriting is on the wall. This soldier will die.

The casualties now claim my heart completely. Hours become days, and there is the sense there will never be an end to where we are or what we are doing. In a matter of weeks, short by peacetime standards but long in a war zone, I'm an "old-timer."

My mother writes:

> You asked me to tell you what's been going on in this world. Well, Winnie, with the way things are going I really think it would be a pleasure to stay in Viet Nam for a while to get away from world problems. . . . Our country is beset with a little bit of everything—beatniks, Vietniks, taxes, topless waitresses, CIA problems, [Adam Clayton] Powell's disgraceful conduct in Congress, Joan Baez and her concerts in Japan. Also the liberals, eggheads and Bobby Kennedy are leading us down the left path to ruin and a decadent country. I'm sorry that Johnson can't be a more positive president, wish he could just bristle up and be another Harry Truman. So Winnie, if you can entertain yourself without news and problems from here you will be happier. I told Frieda that you wanted to know what was going on in the world. She said, oh, I would love to be in some place that's old fashioned. . . .

Operation Junction City, the war's biggest offensive so far, starts the last week of this month. Once again it's against a Vietcong stronghold near the Cambodian border. Once again it's to ease pressure on Saigon. Once again it brings us many wounded. When no beds are left on either side of the ward, gurneys with incoming wounded are rolled between beds in the recovery room.

Blood has been accumulating on one soldier's head dressing as he awaits surgery on a gurney. The dressing covers his eyes, so it's impossible to check his pupils—standard procedure with head injuries. He's alert and moving all extremities, neurologically fine, but I need to try to stop the bleeding.

Cutting through the layers of Kerlix, I lift it from his face. With it comes his eyeball, dangling by a thin strand of tissue. I gasp, backing away from the mangled eyeball. My retreat is blocked by the bed behind me.

Gathering my composure, I pick up the eyeball with the blood-soaked dressing and place it on top of its socket. No matter that it's a useless motion, I haven't the nerve to cut it free, much less touch it with my bare hands.

The soldier's other eye is stuck shut with dried blood. He reaches up to feel his face.

"Don't touch it!" I cry in alarm.

His head turns toward my voice, and the eye falls out of the socket into my hand. I'm trembling as I replace it.

"Will I ever see again?" The voice of this nineteen-year-old soldier is calm, in marked contrast with my own, which has betrayed my horror.

I breathe deeply to control my tremor. "You've lost one eye. The other's covered with blood, so I can't tell about it." In nursing school we were taught never to divulge such information, that it's the doctor's decision to determine when and how much a patient should know. But what we learned then has nothing to do with what we do here. Doctors are scarce, and wounded soldiers won't be put off, insist everything be laid on the line.

"Don't turn your head. I'll get something to wash it."

I fear that I don't have time to do this, that another casualty will go into shock while I diddle around washing off dried blood. But when the eye proves uninjured, and he smiles brightly for still having one good eye, it's worth the worry.

A putrid smell follows another casualty through the swinging doors. I swallow against the nausea creeping up my throat, grab a wrist to check his pulse: weak and very fast. And touching his arm is enough to tell me that he's burning up with fever. The IV is running wide open. Good. I tear down the dressing on his abdomen and find his blood and guts swimming in a mire of green, foul-smelling, maggot-infested pus. This soldier lay too long in a rice paddy before he was rescued.

Dear Lord, when will all this end so we all can go home?

After work I join Alex at the Redbull Inn. He's at a table with Luke, an anesthesiologist with unruly blond hair and a boyish smile who strikes me as too young to be a doctor, much less married with children.

They're having a heated debate about whether or not we belong here, a favorite discussion for passing the time. Alex is adamant that it's absolutely necessary if all Asia is not to fall to the Communists. Luke argues that it's not Communists but Vietnamese peasants that we're fighting, that something is wrong if we have to bomb their villages and shoot their children to save them.

I stay out of it, having long since concluded that there is no end to this conversation. My job is to care for the wounded, not to ask why they exist. Nothing else matters save when the war will end, but that topic is never raised. What is there to talk about? Everybody wants it to end, but nobody sees an end in sight.

CHAPTER EIGHT

MARCH 1967:
Scorched Suns

THE first week in March Sandy comes with me to Singapore. The city sparkles. Its streets are paved and swept, its buildings painted and intact, its lawns sprinkled and mowed. Singaporeans are brisk and scrubbed and well heeled; they even run for cover when it rains as though it matters if they get wet. Tour guidebooks say not to miss the Parliament Building, an edifice to rival the finest of Western architecture, but just the fresh-smelling air and riding around in a taxi, meter included, impress us. And our hotel seems downright decadent with its limitless hot water and clean sheets, chilled fruit drinks, and gourmet meals. A real American breakfast and fresh milk have not yet come to this tropical paradise, but all things considered, we can survive those deprivations.

Above all, it's a relief to be away from everybody wearing uniforms and to shop without a ration card, to take long rides through a tranquil rain forest where houses stand on stilts and birds sing in trees, to meander through city streets without concern of curfew or fear of dark shadows, to be where children play instead of beg and people smile at us, even talk to us.

At lunch one day we talk for a long time with a middle-aged Malaysian man who joins us. He questions our being in Vietnam but, more than that, our tactics. He says his people had a similar situation when the British helped them fight the Communists in their jungles. He also says that we have no business in the jungles, that we'll lose many men and gain little ground. According to him, the only way we can win the war is to form detention camps for the people, then cut off their supply routes and bomb them.

From Singapore Sandy and I take a quick flight to Penang, a large island off the northwest coast of Malaya with a tantalizing mixture of Malaysian, Chinese, and Indian cultures. Our hotel lobby is furnished with massive rattan chairs and huge ceiling fans. Its walls open onto the beach and ocean on one side, lush lawns and flowering bushes on the others.

We spend our last afternoon in an airport, waiting for a flight to Singapore and from there to Saigon. Cows, goats, and an occasional bull graze along the airstrip. A cool breeze stirs through the open walls and sways the surrounding palm trees. Birds chirp and hop around on the chairs and the floor, careful to keep a safe distance from a sleeping cat. The cat, like many I've seen in Asia, has no tail.

In Vietnam every day is too long to think about and too tiring to remember. Here a week has passed in a flurry, and the war was nearly forgotten.

"Do Van Tap is a dirty old man!" chants Corpsman Watson, a lumberjack in his former life.

Do Van Tap nods and smiles toothlessly, pleased with the attention. Pointing a craggy finger at himself, he repeats "dirty old man." He got his reputation when a corpsman gave him a *Playboy* magazine to read. The old man's eyes got big as saucers, and he all but drooled on the pictures.

Do Van Tap is not a casualty but has chronic renal failure that would have a poor prognosis even in the States. He's on ICU because one of our surgeons dragged him over from a Vietnamese hospital for treatment of septic shock from bed sores so deep you can see his tailbone—the result of being bedridden for so long.

Our staff was incensed and demanded that he be sent right back to where he came from—or, at the very least, to a regular ward. When we're busy, we exile expectants to die alone because of shortages in bed space, staff, and supplies. Even when we're quiet, as we were when Do Van Tap arrived, we rush our own men to Japan in case there's a push. Why should this old man take up time and space denied to our own soldiers?

He needs ICU care, the doctor said, and he can't get it in a Vietnamese hospital. Besides, it's good PR.

When the tough old buzzard got better, the doctor grafted the bed sores, and, he claims, grafts require ICU care—no matter that the ward is now so busy that we're out of spaces in recovery room for ICU overflows, and we've gone on twelve-hour shifts six days a week to bolster our staff. He's the doctor; we have no choice but to obey his orders.

My resentment of the old man's presence is reflected in the nervousness of awake casualties, to whom he looks too much like old men Charlies they've seen in villages, and by the corpsmen, who tease him ruthlessly about GIs he's killed and VC buddies waiting for him to get out.

Do Van Tap nods and smiles toothlessly. I wonder if he knows what the VC are.

Operation Junction City, begun the last week of February along the Cambodian border, has put Victor Charlie in a fighting mood. Word has it that he's after Nui Ba Den (Black Virgin Mountain), not far from there.

Those who have seen the mountain say it's beautiful, rising abruptly from the jungle. From its top one can see for miles around—a coveted view. Folklore has it that Special Forces parachuted to its top one night and set up a permanent camp on the upper echelon. Periodically the Vietcong take offense and amass at the mountain's base until they are mighty enough to assault the camp. When they make their move, our men rain fire from the top and new forces are ferried in by choppers to the bottom, trapping the enemy in the middle. The fight ends when Charlie slips away as quietly as he has come.

How can he do that with our forces in way of his retreat? He's a slippery little bastard all right. Can't get him to come out and fight like a man. Does his dirty work at night and runs away at the first light of day or at the first sign of a real fight.

The mountain's name is a favorite source of speculation. I've been told it's a volcanic formation of black soils shaped like the reclining body of a woman. But some say it's named for the soldiers who are still virgins when they lose their lives there.

Either way many men have died for that view. And the Black Virgin's wounded are keeping us busy. We've cleared a bed, so I cross to the recovery room to see which of the overflows we should transfer. The silver swinging doors bang open with a sharp crack about the time I enter. Though it will not be my concern, I look to see what comes through the doors.

It's a soldier whose face has been blown apart. In its place are mangled tissues, dark with mud and clotted blood, and a single tooth garishly gleaming from a bloody mask.

Glum silence hangs over the ward. What is there to say?

From our homeland my mother writes: "Well, with Spring comes the demonstrations. I don't know what would bring our country together again unless 'war' was declared, which is a rather drastic thing as such. Bobby Kennedy is on the rostrum preaching 'Stop the bombing in North Viet Nam and come to the Peace Table.' Well, that slush has been handed out so much by the Vietniks, Reds, etc. and I don't see how he can think this country is so naive as to listen to him. . . . "

Peter is in that world, stationed near Denver and the Rocky Mountains. His letters say he's waiting for me, but it's been so long since we saw each other that I'm uncertain how I feel. I know I hardly ever think of him anymore. Then, again, I don't think much about anything anymore.

In this world Chris drops in to visit about every two weeks. My attraction for him is growing, and I suspect he wouldn't fly all the way from An Khe unless he felt the same. But our friendship and Peter keep getting in the way. And then there's Alex, who is getting more serious than I want. I no longer need him to bolster my confidence at work, but I dread being put on the meat market again. So I tread a crooked path, seeing him more than I want, giving in to amorous hugs and kisses to keep him from straying. At least it's not too often; the one reason to be grateful for lack of privacy here is that we are seldom alone.

The one place for privacy is the Starlit Roof, but I have never mentioned that haven to Alex until tonight, when a padlock on the door barred me and I enlisted him and Luke to wrestle with it. The knife I bought in Malaysia as a present is being ruined in the process.

How dare they deny me my refuge, the only place where the cacophony of the street is muted to a sane level, the only place where the stench of exhaust fumes, human wastes, and death is not suffocating? The only place to remember that stars still exist?

The brass has determined the roof is unsafe because of "enemy encounters in the immediate vicinity." What a joke! Another arbitrary command meant to make my life miserable.

It doesn't take long for my disobedience, openly admitted in a note left with our first-floor guard, to bring a response. I'm brought before some rear echelon mother fucker major and informed that charges are to be brought against me for theft of Army property (the lock), destruction of Army property (the hinge), and endangering fellow officers through willful removal of security measures at an unguarded entrance to our quarters.

I laugh at the very idea.

"Watch it, Lieutenant," the REMF growls, "or I'll write you up for insubordination."

"Oh, that's good!" I answer. "Maybe they'll send me stateside for a court-martial! I could use a change of climate!"

He caves in with an exasperated expression that clearly asks what women are doing here anyway. "All right, Lieutenant. I'll make a deal with you. Just stay away from the roof perimeter where you might be seen." A slight pause. "And no more than three at a time up there."

"Oh, now I get it. You don't care about enemy encounters; you just discovered how rickety the roof is. As if the whole god-damned building isn't just as rickety!"

"Not the whole building. Just the roof! And anyway, it's not your concern!" Leaning on the desk with his fists, he glowers. "Do you or do you not accept the terms?"

Right. I don't want to blow a good thing. Smiling, I bring myself to attention. "Yes, thank you. May I go now?"

He nods that I can leave.

The TV goes right into the combat areas and shows the whole show. It just doesn't seem real. I feel as though I'm watching an updated WWII movie or at least Korean—those boys going into those tunnels and all the fighting—seems to me the cameramen along with those reporters are in an awful spot right in the middle of the action with nothing but a pencil & camera. The VC are young (the prisoners) but some of our men looked like 16 years old—such baby faces and none of them even seemed to be aware of newsmen or cameramen. Oh, boy. Last week it showed our men getting hit and the medics and the helicopters etc. But the whole thing seems as though it should be acting instead of the real thing. . . .

No, Mama. The war's real all right. And those cameramen don't always get away unscathed. We have a UPI reporter, a head injury, on the ward right now.

Our new corpsman groans and calls, "Lieutenant!" I turn to see him holding up a new admission's leg that sags like a rubber hose. Run over by a friendly tank, it's what we term squash meat, not a hint of intact bone, much less a knee. There must be two pints of blood on the gurney under it.

Fascinated, the corpsman lifts the leg first with one hand, then with the other, undulating it like a Slinky toy. The wounded soldier, propped up on his elbows, watches in horror.

"Get a unit of blood." My command carries a calm assurance that there's nothing to worry about. "Hooper!"

The inevitable "Yes, ma'am," comes from behind me as I tighten the tourniquet.

"Ten milligrams morphine for this man." The corpsman returns with the blood. I nod to hang it.

Hooper returns empty-handed. "The card says he had morphine in the field."

"Then give him more!" I snap.

"Yes, ma'am." He turns to lope back.

"And stop calling me ma'am! I told you it makes me feel old!"

"Yes, ma'am." He darts into the nursing station.

"Cut off those fatigues, and put a sheet over him," I order the corpsman as I turn to check on other patients.

"Wait!" cries the Slinky-legged soldier. He stares at me with terror in his eyes, eyes that don't seem to belong in his face—too haunted for someone just out of high school. "What about my leg?" It's a cross between a demand and a plea.

I breathe sharply. The other thing wrong about his eyes is that they aren't dazed as they should be. Where is Hooper with that morphine? "Stop worrying about your bad leg, and be grateful you've got a good one." My voice is without sympathy, though he will surely lose that leg.

His stare burns through my back, but I ignore it. I don't have time to hold hands. The silver swinging doors bang open. New business. I run to meet it.

It's a bloodbath, blood pouring from everywhere. The dressings are soaked with crimson blood; the fatigues are clotted with burgundy blood. Puddles of it ooze over the gurney. More runs from bottles into both arms, but anyone can see they won't be enough. Luke, the anesthesiologist, is with him, pumping oxygen into the endotracheal tube with one hand, blood into an IV with the other. When the casualty coughs, blood spews into the breathing apparatus.

"Get the cart!" I shout at the corpsman. Shit, what I wouldn't do to have Mott or Watson with me. This new corpsman didn't even look up when the doors banged open. "Move it!" I growl at his ambling figure, and he makes a break for the crash cart. No way will he last in this place.

The left leg has a gaping wound with crushed bones. Blood spurts with each heartbeat. Curse the field medic—the tourniquet isn't tight enough.

"Get some O_2," I order the corpsman when he brings the cart. Then to Luke: "Where are the surgeons?"

131

"Went to eat." He suctions blood from the breathing tube. "They never radioed this guy was coming," he says without a hint of his boyish grin. "They left me with a new nurse who went to pieces. I sent her to find them."

Fuck. What a mess. There's blood everywhere. But the right leg is more promising for another IV. "Cut off his shirt." I prod the corpsman. Oh, Mott, where are you now? Watching TV from your dining-room table? The right arm is in good shape. Compound fracture of left arm but no heavy bleeding.

"Two more units of blood," orders Luke. The corpsman looks to me to see if it's okay.

"For Christ's sake, yes!" Easy, Smith. He's new. Precious blood is oozing from hundreds of shrapnel wounds, but there's nothing to do about that. There's no major chest wound, so why so much blood in his lungs? Luke reads my mind, stops pumping long enough to help me turn him onto his side.

His fatigues are so clotted they can't be ripped, and they're slow to give way to scissors. My thumb aches, but instinct tells me I'm getting warm.

"Jesus!" We stare into a deep wound the length of the soldier's back, the blood pouring out. Trembling, I stuff packs of fluff dressings into the wound. When I do, my hand is engulfed by warm, sticky tissue; blood trickles down my arm. Fuck. I should've put on gloves. "This guy's in a world of hurt!" My voice transmits the alarm I feel. "Where the fuck are the surgeons?"

As I feverishly stuff dressings into the welling blood, seconds tick by in small eternities. Open and stuff, tick and tuck, open and stuff, tick and tuck, open, tick, stuff, tuck. Tick, tuck, tick, tuck.

The corpsman returns with two units of blood. Not nearly enough. "Get four more! Run as if your life depended on it!"

No more fluffs will fit into the wound. We turn him onto his back, hoping the pressure will stop the bleeding. Now try for that IV. My shaking stops, and I jam the needle into a whisper of a vein. We have to get more fluids into him.

Alex bursts through the doors, another surgeon close behind. Tape down the new IV; disconnect the oxygen tank. Luke squeezes the ambu and Alex pumps blood as they push the gurney toward the silver swinging doors. Their khakis are already spattered with blood. Looking down, I see my whites are soaked red.

"Call the MPs for fresh blood," Alex yells, and I dash for the phone. I know he's checking the dog tags, wait for his shout of "A-pos" as I dial the number.

Let GIs with type A positive blood beware this night. If they're stopped by MPs as they roam the streets, their blood will be volunteered to save the life of a fallen comrade. I've heard of such waylaid soldiers fainting at sight of the big bore needle in the emergency room. I have never heard of one complaining. Thanks to them, this soldier will live.

In this land the vernal equinox has little meaning other than the fact I turn twenty-three.

Hello Birthday Girl. It doesn't seem you should be as young as you are when I look back on your activities of the past few years.

. . . Am sure you are anxious to get away from Vietnam, am sure it must feel as tho' you are in a hole and can't get out. . . . I sometimes feel that the people there are really hopeless. Then I think about the Japanese—the old beliefs that they had up till and a while after the WWII business. . . . So now Japan has become civilized but Vietnam, especially South Vietnam, has been under such difficult rulers—Japanese, French and even their own war lords etc. . . . Maybe they are their own people and should learn to live together and stew in their own fat, but unfortunately other countries have become involved and who's to say where it will ever end. It will be a while before the U.S. can pull out and leave them to themselves.

. . . I can imagine how tired you are. . . . The most interesting nursing is hard work, routine is so dull. Your days must be filled with the feeling of so much accomplished. I was never in your circumstances but got that feeling in the hospitals I worked in so often—with you it's an everyday occurrence. This must be a good feeling. . . .

As is the way of things here, the war abruptly grows quiet, and the flow of wounded slows to a trickle. Because there's no way to know when things will pick up again, we continue sending patients stable enough for the trip to Japan. As a result, our census is down to eleven in ICU.

This night we've turned off the overhead lights, a luxury for awake patients that's impossible when it's busy. Our luxury is having time to sit in the nursing station and shoot the breeze.

Watson's just told me about the bets taken on how long I'd last when I started to work here. I allow as how I should get the pot since I clearly won the bet. Watson points out that I didn't take the bet, and I'm just about to counter with my never having been given the opportunity when there's a shout from the ward.

We leap in unison and run into ICU. But we can't see worth shit with the lights out.

"Over here! Where the fuck am I?"

It's the Green Beret captain, a triple amputee. When we move toward him, combat reflexes send him diving for cover, and he slams into the side rail. A split second later comes the stricken "Oh, my God! My arm! Where's my arm?" Another split second and, with rising despair: "My legs! What happened to my legs?"

The voice propels horror through the darkened ward, cracks the veneer coating my heart. We stumble forward, then stop in front of his bed.

"Who the hell are you?"

"It's okay." The voice comes from outside myself, perfectly calm. "We're here to help you."

"Everything's cool, man," adds the corpsman. "We're on your side." Unconvinced, the Green Beret searches for his weapon.

"I'm a nurse, Captain. This is an American hospital. You're just waking up from surgery. Everything's fine."

Fine? The cliché ricochets in the back of my head like a bad pun. It'll be months before he's fitted for artificial legs. And then crutches will be a problem with an artificial arm.

Suddenly the ward is brightly lit, all of us blinking and frowning at one another. Good thinking, Watson.

"Where the hell am I?" The captain's breaths come in gasps,

and it's easy to see that he's feverish. Bad signs so soon after surgery.

"Third Field Hospital. It's safe here. You can relax."

His attention shifts to his bandaged stumps, where legs were just a few hours ago. "What about my legs?"

I can feel every awake patient listening. "You were hit by a rocket." The tone of my voice says clearly that there's nothing more to talk about.

"What about my arm? Where's my arm?" His voice demands an answer, but I can think of none. "I want to know, Lieutenant, what you did with my arm and legs." His words have the sharp edge of steel, his eyes the level gaze of a commander. He has switched our roles from patient/nurse to captain/lieutenant.

"I didn't do anything with them." Still, my voice does not betray me. "This is the ICU. You came here after your surgery."

His eyes tell when the words sink down deep. As weak as he must be, he sits up to reach for his leg stumps. He loses his balance and falls over, causing the thigh to flap helplessly. His eyes fill with horror at the sight, and the flapping grows to a frenzy.

We just stare, unsure how to help him, until he begins beating his stumps on the side rail. We jump into action, Watson moving to pin him down, I running for Librium.

"What's that?" he demands when he sees the syringe.

"Something to help you sleep."

He recovers his captain's authority. "Get away from me. I will *not* be doped up."

"Please," I coax in my best nurse's voice. "You'll feel better with it."

"I said, Lieutenant, to get away from me. It's my body!"

I take a step closer.

"Stay away from me, you bitch. And call this mongrel off. You're not going to dope me up! Goddammit! I said keep away from me! I'll get you court-martialed for this!" The leg stumps flap frantically as he tries to kick me away.

"Please, I'm trying to help you," I say, plunging the needle into his arm.

He spits on the floor with contempt. "You bitch."

Silently I beg him not to hate me.

"Fuck you." His voice cracks. "Fuck all of you! Get away from me, you mother-fuckin' shit-eatin' ass suckers!"

Watson and I pull him up in bed, check his dressings, and straighten his sheets. I can't meet his challenging gaze. He has won, in a way.

The other awake patients stare at me as well. Only their expressions are blank, dazed.

Fuck it. Why can't he just let us dope him up like the others do, put off facing what he has to face? There'll be plenty of time for that later. But I know I'm wrong. It's quiet, and I have time to talk if he's ready for that.

Whatever happened to the nurse in Japan who cared about patients as people, not just as wounds? The nurse who didn't give Seconal to keep them quiet?

I turn away from those questions, busy myself with cleaning out the medication cabinet and tidying the nursing station. Then I mix bags of IV antibiotics for the next twenty-four hours, a night shift chore. It's so quiet I have to pinch myself to stay awake. One more bag of fifty million units penicillin to prepare. One more night and then my day off. Just one more night—

A resounding crash shatters the quiet.

Watson beats me to the Green Beret captain. "What the fuck do you think you're doing?"

"Getting your attention" is the slow, deliberate answer.

"Well, you got it! Now what the fuck do you want?" At six feet two-inches and two hundred pounds, Watson towers over the bed. The Green Beret captain is undaunted, ignores him.

"Well, if it isn't the long-legged, yellow-haired, blue-eyed, wickedly armed nurse lieutenant. Where's your weapon, Lieutenant? Behind your back?"

"What was that crash?" I ask Watson.

"The urinal." He nods toward the dressing cart. "The son of a bitch threw it."

I slump perceptibly, nod for Watson to start damage controls. We can't do morning dressings until the cart has been restocked.

The Green Beret captain is smiling. He has created more of a stir than he expected.

"Captain, please understand. Supplies are not plentiful, even in Saigon. And contrary to what you seem to believe, we are not the enemy." When there is no response, I sigh. "I'm here, Captain. What can I do for you?"

"Get me some water. I haven't had a drop to drink since I got to this place."

I dread what's coming. "I'm sorry, but we have to be sure you don't have any internal injuries before you can have anything."

"I don't have any internal injuries, Lieutenant. Get me something to drink."

"You'll have to wait until the doctor examines you."

He tenses. "Then get the doctor."

"Captain, I can't. The doctors need to sleep while the hospital is quiet. They make rounds at 0600 hours."

"And what about my men?" he explodes. "Do you think they're sleeping? There's a war going on in case you didn't know!"

I stare at him a long moment, then nod toward the ward. "I can see the war all around us, Captain. And if your men are brought here, our surgeons will be prepared to help them because they've rested tonight."

I can look him in the eye now, meeting his gaze until the menacing captain struggles to hold back tears.

It's been twelve hours since he went into surgery. Surely he would have signs of a hot belly if injuries had been missed during his surgery. He has a fever, but I'm developing a sixth sense about these things and feel certain it's from his lungs—not uncommon after a long anesthesia. I put my stethoscope to his abdomen to make sure his intestines weren't put to sleep as well. His bowels growl.

"Truce?" I ask, handing over a small cup of water.

Squinting at me warily, he rolls a sip on his tongue.

"Take it as though it had to last all day."

He smiles with tight lips. "I can handle that."

Thinking to do him one more favor, I grab a sheet to cover his

137

stumps. When we're busy, there's a shortage of sheets. But we're quiet.

It's a flag waved in front of a bull. Throwing it to the floor, he shouts. "They're my goddamn legs, and I'll tell you if I want them covered!"

Watson comes on the run, ready to deck the guy. I hold up my hand. "Everything's under control. Just a misunderstanding."

The captain cries as I give medications, change morning dressings, and clean tracheostomy tubes. I can't shut out his quiet sobs or his words, spoken over and over again: "What am I going to do? What am I going to do? What am I going to do?"

Awake patients listen, too, staring at the ceiling. A few cry with him, their tears falling in the gray morning light.

Skip breakfast. It's been so damn hot this week that I'm better off going straight to bed, getting as much sleep as I can before the generator is turned off and our Casablanca ceiling fans shut off with it. Only my sleep isn't long in the making when somebody blows up the paint shed of the Lambretta factory.

It's attached to the hospital, in full view of our Sunbaked Roof. All the maids run to watch the action, their singsong chirping over my head. I can't sleep, so I traipse to the first-floor refrigerator for a tray of ice—worth the six flights even though the ice will melt before I've finished my first drink. Sipping on a rum and Coke, I daydream about spending this Sunday morning at home— a cup of coffee over a newspaper, all the doors open with a cool spring breeze and birds twittering.

The slow spell drags on, wounded coming by ones and twos, sometimes none at all for several days in a row. Most go to wards from the recovery room, and the ICU census slides down to four patients. A breather, during which we can take lunch breaks and go back to eight-hour shifts.

Without work to exhaust me, I become restless. Visits to warrior buddies up north are out; things are hot up there, and they can't get away. And it's been so long since I've been to the orphanage that I'm too cowardly to face the nuns. So I sign up for the medical civil assistance program, "Med Cap," for treating Vietnamese villagers.

Evidently some muckety-muck thinks more highly of this activity than of orphanage trips. We travel in Jeeps rather than a deuce (my back thanks him), and we have an armed escort. We pass through landscape that looks like some huge construction site after the bulldozers have torn through and before anything has been built; the earth is scarred and brown, glaring under a blistering sun. No one tills the land, no one peeks from a farmhouse, and only a spattering of children run through village streets.

I'm beginning to worry that we have somehow gotten lost and strayed into VC territory when they appear—a long line of what must be everybody for miles around, waiting for us at the only adobe building I've seen since Saigon. Children tumble over our vehicles before we've come to a complete stop.

"Cigarette, GI? Cigarette?"

"Get out of here, kid. You're too young to smoke."

The makeshift clinic is a single room, bereft of furniture except for an examination table, a stand for operating instruments, and a big wooden desk with a straight-back chair. A blackboard on the far wall indicates this is a school, but there are no desks or books and, not surprising, no running water or electricity.

The desk serves as our triage area, where prospective patients get a cursory exam while they're interviewed by a doctor and interpreter. They are then directed to the appropriate "station." One station, basins of soapy water, is for scrubbing the lice-infected scalps of children—something we did for children at the orphanage as well—and infected "jungle" sores on their legs. Outraged howls of babies occasionally pierce the room, but children over two are remarkably quiet.

Another station, an Army green box, is for dispensing medicines: vitamins and malaria pills for everybody; antibiotics and Kwell for just about everybody; tetanus shots and vaccinations for many. More unhappy babies, but lollipops make for smiling children. A third station, a sheet on the floor, is for examining pregnant women, although judging from all the kids in this country, I'd say they don't have much of a problem in that department. Last but not least is a station with the examination table and instrument stand for performing minor surgeries.

Everywhere there are flies. Wherever you go in this country, there are flies. They pass through screenless windows and open doors, ignored by the natives while we foreigners futilely whack at the air. They flit and hover around the stations, buzzing and whining. The minor surgery station is a big hit; flies go into a near frenzy when pus is drained from an abscess. Surgical instruments are a frequent landing site.

A woman with shrapnel popping through her skin has come to get the fragments pulled out. A young boy who lost a leg to a land mine has come to get it debrided and dressed. A skinny old man has come to have a bullet removed from his leg. We have no anesthesia, so he gamely bites down on a piece of cloth with true John Wayne grit. The bullet was "Made in the U.S.A."

We don't ask any of the obvious questions. If we did, no one would come back. We just watch the old man limp out on his walking stick with enough clean dressings in hand to last until our next visit.

Young men and women, other than those pregnant or with a child in tow, are conspicuously absent. It's not surprising. Everybody knows that these villagers are Vietcong, that only those too old or too young (and those needed to care for them) are left in the villages—and that the dressings and medicines we hand out will wend their way to our wounded enemies.

"How can they be so two-faced as to take our help in the day and kill our men in the night?"

"Why not, if we still offer our help in the day when they're still killing our guys at night?"

Another riddle to forget about.

CHAPTER NINE

APRIL 1967:
Where No Birds Sing

OPERATION Junction City is back in action. The push is on

The corpsman and I are changing the bed of a soldier racked with pain and high fevers, whose eyes gaze emptily at the ceiling. Rubber catheters have been inserted into his abdominal abscesses to flush out pus. Every four hours we attach IV tubing and run in an antibiotic solution. After thirty minutes suction is attached to the catheters to suck up whatever has not spewed out of his open incision. By then he's soaked in green putrid mire and smells like decayed stems of flowers left in a vase too long.

Gloves are too precious to waste on niceties, and the pus makes our hands slide on the sheet. But it's not the sickening smell or the slime that concerns me this early morning. It's his respirations, shallow with nostrils flaring on inspiration. I grab an oxygen tank and setup for the corpsman to put on him and dash over to the nursing station to call for a portable X-ray and leave a message for the doctor in the ER. Back on the ward I check pupils on a head trauma to see if Mannitol has helped; they're still dilated but now sluggishly reactive. Then I check a back dressing we reinforced to see if the soldier is still bleeding; a small patch of bright red has broken through, but it doesn't look bad. The double amputee in the corner is crying from phantom pain, but his pain medicine will have to wait; the portable X-ray machine has arrived.

I hurry over to tell the X-ray technician it has to be done with the patient sitting up, no matter how much of a problem that poses. The soldier's respirations are still shallow, but his nostrils are no longer flaring; the oxygen is helping.

Next, suction that gurgling tracheostomy before grabbing the 0600 IV antibiotics to hang. I'm at the medication cabinet when I hear the sound of glass breaking and a loud "Holy shit!"

Running back onto the ward, I see the portable X-ray machine has crashed into a chest tube bottle. When I start to clamp the chest tube to prevent more air from getting into the chest cavity, I find the tube has been yanked out of the patient's chest. "Christ! Get me Vaseline gauze!" The corpsman runs for the new dressing as I tear off the old. Glancing at the patient's terrified eyes, I smile a reassurance I don't feel—something I'm quite good at by now.

Chest tubes are normally inserted by surgeons, but all of them are tied up in the operating room. I've never done it before, but this man's chest produces enough pus to fill a gallon bottle every day. If it's not suctioned out, he'll drown in it. Besides, the incision and route for placement have already been established. I tell myself I can handle it.

The corpsman is reading my thoughts, runs for the new tube on my nod. It slips into the chest like a well-greased rod, though I'm not certain it's in the right place. I have the technician take an X ray, so one of the surgeons can check it along with the abdominal abscess patient when there's a break in the operating room. That'll be after my shift ends. Now it's time to gather numbers for morning report.

I'm in the middle of report when James Garner stumbles into our utility room. No one has to tell me who he is. For those who don't recognize him, the fact that there's no rank on his spanking new fatigues and that an entourage trails close behind him are good hints that he's a big shot of some sort.

"Pardon me," flashing a Maverick smile, "I was told I could smoke in here."

There are too many of us for him to maneuver to the sink, so we nod toward the closest ashtray—the bedpan flusher. Then, uncertain whether or not to continue with report, we silently stare as he lights up. The Army can be funny about such things.

"Am I interrupting something?" he says as though it has suddenly dawned on him that we might be here for some reason.

We assure him it's no problem; we understand about nicotine fits. He makes stabs at conversation—how hot it is for such an early hour, what a problem it is to find a place to smoke, how the folks back home sure do appreciate the fine work we're doing. We say nothing, just nod and smile politely. We've been in-country too long for small talk.

With an uncertain grin, he throws the half-smoked cigarette into the hopper, thanks us, and is gone.

I trudge back to the tower, climb the six flights, throw my uniform on the floor for mama-san, and take a squat bath. I go over the hump this week. It doesn't make the days or weeks any shorter, but passing the halfway mark is reassuring. If I can make six months once, I can make six months twice.

My mother writes: "Looks as tho' a lot of changes are being made in Vietnam. Hope they step it up and get it sort of on the way to the finish. From what I see & read we are on the plus side now, altho' with it we are really having a lot of casualties. How do the patients feel about being out there, are they for or against? It seems the debates are getting hotter in this country. . . ."

The patients? Most are too sick to feel much of anything. The rest care about their buddies, not politics.

If I could, I'd be a man. Then I'd be a chopper pilot and fly every day. Up there are no thoughts, only sensations—the cool air rushing past and the serenity of a blue-green world unfolding far below.

Chris and his Good Buddy have whisked me away to a party at An Khe. We flew at three thousand feet, safe from enemy fire, which is standard procedure with a woman aboard. When we land, the pastel shades of sunset have faded into the gray of dusk. The base is hot and dusty and smells as if its outhouse refuse is being burned.

"Is it possible to go for a walk?" I ask Chris, gazing at the tree line beyond the perimeter. It's so inviting, so lush and cool-looking, it seems worth asking.

"What? Out there?" He smiles, and his pale blue eyes crinkle. "Now, why would anyone want to go out there?" he says with that exaggerated midwestern drawl.

"To sit under a shade tree and listen to the birds."

His gaze follows mine, lingering at the tree line for a while. "Not here, little lady. You know what happens to ground pounders going for walks in the jungle. Besides"—he smiles through serious eyes—"there ain't no birds out there."

"I thought there were lots of birds in the jungle."

"Not here."

"Too hot in these parts," Good Buddy says. "They don't like bein' shot at, so they flew the coop a long time ago. It's the perfect cure for crows." His dark eyes glint. "Problem is, folks back home just wouldn't appreciate it."

They laugh at the little joke as I scan the tree line. No birds in all those trees.

"Cheer up," Chris says, squeezing my shoulder. "The only bird that matters is that big silver Freedom Bird to take us home."

"A birdcall I'm gonna hear real soon," adds Good Buddy. He's now officially a short-timer; he's got less than two months left here.

The club is already crowded with officers, and among them are two American women. Thank goodness, for they'll relieve the pressure on me to entertain the troops. Not that I mind so much, just that I prefer spending time with Chris and Good Buddy.

We women are meted out one per table, dining scrumptiously in true First Cav form. After dinner I nudge Chris by the elbow and nod toward the door. He reads my message loud and clear, leaves with me to stand guard while I'm in the four-holer.

As it turns out, it's occupied—and for a long time. "I thought women were the ones that take forever," I say woefully.

"Sounds like they got a regular coffee klatch going, all right. Want me to clear 'em out for you?"

I shake my head. I haven't outgrown the modesty I learned as a child. I don't want everyone to know I'm going to the bathroom. "Are there any friendly bushes around?"

"No bushes. But some tall grass in an overgrown rice paddy. Will that do?"

We head for the other side of the outhouse. On the word "go" I race to get out of earshot, tearing at buttons on my fatigues along the way. I hear Chris warn that I shouldn't go too far, squat behind a clump of grass, and let go.

A low-flying chopper barely catches my attention—choppers are liable to pop up anywhere at any time—but the flare it drops sure does.

"What next?" I hear Chris groan.

Then comes a sound I've heard before—on those tapes our patients in Japan recorded: the *thwhoop* of an incoming mortar.

I'm listening with mild fascination when the whole world explodes and I'm thrown backward.

There's another *thwhoop* as I scramble into my pants. Chris is calling, but I'm too terrified to answer him. Oh, Jesus! I've got to get out of here, but I can't move, can't even crawl!

The next explosion changes that. I bolt like a scared jackrabbit and run smack into Chris. He yanks me back to the ground and snaps, "Move it," as he drags me along.

Thwhoop! The world shifts into slow motion, every blade of grass blazing a small eternity into my mind. Chris is saying something about a bunker.

Oh, yes. Please, dear God, a bunker.

He shoves me down three steps into a hole with a dirt floor and sandbag walls above waist level, populated by two other soldiers and the other two nurses. Blessed be the bunker. Outside, the hillside is erupting with guns, cannon, mortars, and rockets. Choppers tear at a sky blazing with flares.

I can't stop shaking, can't even take a deep breath. Chris is asking if I'm okay. I nod numbly, wondering vaguely if I'm bleeding from someplace—like those casualties who never saw it coming, didn't feel a thing.

Chris has to leave, but the two soldiers stay. Everything, everyone flicker in the orange-yellow of flares, float eerily in and out of shadows. The soldiers peer past their weapons, which poke through the crack between sandbag walls and roof. They wear the comforting deep tan and well-worn fatigues of warriors who have been in-country for a while. One draws from a cigarette hanging at the corner of his mouth, not bothering to flick the ashes. Both lean against the sandbags in an easy manner that says we're too far from the action to worry. My attention shifts to the other nurses. None of us says a word. I wonder if I look as terrified as they do.

My shaking subsides, and when I'm no longer thinking about it, a deep breath fills my lungs. The noise abates to sporadic bursts of machine guns and the roar of low-flying choppers. The flares persist for a while. When one guard props his rifle to light another cigarette, I know the attack is over.

One of the nurses is crying softly while the other chatters giddily. A stinging in my arm draws my attention to an abrasion coated with dirt and dried blood. When I move to check it out, my whole body aches. The other guard now props his weapon against the wall to light a cigarette. Their eyes are still riveted on the perimeter, but it's obvious from their relaxed poses that they don't expect to see anything.

It occurs to me maybe I should see if they need my help out there, but it's a cinch I'm not going to. Why am I flashing on patients at Camp Zama? Why not Third Field? Speaking of which, I'm off limits. Fuck. I'm in trouble deep if I can't get back in time for work.

That nurse has stopped crying—thank goodness. What is there to cry about? And that other nurse has stopped yapping. A good thing. If she'd gone on much longer, I would have told her to shut up.

Someone opens the small door above the steps. Chris is smiling down at me. I try to stand but am too weak. He leans to help, easily pulling me to a standing position. His strength flows into me.

The party resumes as though nothing ever happened, save the added attraction of a spectacular light show through the picture plate glass window. Flares glow brightly when they burst, flicker surrealistically as they dim, throw dancing shadows in the hillside as they falter and fall before the next burst. It's enchantingly, disarmingly beautiful.

Back in Saigon, back on nights, I bless our *Casablanca* fans that let me sleep through at least part of the steamy days. But when the generator is turned off at ten o'clock sharp, sweat tickles me awake. I lie in my soggy bed too exhausted to get up but too miserable to sleep until two, when the generator resumes work and the fan's breeze dries me off and its whirring lulls me back to sleep.

We once had a cold snap, temperatures plunging into the sixties, and as luck would have it, I was working days and sleeping at night. When we realized there was no switch to turn off the ceiling fans, everyone ran around scrounging up wool blankets and fatigue jackets. I wasn't fast enough to land either and just shivered through the nights. As for the Vietnamese, they vanished into thin air. Those who dared to venture out of doors scurried hunch-shouldered from one cover to another. Too bad they can't just put the whole goddamn country into a deep freeze. We could all go home a lot faster.

We've long since come back to steamy tropical days, but now some VC have gone and blown up the generator. Naturally I'm working nights and sleeping in the day. The big brass are all up in arms, can't understand how this could happen, but we're not surprised. This is Claymore Tower, so called because it's been mined so many times. And from his position at our gate, the MP guard can't see what's happening on the other side of an eight-foot-tall generator situated on main street where hordes of gooks pass at all hours of day and night.

Ah, well. The MPs don't talk to the brass, and even if they did, our leaders don't listen. Once the generator has been fixed, it'll all be over and forgotten. But that won't be for several days. Right now I am staring miserably at the useless fan from my bed when Sheila comes in to say our bicycles have arrived.

It was she who enlisted buyers for the bikes at ten bucks apiece, including pumps. Sandy and I jumped on it, envisioning the end of haggling with pedicab drivers and beggar urchins.

Forthwith five of us climb upon the beasts and head down a back street, giggling and teetering precariously. Vietnamese stare in amusement.

Our merriment is short-lived. Little by little and one by one, our tires deflate. Worse yet, the pumps don't work. We're furious, our anger spurred by the natives laughing at us as we lead our crippled bikes back to where we bought them. We mean to kill the dirty little yellow low-down bastard who sold us the bikes, but of course, he's nowhere in sight, and no one knows where to find him.

For three days I ride the monster to the swimming pool anyway, pumping its tires going and coming. Finally I pass it off on a street urchin. Both of us wear big smiles as we go our separate ways.

I'm sure you make quite a happy picture biking to swim. I know you have to work hard and you are in a serious business and I'm so glad you can take time to really enjoy yourself, have fun. The serious part comes later when you get in the slow down part. . . . I don't like your being in Vietnam but I would like less for you to be in New York City. . . .

Saturday's "Peace March" was such a disgrace to this country and I'm ashamed that this thing happened to be exploited all over the world. . . . I think Martin Luther King has let everyone see his Communist side. As I told you, the FBI has pictures of him attending the Communist school many years ago. As far as the Nobel Peace Prize—like everything it seems it means nothing anymore. . . . Martin Luther trying to make the Civil rights and get out of Vietnam theme the same has really set the most dependable Negroes and whites against him. . . .

Nancy Sinatra is here in miniskirt, high-heeled knee-high boots, and heavy makeup to cheer up the troops. I hate her flaunting herself to sex-starved soldiers, but the corpsmen and awake patients are eating it up, grins spreading as she clacks down the ICU aisle, bending at each bedside to kiss a cheek, with her long hair tumbling down and her miniskirt hiking up.

She acts embarrassed by the men's scant covers, eliciting an apology from one patient for his state of dress. She gazes too long at one of our amputee's stumps, causing him to joke that he never liked shopping for shoes anyway. When I explain that a patient on a respirator is unable to speak, she squeezes his hand sympathetically with a wavering smile. When she speaks to a head injury, I explain he's in a coma and can't answer her. Her smile disappears, but she continues gamely to the next row of beds, skipping those with head dressings. When she kicks a urine bottle, I gasp. She backs away in alarm, hands flying to her face. I apologize for scaring her, say just to be careful of bottles on the floor.

She's starting down the third row when eyes brimming, she turns and makes a hasty retreat through the silver swinging doors, her attendants close on her heels. Awake casualties call to her not to worry, that they'll be okay. But once she's gone, the ward is more subdued than usual.

Now I'm really pissed. If she couldn't handle it, she shouldn't have come. The last thing these guys need is more worry about how their mothers and sweethearts will react when they get home. She drops into this stinking hellhole dressed to the hilt and chauffeured around in a sedan, sleeping in an air-conditioned hotel and eating at French restaurants. After a few days or weeks she'll hop a jet back to the States, and everyone will say what a great thing she did. I want her to stay for a year, to climb six flights of steps every day and sleep in one-hundred-degree weather, to wash her hair in a trickle of water and eat at the Redbull Inn, to ride around in Jeeps under the broiling sun over stinking roads. I want Miss Nancy Sinatra to walk through mud puddles in those boots, wear that makeup while sweating it out on the ward, parade around in that miniskirt without a private car and attendants to protect her. I want her to see wounded straight out of the field with pussy wounds or blood pouring, expectants behind the yellow-curtains screen, the body of a soldier you've tried hard to save ready for graves. Then, if she still could, she might have cause to cry.

* * *

Though I'm assigned to the recovery room today, all the routines have been cleared and no incoming are expected. The war is taking a break, but the ICU is jumping, so I've crossed over to help.

A Bouncing Betty shredded this soldier's groin. After being treated at Cu Chi, he was taken to Tan Son Nhut to catch his Freedom Bird, but the flight nurse found his temperature too high and his blood pressure too low. She forwarded him to us.

Baby flies hovering over him tell part of the story. Under the dressing, where his genitals should be, a pus hole wriggles with maggots. The Cu Chi hospital must be catching hell to evacuate such a wound.

I tell myself not to think about what I'm doing. Just scoop them out, sop up the pus, irrigate the wound, and hide it under a dressing.

"Jesus! Is that what my legs look like?" another patient cries, noting the tiny flies hovering over his leg casts.

"No way," the corpsman snickers. "Your legs are bonier."

I shoot the corpsman a glare. Though we're inured to bare bones, they're not our bones. And the casualty may not be ready for our brand of humor.

I'm distracted by the sharp bang of the silver swinging doors to the recovery room. Business for my side, and I hasten over. I slow to a measured stride when I see only a corpsman with the gurney. Any hope of saving the man, a pre-op with blood-soaked field dressings on his head, would have brought doctors with him.

"Fuckin' yellow-bellied bastards!" the corpsman fumes, swinging left toward the yellow curtains. "Stinkin' cowards shot him from the back, and he wasn't even armed! Fuckin' yellow—"

"Not there," I break into his deprecations. "Here." I'm standing in an empty space on the empty ward.

The corpsman shakes his head, pointing at the bloody head dressing as if I haven't understood, or the casualty might hear if he spoke.

"Yes, I know. I want him here," I nod. Shrugging, he swings the gurney in my direction.

"You busy in ER?" I ask, and he shakes his head no.

"Good. Help me get some clean Chux and pads under him."

"You feelin' okay, Lieutenant?"

"I feel fine. I just want to clean him up."

The corpsman grimaces as he lifts the expectant from the blood-soaked sheets, first on one side and then the other, while I cut off the clotted fatigues and spread pads the length of the gurney.

I thank the corpsman and nod that he can leave. Before he does, he takes a last look at the expectant's face, the empty fixed and dilated pupils, a warrior shot by a Vietnamese cowboy haunting the red-light district for prey.

"Such a shame! He never even had a chance to take the slimy little bastard with him!" is the corpsman's parting shot.

I wonder vaguely if it would be less of a shame if he had but say nothing.

I begin meticulously to wash away the blood and grime from his face. He strikes me as a Yankee though I can't say why. I rewrap his shattered head in clean white Kerlix, change the pad under his head and shoulders. I see by the look of those soft muscles that he hasn't been in Vietnam very long. I cover him with a clean sheet. As I do, a corpsman from ICU steps into the ward to see what's taking me so long.

"Are you crazy, Lieutenant? They'll just undo all your work at graves."

I dart him an icy glare. He shakes his head and leaves.

When I turn my attention back to the casualty, I realize he's not breathing. Sigh. I hadn't wanted my work undone quite so quickly. I fleetingly wish that his family could know he has not died alone, then vaguely remember that before I came here, I assumed they never did.

Before returning to the ICU, I head for the latrine outside. Sheila is climbing down from the deuce; this must be Tuesday, and they're returning from the orphanage. She flashes her dimples and waves that she has something to tell me.

"The nuns have asked that you see Le Ly," she says when she reaches me. "She hasn't eaten in several days. They're hoping a visit from you will cheer her up."

I never consciously decided to stop going to the orphanage. Every week I heard from those who went that Le Ly had been waiting for me with her sketch pad in hand, that once everyone had climbed out of the troop carrier, she forlornly walked away. Every week I thought I'll go back next week.

Then one week she didn't bring her sketch pad to greet the carrier. The week after, she didn't greet the truck at all, and the nuns said she was more withdrawn than ever.

My heart constricts, remembering her arms around my neck, her silence, her serious eyes and shy smile. But I don't cry. I never cry anymore.

The following week I'm back on evenings, and on Tuesday I climb aboard the troop carrier for the orphanage.

When Le Ly hears I've come, she runs away.

She is never again seen at the orphanage. Nor am I.

Another week has passed, and I'm back on nights, when Retta flies down from Qui Nhon. Fuck the gawkers. It's too damn hot to go anywhere else, so we've come to the officer quarters' pool.

Retta is much thinner now, too thin for her wide mouth and wide-set eyes—eyes that are much older than before. And her lightheartedness is gone.

"Sometimes I try to imagine what Miss Novicky would say if she saw the way we do things here!" She chuckles bitterly, drawing deeply on her cigarette.

She's talking about her old nursing instructor, whom she has described to me before—the prototype for the ever-professional nurse with just the right amount of makeup, every hair in place, stiff starched uniform, and nary a scuff mark on her shoes. To her, appearance was every bit as important as medicine. I laugh. Miss Novicky would have a shitfit over my hair popping out of its French twist, my yellowed whites with adhesive tape holding seams and hems together, my cracked dusty shoes, and worn-out shoelaces held together with knots.

"Our instructors used to have a dipshit if we threw dirty linen on the floor," I recall. "Here, when we're busy, I throw dirty dressings on the floor, and they just lay there until someone has time to pick them up."

"Shit," Retta laughs. "When I'm marking chest tube bottles, I just sprawl out on the floor. Sometimes it's the only time I get to sit down for the whole fucking shift."

"Maybe I should try that in my whites." I laugh.

We're sitting at the edge of the pool, sipping on warm rum and Cokes that we've mixed from a full bottle of rum and a six-pack of Cokes brought with us.

Our laughter fades. "This place sucks," I say, stamping out one cigarette and lighting another. "My family writes that I should enjoy life and make the most of it here. They think this is some kind of vacation."

"The Real World." Retta sighs. "Girls in my hometown are jealous because we've got all the men over here."

"You've got to admit, the odds are in our favor. I'm dating four guys right now." Squinting at the sun's reflection glaring off the pool water, I add, "Only I still feel so goddamned lonely."

"I know what you mean. You don't dare get too close because you never know from one shitty day to the next if you'll ever see them again. And when you do, there's no way to know how they'll feel about you back in the World."

We don't speak for a while. Retta lights up again. I finish my drink. Several officers who live here are splashing in the pool, clearly trying to attract our attention. We ignore them.

"When we were busy," I think aloud, "I thought my pissy moods were because I was always so tired. But now that we're quiet, I'm more depressed than ever." I take a long drag on my cigarette, blowing rings as I exhale. "What I hate most about quiet spells is spending our time and equipment on the gooks. When I came, I had all kinds of ideas about helping these people. Now I fuckin' hate them so much that it turns my stomach to have to take care of them."

Retta nods. "War changes the way you think and feel about everything." She holds her cigarette smoke for a long while, lets it out with a sigh. "I'm not sorry I came to this stinkin' excuse for a country, but I'll sure be glad when my year's up."

"Yeah, only when I think about going home, I wonder if I can ever get back to who I was before I got here."

We fall silent again, swinging our legs in the pool.

I pour myself another drink. "Sometimes I don't give a shit what anybody thinks. I figure if a guy doesn't like what I have to say, he can take a hike. Other times I lead a guy on when I really don't give a damn if he ever comes back."

"All part of growing up in this hellhole," Retta says, emptying the rest of the rum into her glass. "I see the changes in everybody. At work and the club. In guys we knew in Japan."

"Especially in the grunts," I agree. "You can see the year's toll right here—between the nineteen-year-old coming and the twenty-year-old going."

We are quiet, watching the sun's rays lengthen and deepen over the pool. As they always do in this country, our thoughts turn to the dream of going home, back to the Real World—a place where there will be no more wounded, no more death, no more war. Please, no more.

CHAPTER TEN

MAY 1967:
My Soul for a
Soldier's Life

THE silver swinging doors burst open. New business.

We jump to find out what it will be, but I know long before we reach the gurney, my stomach churning with the smell of charred hair and flesh: a crispy critter.

Fighting back the dread, I help roll the soldier to the space closest to sterile supplies, the place saved for the critically wounded who are given every chance to live.

"Phosphorus flare backfired in a chopper," Alex states flatly, his right eye batting in a frenzy.

At least it's not napalm, I think, not realizing that phosphorus does not self-extinguish but keeps burning deeper unless cut out. It's as bad as, if not worse than, napalm.

My nod to Banks, the corpsman I never thought would make it in this place, is all it takes to send him running for a respirator so the anesthesiologist can return to triage. Alex is already plucking out pieces of fatigues from the soldier's chest.

I'm mesmerized. In go the forceps, clamping shreds of cloth

and charred tissue. *Clack,* as the forceps drop barbecued meat stripped from the bone, into a silver basin.

Alex orders, "Wescodyne and scrubbing brushes."

Banks goes for the supplies. I'm unable to move; I can't even remember what I'm supposed to be doing. I tell myself not to watch, but my self doesn't listen.

"Tell the pharmacy we need three percent IV saline solution," Alex says, not looking up from his work.

Banks has gone for the Wescodyne; the other corpsman is caring for the routines. Still, I don't move. The forceps go in again, out again. Another bit of fatigues and strip of meat clacks into the basin with unnatural slowness. It's a horror show in slow motion.

"*Smith!* What the fuck's the matter with you!"

Tearing my eyes away from the forceps with a piece of meat dangling at the end, I look at Alex. He's frowning, worried that I'm having a breakdown. I take a deep breath to steady myself, but the stench threatens my equilibrium. This is no time to fall apart. I snap out of it. I call the pharmacy, then gather sterile supplies. Don't forget an IV bottle for the almost empty one hanging. Get another IV started; he needs lots of fluids.

All the burns are above his waist. Banks cuts off the pants to insert a Foley catheter so we can measure urine output. The blood pressure is low. We remove the boots and start IVs in both legs. Blood pressure better. Draw bloods from the femoral vein for hematology and chemistry. I'm grateful the patient is unconscious.

The swinging doors burst open again. Luke is pushing through another burn victim. This one is not unconscious. He's screaming silently around a breathing tube in his mouth, writhing in pain. His face is charred; his nose and ears are burned off; his wild stare is clearly sightless. I yell for Hooper to bring us some morphine, but he can't hear me from the ICU.

Burns on this soldier extend to mid-thigh. Banks cuts off the fatigue pants to insert a Foley. Blood pressure is low. We take off the boots and start IVs. The blood pressure improves. I yell louder for Hooper. I draw bloods for hematology and chemistry.

Luke is squeezing air and pumping blood into the second soldier. He tells us there are more burns in triage, and one is in bad shape.

"Fuck. We can't save all of them," Alex says, swiping unconsciously at beads of sweat on his forehead. "If we try, we won't save any of them." His voice shakes in marked contrast with the calm efficiency of his hands, never pausing in their work. Crimson mingles with the dark brown of Wescodyne, dripping from gurney to floor. The metallic smell of blood combines with the sickening odor of charred hair and flesh.

"This one's breathing on his own, but there's nowhere to tape a tube," Luke says. "If you whipped in a trach, I could get back."

For a moment I don't think Alex is going to answer.

"Fuck it," he finally spits out, ripping off his gloves.

I run for the tracheostomy tray, then open it on a bedside stand. Luke motions for me to hold the breathing tube, but the patient is thrashing around, needs to be sedated.

"Hooper!" I scream, determined he will hear me.

"Yes, ma'am," he answers from the nursing station.

"Morphine now!" The second burn jerks, and I instinctively grab his forehead to keep his head still and protect his airway. My hand slides across the charred skin, tearing away slimy tissue. My stomach churns. Steady. Don't look at his face. Don't look at your hand. Don't take a deep breath.

I motion for Banks to hang another IV bottle on the first burn patient. Hooper shoots the second with morphine. Banks is starting the Foley on the second soldier, his face gray as he fingers the charred penis. I feel like I'm going to faint. Look up. That's better. If only I could take a deep breath!

Alex is ready to do the trach, nods for me to hold the soldier down so he can't move.

Ready, I nod back. I will myself not to think about the smell or the slippery, charred head. At least he's quieter with the morphine on board.

We can hear the third burn's screams of agony before the silver doors swing open, the bang of the incoming gurney in unison with the hiss and bloody cough of the tracheostomy. I tie the trach tube around the soldier's neck, then pull the breathing tube out from between his charred lips.

Hooper has heard the new screams and runs over to help with

this third admission. The pint of blood on the trached second soldier is almost gone. I wipe my slimy hands on my uniform so I can pump in the rest of the blood and hang saline. The corpsman caring for the routines takes time to check vitals on the second burn while Banks runs for another oxygen tank for the screamer. At least this third burn has three IVs and a Foley already in place. I wonder if his bloods have been drawn.

The doors slam open again. Please, God, not another burn!

But God has long since forsaken this place. This one looks shocky. Check his blood pressure. None! I send the remaining corpsman for six pints of blood while I pump in plasma. Where's all the blood on this gurney coming from? Alex comes over, finds a huge gash in the soldier's leg, puts on a tourniquet. Corpsman Banks comes back with the oxygen tank only to find we need yet another. What's taking the other corpsman so long? Hooper has given the screamer morphine, and he's quieter. Good. Here comes the other corpsman. Hang blood on everybody—two on the one in shock and two on the one Alex was debriding.

The doors bang open again. Despair clutches at my throat. We can't handle any more. I look up to see Luke—alone. The last burn must've bitten the dust. Guiltily I realize I'm grateful he's dead. I've traded my soul for one less soldier to worry about.

"Ready for the OR," Luke says, and Alex tells him to take the one in shock. They're rolling him out as Banks returns with the now-unneeded oxygen tank. Hooper has to give antibiotics on the ICU side but will be back. The other corpsman goes to check the routines. Hang more IVs and get the bloods drawn. Banks is checking pressures, so I sign out another post-op. We've settled into push gear, each of us part of a well-oiled machine.

No more pre-ops arrive, the routines are cleared, and the last of the burns is rolled to the operating room before the first post-op returns. I should eat while I can, but I'm not hungry.

Sheila's on the ICU side, starting an IV. Sometimes it feels as if we spend half our lives starting IVs. We decide to keep the burns in recovery, so our work loads will be more even. If there are more incoming and the recovery room can't handle them, we'll rethink what to do.

Shit. We're barely halfway through the shift, and I'm already tired. It's going to be a long night.

No matter how tired, we must eat. After the shift, at breakfast in the Redbull Inn, I'm joined by a dustoff chopper pilot who wants to know how the burns are doing.

It was his chopper that responded to a call from the Special Forces team for emergency evacuation of a severe chest wound. When he set down, the jungle erupted with Vietcong, and the whole team jumped into his chopper. They lifted out of there, but at several hundred feet, about the time they thought they were home free, a phosphorus flare misfired inside the chopper. He thought they were all goners until one soldier grabbed the flare and jumped—ablaze as he plummeted to the black earth.

"Damn crazyass fool." The dustoff pilot sighs. "All he had to do was throw it out the goddamned door." Then, with a slow shake of his head: "But he saved my sorry ass right along with theirs."

I can't think of anything to say. People hardly ever say I'm sorry here. There's always something to be sorry about, and once you started, you could never stop. "That's war," people sometimes say, but he doesn't need me to tell him that.

"I'd sure appreciate your gettin' that soldier's name from one of his buddies. I'd like to pay my respects when I get back to the World."

If you get back, I think tiredly.

After breakfast we repair to the bar, where I gulp down a Rob Roy. Then another for good measure and another to keep dreams at bay.

At work the next day there's an IG inspection. We sneered when they told us to get ready for it. Now we're furious. The inspector general has disallowed our use of silver nitrate, on the ground that it mars the walls and floor with black spots.

We explain that patients do much better with silver nitrate than with copper salve, our previous treatment for burns. There are fewer infections and no renal shutdown, which used to happen from copper poisoning.

Where are the scientific papers to that effect?

We don't have papers. We know from experience that the patients do better.

That's not good enough. The inspector general needs proof.

We turn to the dialysis team to support our word that copper salve causes renal shutdown. Their word isn't enough either. In the end silver nitrate is allowed on the condition that messy burn patients are hidden behind curtains in back of the recovery room and that we protect walls and floor with tarps. Oh, and cultures of the tarps must be taken and come back negative—free of any organisms. We're in the Army and must comply, but at least we've bought some time to find the papers.

Back at Claymore Tower, our fans are on the blink again, and I can't sleep, so I pick up a *New York Times* Sunday paper that arrived with a letter from my mother. According to the *Stars and Stripes,* we're winning battles and our casualties are light. But the scuttlebutt among soldiers is that we're not winning much of anything. And one infantry officer told me that tallies of casualties are based on total number of men in a battalion. Very tricky. A whole company may be wiped out, but casualties for the *battalion* are light.

To my amazement, the *Times* has nothing about the war on the front page. Yet there's a whole section on fashions. My romantic notions about war have fallen by the wayside, and now my love for my country is slipping away.

My mother writes:

"It is such a monotonous life, day in & day out in the house with a dog & cat. Sure would love to go back to nursing, but working in N.J. hospitals would be impossible for me. Around here the patients are fed in paper plates and cups, and I'm sure a lot of other things would bother me. I wouldn't mind working in N.Y. part time, but I'm afraid of traveling around the city. . . .

"I guess it's well that you are in nursing, Winnie—it seems such a problem for teachers these days. Honestly, the teacher strikes, the children today are such a breed—I'm so glad I don't have any children in schools. . . ."

Winter, or what passes for it here, is on its way. Every morning and afternoon come freshening rains. I'd forgotten how green the palm trees are without layers of dust, how sweet and cool the breezes of tropical storms. The stars are brighter than they have been for months, crickets and lizards sing their hearts out, and baby geckos scamper across walls after mosquitoes, doing their job, saving us from bites and keeping down malaria.

The big drawback to winter is walking through an inch of mud instead of dust. My white shoes and nylons are a joke by the time I get to work. Today my starched whites are a joke as well, thanks to some smartass driver who thought it was funny to splash me with his Jeep.

Right now none of that concerns me. Corpsman Banks has just checked the blood pressure on a routine and is giving me a look that says trouble.

The first step is always to speed up the IV, but goddammit, it won't speed up. Banks goes for equipment to start a new IV while I search for a vein. The casualty is so swollen I can't see or feel anything. Why is he so swollen?

When all else fails, we go for the jugular. "Blood," I order tersely when Banks returns, not looking up. "And tell Hooper to call ER and have a doctor come check this guy out."

I glance in the other corpsman's direction. His row looks good. I stick the needle in the casualty's neck, slide the catheter into the vein, and tape it in place. Hang the blood. Now Banks can help me turn him onto his side for a look at the back wound mentioned in report.

Shit! There must be two pints of blood in those dressings. Banks holds him as I run for nitroglycerine sticks to cauterize the bleeders. I yell to Hooper to see if a doctor is coming. He yells back yes. Back to the casualty. Take down the dressings to locate the bleeders.

The silver doors swing open, but there's no urgency in the bang. It's Alex with a routine. He flashes a smile, heading in my direction. "You called?"

He checks out the wound, deftly cauterizes bleeders. It's not helping enough. I slide past him for suture materials.

"This guy needs ICU." His right eye twitches.

Banks returns to our other patients. I inform ICU of an upcoming admission, check out our new routine, come back to see if Alex needs help. Everything is under control. There's time to change dressings on that burn patient.

I begin unwrapping Kerlix dressings around his hand. A maggot wriggles into view, then wriggles back under the gauze. My stomach churns as it always does when I'm confronted by those slithery larvae. I stand back as though they could jump out and get me, unwrapping the rest of the dressings with my arms extended. The top of the hand is ulcerated with a pocket of pus squirming with maggots.

"Get rid of those things," I demand of Alex.

"They're the best thing for him," he says. "They clean the wound by eating pus. And they make your work easier; you don't have to change the dressings as often."

"Maybe," I reply, "but I can't stomach them. I'll change his dressings every two hours if that's what it takes."

So he plucks them out, one by one, with a pair of forceps.

The next day they're back. Alex refuses to spend more time for the sake of my weak stomach. Goddamned slithery little fuckers. How the shit can they survive all that silver nitrate?

Sliding behind the yellow curtain screens, I see one expectant gazing calmly at the face of another expectant on a gurney next to his. Has there been some dreadful mistake? I take the man's blood pressure: eighty systolic. What's he doing behind the screen? I speed up his IV, pull back the sheet to check out his wounds.

At first I see only one arm missing at the shoulder. Then I see why he's here. Where there should be chest wall are only dressings saturated with coagulated blood.

The soldier watches with a look of vague curiosity. I replace the sheet.

"Water," he whispers.

"Sure. Anything else?"

"Hurts. Hurts like hell."

"I'll get you something for it."

I'm so tired. I wish I could take a break, but as I come out from behind the curtains, I notice an IV that's almost empty. And I remember that one routine has poor urine output and see another's leg dressing is saturated with blood.

I find Hooper in the medication room. I ask for fifty milligrams of morphine.

Hooper raises an eyebrow to ask if I'm sure.

I'm sure. I slip back behind the yellow curtain, hold the expectant's head so he can sip the water. He runs his tongue over his parched lips, nodding gratefully.

"Sorry, no ice," I joke.

"No sweat, Lieutenant. Thanks." He smiles weakly.

"This is pain medicine," I tell him, sticking the needle into his IV tubing.

He smiles again. "You're an angel, Lieutenant. Maybe now I can get some rest."

My hands tremble slightly, but I do not hesitate.

When I look into his face to say a last good-bye, his eyes are already closed.

Oh, what I wouldn't give to sit in the shade of a tree with a tall glass of iced tea!

As busy as we are, there's a command performance in ICU. A general is here to pin Purple Hearts on the patients, something none of us has seen done before. The journalists love it. So does the general, smiling benevolently upon wounded soldiers as he angles Purple Hearts to be conspicuous in photographs.

He starts at bed one, ceremoniously reads off name, rank, and serial number as if he were playing a part in some cornball flick. Only there's a glitch. The general can't pin the medal on because the recipient wears no pajamas. Seeing the general's fluster, the wounded man holds out one hand, nonchalantly salutes, and smiles.

As the general approaches the next patient, the general's aide hisses, "Straighten up, soldier!"

"Yes, sir!" barks the soldier, whipping out a brisk salute.

We grin, give him the thumbs-up. But the moment is lost when the general passes up his buddy, wounded a few days later in another skirmish.

"Hey, you forgot the Dude," he calls.

No, someone says, they haven't forgotten. The Dude was hit by our side. There are no Purple Hearts for those wounded by friendly fire.

The next recipient has not been in-country for long, easily seen by his lack of a tan. Racked by high fevers, horrified by the green pus oozing from his belly, and terrified of dying, he believes the general is a priest come to say last rites. Eyes wild, teeth bared, he swipes eratically at the IV bottle hanging between them.

The general is obviously ill at ease. He hands over the medal and backs away, glances with irritation at the bedside fan blowing over them to reduce the soldier's fever. He runs his hands down his chest to his waist to straighten his uniform, then squares his shoulders.

On to a head injury, trached and on a respirator, who gurgles while the general is making his spiel.

Enough of this bullshit. Breaking ranks, I roll a suction machine to the bedside and turn it on. The soldier's secretions slurp through the catheter into the tubing. I rinse the tubing with water, turn off the machine, and replace the catheter in a bottle of Wescodyne.

"Is he all right?" the general asks anxiously.

The soldier's right frontal lobe has been blown away. If he lives to get back to the States, he may never get out of the hospital. But I say nothing of these things. I focus on the patient rather than face the general. Answer: "Yes, sir."

We're way behind in our work when I return to the recovery room. I admit a routine rolling through the doors, check his IV, grab a bottle for his Foley, suction his trach, hook his chest tubes up to suction, note his dressings are dry and intact, insert a stomach tube, change the oxygen tank.

The corpsman says something about a falling blood pressure on the middle third bed, and I can see from here that the shoulder dressing is soaked. I grab some silver nitrate sticks and take down the dressing to cauterize the bleeder. They're rolling in another patient from the operating room.

It's too much for us, see if the ICU can take one of the overflows. They don't have an empty bed. To make space, they roll one of their patients behind the expectant screens.

Did I blow the whistle too soon? Could one of the other nurses have done better? It doesn't matter. I'm the only nurse here.

I step behind the curtains to see whom I have banished to certain death. Another soldier with fixed and dilated pupils.

I jump and whirl at a touch on my shoulder. "Has he slipped away yet?" Sheila asks matter-of-factly.

"No." I'm ashamed to be caught just standing here after having asked for help.

"I come here, too," she says quietly. "I hate them dying alone."

A few days later the war is temporarily called off in our neck of the woods. After a week the time-out catches up to the ICU. Going back to eight-hour shifts would get us nowhere, so we opt to stay on twelve-hour shifts and take more days off.

By luck of the draw, I'm the first to have three whole days off. Sandy and I visit the Central Highlands, a world apart from Saigon's steamy flatlands.

Yesterday we delivered supplies pilfered from our hospital's stockpile to the Army hospital in Pleiku. The war is hot up here, and the hospital needed anything and everything we could scrounge up. We would've done it for nothing, but such is not the custom. Our bartered agreement has landed us cooler jungle boots, small sizes being abundant here while there are none available in Saigon.

Our tour of the Army hospital was followed by a trip to downtown Pleiku—a typical GI town with bars, bars, and more bars. Then a quick stop at a hospital for Montagnard villagers, run by foreign civilians. Converted from an old French villa, the single ward is a dingy room with tiny windows in thick adobe walls. Most patients, including one with her nursing infant, lie on cots. Patients in traction have World War II hospital beds with reed mats laid across the springs instead of mattresses. Casts are old and dirty by our standards, dressings untaped, and uninfected patients have no sheets—all to conserve precious supplies. About the only thing they have in abundance is flies.

I asked why a hospital just for Montagnards. I was told the Vietnamese won't admit them to their hospitals and the Army won't let them into ours unless they are war-wounded. They are natives here but are unwelcomed by their rulers—official and unofficial. We hear stories of South Vietnamese pilots dropping leftover bombs on their villages.

Today we are driven by Jeep through forested hillsides with no one but ourselves in sight, on our way to a Montagnard village. The visit was arranged by a Pleiku nurse to see one of her former patients, the six-year-old son of the village chief. The boy had been riddled by machine-gun fire during a VC attack.

The village is nestled in a valley with tidy gardens enclosed by stake fences. Homes are raised on stilts built mostly of bamboo and covered with thatched roofs. A few are milled lumber with corrugated tin roofs, a clearly American influence.

Children's laughter floats through the village. Leaves skip across the ground in breezes. Villagers come out to greet us, waving and calling to Pamela, the nurse from Pleiku. I'm a head taller than Pamela and Sandy, and they are that much taller than the villagers. I'm so tall, explains Pamela, that they thought I was a man until they heard my voice. A barefoot woman with short-cropped gray hair, smoking a big fat cigar, asks the chief to stand back to back with me. He refuses, causing more laughter.

Back from the crowd, village life goes on. A lean, muscular old man wields a machete, notching a post that will be used as a ladder. A young woman with an infant slung across her bare chest works a loom, weaving a bright colored intricate design much like the sarong she wears. Young men dress in American fatigue pants, belong to the Civilian Irregular Defense Group that fights beside our Special Forces.

The chief's son bears a scar the length of his chest and abdomen. He leads our procession to his house, built of split bamboo. When his mother sees the Pleiku nurse, she smiles warmly and invites us to come in.

Daylight filters softly through the walls, and it's surprisingly cool. Bedding, baskets, and pottery are neatly stacked along the room's perimeter, creating a sense of spaciousness although the room is small. The fireplace is central to the space, with an iron kettle hanging over simmering coals.

The chief's wife produces a ceramic pot that causes an excited stir among the crowd in the doorway. We are about to partake of rice wine, rarely shared with outsiders, in honor of Pamela, who helped save her son.

The four of us—Pamela, Sandy, our driver, and I—sit in a semicircle around the jug with our hostess kneeling opposite us. Every child in the village must be in the doorway, shuffling positions to take turns watching. When the plug is pulled, they cheer—perhaps for the horde of cockroaches that spews from the jug and scatters wildly across the floor. I resist the urge to bolt upright, watch with relief as the roaches fall through the cracks in the floor. When I risk a glance at my companions, they look as alarmed as I must look, and we all burst out laughing. Delighted, the chief's wife and onlookers join in.

Next, she punches a fist into the jug to push down the grain. Roaches scramble up her arm and tumble down her back. When she's satisfied that the fermented grain is sufficiently pressed, she adds water to the top of the jug. Then she inserts a hollow reed to the bottom of the jug as a straw and places a stick with an inch-long perpendicular branch over the top of the jug so it penetrates the brew. Smiling with a slight bow of her head, she nods for Pamela to drink through the reed.

Pamela takes a cautious sip and smiles wanly, turning to pass the reed to Sandy. No, no, our hostess shakes her head. She must drink to the end of the inch-long measuring stick.

As Pamela bends to the task, our hostess encourages her to drink quickly. This time, when Pamela passes the reed to Sandy, her smile is anything but wan.

Our hostess replenishes the jug with water until the rice wine again reaches the brim. Sandy takes her turn, wearing the same grin as Pamela when she passes the reed to me. It's a long, hard draw to get the wine from the bottom of the jug. No one has to tell me that I'm wearing the same silly grin as Sandy and Pam when I pass the reed on to our driver.

Hours go by. My sides hurt from laughing so much although I haven't the slightest idea what's so funny. After too short a day our driver notes with alarm that sunset is upon us. In this land dusk is short-lived, and the Vietcong come out to play in darkness. We rise hastily.

The evening air is fresh and dewy. I'm flooded with the memory of summer evenings in North Carolina. What is it that makes me think of Tom? And Japan—romping on the beach with Peter, a big red sun setting over the water. His face vanishes, and I'm a barefoot child who has never known war, chasing fireflies in the backyard.

The next morning Sandy flies back to Saigon. Head in hand, I hop a flight to Qui Nhon to spend my last day with Retta, celebrating the marriage of her hoochmate's brother (any excuse for a party will do). I've brought a suitcase of champagne, unavailable there but plentiful in Saigon.

Celebrations are under way when I arrive, rum and Cokes before lunch and champagne after. Sprawled across Retta's bed, I confess I envy their quarters—ground-floor accommodations twice the size of our room and a refrigerator as big as the one for all of Claymore Tower. Most of all, I savor the smell of ocean.

It's close, they say, but not *that* close. Still, they have to agree it's not such a bad life.

The next day I return to Saigon's steamy flatlands. Evening finds me back with the casualties.

One of our soldiers' names is Guerrero. It means "warlike," but it's a misnomer. He's slight of stature, bloated and racked by high fevers. Delirious and terrified, he's more like death warmed over.

Pus so inundates his abdomen that wire sutures have been sewn to the wound edges to keep his intestines from spilling out. They are clearly visible through the gaping incision, awash in green putrid-smelling mire. So far antibiotics haven't worked. We must irrigate and suction to keep infection at bay.

If the wound isn't enough to kill him, his pneumonia may be. His lungs are so clogged by yet more of the green pus that a respirator cannot deliver him sufficient oxygen for more than fifteen minutes at a time. Forty-five minutes out of the hour we breath for him with an ambu bag, taking turns when our hands ache and cramp, until the dusky color of cyanosis subsides and his terrified gasps give way to a few minutes of blessed sleep.

When awake, he is in constant pain, but we dare not give him pain medicine, fearful he might not wake up. For we have determined this man will *not* die.

It's his good fortune that we're not busy or we could never devote so much time to him. And he does get better. From forty-five minutes we wean him down to thirty, then fifteen, then five minutes an hour on the ambu bag. Rejoicing that he has been saved, we evacuate him to my old stomping grounds in Japan.

Friends there write to tell me when he dies.

CHAPTER ELEVEN

JUNE 1967:
Emergency Room
and Triage

By the first week of June even the trickle of casualties from land mines or booby traps has ground to a halt—partly because the war is quiet but mostly because we've been dropped to the bottom of the lineup for receiving wounded. Two new hospitals with their own helicopter pads have opened in Long Binh and taken our old position.

Our ward doesn't require two nurses, so I've come to relieve the emergency room nurse for lunch. As they don't have *any* patients, the sarge has gone to eat as well. It's downright eerie not to have another living soul within earshot, never mind sight. Even the walkway beyond the silver doors, left open for ventilation, is empty.

I'm seated at a wooden desk that serves as the nursing station, reviewing the latest letter from my mother:

> . . . I guess things are the same in Saigon—I still get a laugh when I think of your crazy mixed up place of living.
> The U.S. certainly has its problems, but then I guess with

everything in disorder—politics, religion and crime, etc.—
we are in pretty fair shape. This country has more or less led
in the scientific and all other progressive education, and it
will take time for our country as well as the more or less
primitive countries to catch up. I do think if we didn't have
so many eggheads around trying to press all this on the masses
we could get along better—

"Where's the sarge?" startles me from my reading. A field sergeant, whose fatigues are coated in a thin layer of red dust, eyes
me uncomfortably.

"At lunch. Can I help you?"

"Anyone else here?"

I shake my head. "I'm afraid you're stuck with me for an hour
or so. Everyone else is at lunch."

He glances around the room uncertainly, shuffling his feet.
Then, speaking so softly I can barely hear him, he says, "I've got
the drip."

"The drip? What kind of drip?"

"Look," he says, "I gotta talk to the sarge. Or a doctor."

Alex is just around the corner in ICU. He has less than a week
left in-country, a short-timer, and his feelings are mixed about
the distinction; he worries stateside medicine will be boring after
the work we do here. My feelings about his leaving are mixed as
well; although our relationship has gone farther than I want, I'll
miss him.

When I relay the drop-in's problem, he laughs uproariously.
"How," he demands with an incredulous shake of his head, "did
you ever manage to get this far in this man's Army?"

"Just cut the crap," I fire back, "and tell me what's so funny!"

"The drip," he explains, stifling his laughter, "is what the men
call gonorrhea."

It's a side of the war we don't see in ICU, but it's commonly
treated in the ER. I follow Alex's instructions and give the young
sergeant a hefty shot of penicillin, not bothering with records.

As planned, Chris and Good Buddy are waiting for me at the
Redbull Inn when I get off duty. We're headed to An Khe for

Good Buddy's farewell party. His Freedom Bird flies in two days.

Good Buddy has bad vibes about this trip, and superstition is a powerful god of warriors; premonitions are not disregarded. He's riding it out as a passenger, facing me with his back to Chris and a new copilot. As the chopper fires up, he gazes out the open door. His dark tan and easy grace are just as they were when I met him. Yet he's changed: The daredevil glint in his eyes now replaced by the look of someone too worn-out to hope for the future. It's good he's getting out of this shitty excuse for a country, and as much as I'll miss him and trips to An Khe, I'll be glad when Chris leaves, too. That won't be long, another two months.

Shifting my eyes to watch the ground fall away, I empty my mind to enjoy the sensation better. This will be my first night flight; the sun is already low in the sky. The Huey's hum and vibrations feel like old friends.

We're barely up when there's a sharp *thwack*. We've hit something! The world whirls out of control until we collide with the ground, jolting to a stop.

I clutch my seat, vaguely aware of the whine of a dying engine. I look to Good Buddy for an answer.

Blood streams down his face, his eyes staring in startled disbelief. He's a death mask with eyes that still live for a moment, then falter. I can't move, can only stare back at the now-vacant eyes.

Ever so slowly his body slumps forward. Tiny geysers of blood pump out of the top of his head. It takes long seconds for my mind to see what my eyes tell me. The top of his head is missing. I want to scream, "Stay away from me!" But I can't make a sound.

In slow motion the topless head rolls forward. I pull my feet up to the seat in an effort to get away from him.

Blood spills from his head and puddles on the floor. When his body topples, his face lands in the puddle. His profile stares unblinkingly, his mouth is agape.

A voice calls, "Lieutenant," from far away. I want to move toward it but am afraid of falling. The voice says to do something, but I can't make sense of it. Another voice calls, "Winnie," but I can't answer. Then someone lifts me out of the chopper.

The voices speak through a long, hollow chamber: about hitting another chopper—the rear rotor blade shorn off and whipping back. How his head barely slowed it down.

My moan rises in a long wail. I feel it ripping at my heart. I hear it from outside my body.

Darkness falls on a world that holds neither light nor warmth. I'm shivering as I climb down from the Jeep in front of Claymore Tower. I try but can't remember the last time I felt cold. Chris asks if I'm okay. I nod numbly and turn to climb the stairs.

Sandy isn't in. I'm glad because I don't want to talk to anyone. I gulp down a full glass of straight rum, turn off the lights, and go to bed.

At sunrise I'm frozen in our window, watching street traffic below and air traffic over Tan Son Nhut. By midafternoon rain clouds have gathered. Their dark shadows dance over the field, and the palm trees along main street sway fitfully. Everything is washed in an ominous yellow.

Suddenly the afternoon is as dark as night. A bright flash throws the landscape into white light just as thunder cracks the air. There's a sweet breath of rain just before a pelting of enormous drops, then driving sheets of rain that whip the land.

In one instant the world is clean, and the war stands still.

When the storm quiets to the patter of raindrops, the light turns soft gray. Street sounds below are punctuated by the passing of cars on wet pavement, the cracks of jets, and *whop-whop* of choppers from Tan Son Nhut. An old man washes his water buffalo in a mud puddle not far from the old French fort.

I have to get away from rip-off pedicab drivers and beggar street urchins; away from the singsong Vietnamese pretending to be on our side while they shoot American GIs in dark alleys and blow up American compounds in broad daylight; away from two-cycle engines buzzing like lawn mowers, fouling the air right below this window. I have to get out of Saigon.

The chief nurse doesn't ask why I want to transfer to another hospital. And without batting an eye, she grants my request to take leave in Japan. She probably thinks I'm pregnant, but I don't give a damn.

My orders are cut by the next day, but getting on a flight roster

173

takes more time. In early morning I walk to Tan Son Nhut to fly
out space available. Nothing here has changed since I came in-
country. I'm still the queen bee, and there's still nothing to eat or
drink, not even water. At lunchtime, then suppertime, I consider
running over to the Redbull Inn, maybe catching Alex for a last
meal; he returns to the World this week. But missing a flight means
having my name dropped to the bottom of the list. Besides, I
don't want to talk to anyone.

Midnight comes, the list of names ahead of mine shortening at
a dishearteningly slow rate. There are plenty of planes taking off,
but most flights must be military missions at this hour. By now
the mobs waiting for transportation have dwindled to a few dozen,
and the terminal is quiet. Rats, a foot long and stuffed like sausages,
sniff sluggishly along the walls and venture beneath benches on
which soldiers sleep. I've heard that GIs in bunkers wrap up tight
in their ponchos so rats won't chew on their fingers or toes or
ears or nose. I'd feel safer with my feet up, but I'm wearing a
skirt.

Two o'clock. I maneuver the narrow, dimly lit path to the one-
holer in my unaccustomed high-heeled shoes. Inside the tiny cubicle the light is so dim I can't see my feet in my shadow. But I
do see the tarantula, black and hairy and just inches away on the
wall. Is it true that tarantulas can spring on their quarry from five
feet? The unreasonable fear of its coming after me chases me down
the path toward the terminal. Never would I have believed this
place could look so good.

Four o'clock. The hell with propriety. I put my feet up on a
bench like everyone else. Half asleep, I hear an announcement for
space available to Japan. Grabbing my bag, I join the line forming
up. Shit. Where did all these guys come from? I'll never make it
on this flight.

The announcer adds that anyone with objections to riding with
human remains aboard need not step forward. The line dissolves,
the soldiers drifting away. In the end only three of us are willing
to travel with corpses.

I brace myself for the stench of death as we climb aboard, but
there is none. I anticipate piles of body bags, but there are only

twelve aluminum coffins stacked at the front of the plane.

We passengers strap ourselves against the hull. There's the familiar surge of jet engines, the bumpy ride down the runway, the sharp lifting away, and we're droning through unseen night skies.

One of my companions is a captain, and the other a corporal. Conversation is awkward, and my being a woman doesn't help matters. There's no telling how long since either of them has spoken to a round-eye, and I'm not in the mood to talk.

I find myself staring at the coffins, squinting at the nameplates nailed to their ends. I stand abruptly. I have to know if, by some quirk of fate, Good Buddy rides with us. Oddly I can't remember his last name although it was imprinted on his fatigues every time I saw him. I do remember his first name although I never used it. Antonio.

I read the first name, Gary, wonder if he came from Tennessee or Massachusetts or California, pass on to the next. There is no Antonio.

My companions watch silently as I read the names. "Anybody you know?" the captain asks when I return to my seat.

I shake my head, embarrassed by my performance.

"Never is," he says. "Probably just as well."

The Sanyo Hotel in Tokyo caters strictly to American officers. It's reputed to have the best food in Japan if you're a homesick American like me, and I take full advantage of it. I also take advantage of the bathtub in my room—three times daily—and the cocktail lounge. Everything I need is in the hotel, and after my first day here the hotel is where I stay.

That first day I went to the cozy corner at Camp Zama's officers' club. I was searching for camaraderie in the old haunt, but there were only strangers. It's been nine months since I left, and I no longer belong.

I had hoped to recapture the part of me who laughed and played before I went to Vietnam, but the place was haunted by memories of warrior buddies in a happier time. And, I realized, I haven't the courage to make new friends. To protect myself, I've learned to stand alone where there is no risk of disappointment, no need of anyone—and, though I do not see it yet, no hope for happiness.

175

My last day in Japan, June 21, 1967, begins the countdown for my last one hundred days of this tour—the milestone awaited after the six-month hump. I spend it in the Tachikawa air terminal waiting for space available to Saigon.

The smell—that familiar putrid smell, held close to the earth in the oppressive humidity and as unpleasant as ever—assails me as I climb off the jet at Tan Son Nhut.

"Home again, home again, baker's man," rings in my head, driving me crazy because I can't remember the rest of the jingle.

No one has to tell me the war is on again. The easy pace of the air base has quickened with soldiers and airmen; planes and choppers are roaring in every direction. Noise. That's what war is. Noise.

It shouldn't be a problem to commandeer a Jeep for the two-minute trip across the street, decked out as I am in summer cords with nylons and heels. But as I round the terminal, it's not Jeeps I find but bodies, wrapped in the ubiquitous black bags and dumped on a flatbed truck to await processing by graves registration. The stench gags me. Fuck it. I'll take a Lambretta.

The Army should make something to turn noses on and off. Then it could work on the eyes and ears.

A line of Lambrettas is attended by scrawny old Vietnamese men just waiting to rip me off. Shit. If I were in fatigues, I could walk. I'd even walk in these fucking ridiculous shoes if I didn't have this goddamned suitcase.

A horn blares. Fuckin' A. How I hate the bastards honking at me. I turn toward the sound ready to raise a finger, until I see it's an ambulance.

"Hop in, Lieutenant." The driver smiles, banging for the corpsman in back to open up.

Hoisting my suitcase into the dark interior, I step up. It's an inferno, reeking with the metallic smell of blood.

"Third Field Hospital?" inquires the corpsman. I nod, hanging on to the racks as the ambulance takes off. It's very dark after the bright sun outside. "You'll be sorry," he observes, securing an IV that swings haphazardly as we bounce along. He must think I'm arriving in-country for the first time.

176

"I already am," I concede, wondering how long he's been here but not curious enough to ask.

Reflexively I evaluate the wounded. One on a bottom rack is a head injury, and from his stiff posture, I'd take bets that he won't make it. The man above him is wrapped in the poncho used to carry him out of the field. His helmet is missing, but it has left strap marks on his dusty face and matted his hair with dirt and sweat. He disturbs me. There's no sign of a head injury, but he's sleeping very soundly.

I reach for his pulse; it's barely palpable. Goddamn. He could be bleeding to death, and nobody would know it while he's wrapped up like that. I turn the IV wide open, then reach to throw off the poncho, but the litter strap is in the way. I start to loosen it.

"Hey, what're you doing!" demands the corpsman.

"This guy's bleeding."

He grabs my hand. "They'll take care of it at Third Field."

"There might not be time," I snap. "Be useful and hang some blood!" It never occurred to me he might question my actions.

"There ain't none." There's a change in his voice. He's realized that I'm not new in-country, that I know what I'm doing. Now I worry if he does.

"Then hold the litter."

When I loosen the strap and pull back the poncho, blood spills over us onto the floor. I sense more than see near panic in the corpsman. There's a dressing over the soldier's groin. I press down where the femoral artery should be, praying that's the problem. I can't see worth shit, and there's no way to turn him over to make certain.

The corpsman retightens the strap. At least he can think straight. When the ambulance lurches, I slip in the blood and fall to my knees. The corpsman presses on the soldier's groin, so I can stay on my knees. When we reach triage and the doors swing open, an emergency room corpsman gasps at the sight of me. With so much blood on me, he thinks I'm wounded.

Scrambling out of the way, I point to where the blood is coming from, then leave before I get snagged into helping. I'm dog-tired, and the six flights of steps seem much longer after a week. I take

177

them slowly; I'll never make it in time for lunch anyway. I pull off my clothes, thinking how mama-san will have a shitfit when she sees them, then sit on the end of my bed, staring dazedly at the bloodied pile. For some reason it makes me want to cry.

Starting the next morning, I'm assigned to relieve the emergency room nurses on their days off. An ambulance is pulling up to triage as I report for duty. It must be busy inside, as only one corpsman comes to help out.

There's an unfamiliar patch on the wounded men's fatigues, a four-leaf clover.

"What outfit are you with?" I ask the first soldier as I check under his leg dressing.

"Ninth Division." He grimaces.

I've never heard of it. "New to this part of the country?" He has a compound fracture, but the bleeding is under control.

"New in-country."

A new division in-country. Somebody should inform the newspapers that keep reporting the war will be won in no time.

He props himself up on his elbows, surveys the damage to his leg. "How's it look?" His face shows no emotion, but his voice is tight.

"How long do you have left on your tour?"

"Nine months."

"Well, you'll have to come see us again if you want out sooner."

He lies back down. "Just so long as I keep my leg."

I move on to another four-leaf clover. Below a tourniquet this soldier's arm is black from lack of circulation. When I loosen the tourniquet, blood gushes from the wound. Reflexively replacing it, I call for the corpsman. "OR right away," I order, "so they can save that arm." It is at such times I feel good about what I'm doing.

By midmorning the tropical heat has begun its wilting process. The early incoming wounded have been cleared from the emergency room, but Tan Son Nhut has radioed there are dust-off choppers on their way with seven wounded—none of them critical.

We gather outside, sit on gurneys with our legs dangling as we smoke cigarettes and shoot the breeze, waiting for the first ambulance.

Two walking wounded—more clover leaves—step down from the ambulance. A corpsman accompanies them into the emergency room.

Dressings swath the upper torso of the first litter wounded, his right arm missing at the shoulder. There is a notable but not alarming amount of fresh blood. Then I notice the missing arm, lying across the man's lap. Somehow I've never wondered what happens to limbs in the field.

"If I die, my arm goes with me," he says in response to my look.

I shift my attention to the dressing. "Fine by me."

Another litter wounded is lifted from the ambulance. A thigh wound, no fresh bleeding. Satisfied that the missing arm needs me most, I help a second corpsman push his gurney into the emergency room.

"Can you sit?" the surgeon asks. If he has noticed the arm, he doesn't show it.

By way of reply, the soldier swings his legs over the gurney and sits up easily, despite a dismembered arm and sizable blood loss. The surgeon and I exchange glances to say we're impressed. Humping in the boonies makes men strong.

The first corpsman stops dead in his tracks, staring at the arm in disgust. "What are you?" he demands. "Some kind of ghoul?"

The grunt instinctively reaches to his side with his good arm, the motion of going for his weapon unmistakable. Then he spits, "You goddamn bastard," grabbing the arm from his lap as he lunges for the corpsman.

"Get the fuck out of here," I snap at the corpsman, but it's hardly necessary. He's already backing away from the dismembered arm being waved in his face.

"You're not going anywhere," the surgeon says, pushing the grunt back on the gurney. I'm already there, holding a syringe to draw bloods.

"Is that necessary?" the soldier asks in alarm.

I assure him it is, and he turns his face so he won't have to watch. Amazing. They come straight from the field, shot up and blown to pieces, then act as if they're going to faint at the sight of a needle.

The surgeon removes the bottom half of his dressings. Blood oozes from multiple fragment wounds, a significant loss but not dangerous. "Blood here," calls the surgeon, not looking up.

The upper half of the dressing now falls away under his careful touch. Above the nipple line, muscle tissue has been shorn from the chest, exposing part of the ribs. Not a word now from the soldier who flinched at the sight of a needle as he pulls back his head to stare down at his chest.

Blood is hanging by the time the dressing is fully removed. All that is left of the field dressing is what has been stuffed into the shoulder joint. "We'll do the rest in OR," the surgeon says, and leaves to scrub.

That's my cue to wash the soldier's chest and back with Wescodyne, have the second corpsman remove his boots and cut off his fatigue pants. In the process the dismembered arm falls off the gurney. I hesitate a moment, repulsed by it, then pick it up. It's cold to the touch, has a doughy quality, and is already getting stiff. I hand it back to the grunt.

"Thanks, Lieutenant," he says as the second corpsman rolls him into the operating room.

The first corpsman has the thigh wound under control. I swipe at sweat on my nose, decide the rest can wait until I've had a cigarette. When I step outside, another ambulance is pulling through the gate. Shit, I really wanted that cigarette.

The afternoon is long and hot, but I'm more at home here than in Japan. I've grown accustomed to the noise, the sickening stench, the thick, oppressive heat, the bloodied bodies. This is where I belong now, no matter how much I hate it.

After work the grapevine at the Redbull Inn says the Ninth Division is catching holy hell because of inexperienced officers and men. Word has it that even the 1st Cavalry, the gung ho outfit that has resorted to taking draftees, is a luckier draw than the Clover Leaf Boys.

*   *   *

When my day off comes and I still haven't heard from Chris, I know I never will. Sheila finds me wandering aimlessly around Tan Son Nhut terminal and calls the hospital to get orders cut for me. She takes me to Chu Lai.

The base is up north, along a breathtaking coastline where white sands stretch into the mountains from an azure sea. But the Army is inescapable even here: Concertina wire and bunkers line the roads; scrap metal stockpiles and stark wooden barracks dot the landscape; Army vehicles and their choking dust are everywhere.

It seems a shame, but I do not doubt their necessity, for I no longer question whether the war is right or wrong. All the maimed bodies and souls I've seen make it unthinkable that we could be wrong.

Back in Saigon, my shift in triage is drawing to an end. The late afternoon brings the daily tropical rains, cleansing and cooling. It's calm now with only one casualty left. At his request we've left him outside so he can watch the storm. Multiple fragment wounds dot his arms and chest, and I'm picking out the superficial pieces of shrapnel while we wait for a surgeon.

This soldier does not hide his pleasure at having a round-eye to talk to. I'm the first he's *seen,* much less talked to, since he got in-country. He speaks of his little sister, now twelve years old, who keeps writing how much she misses him. And of his girl friend, waiting for him back home.

For some reason, talking is making him short of breath. His blood pressure is stable, so maybe it's just excitement. A surgeon arrives with X ray in hand. "There's a lot of blood in your chest," he pronounces. "I need to insert a tube in there to drain it."

"It'll help your breathing," I add, to inform the doctor of his shortness of breath.

The casualty nods. "Whatever you say, Doc." He smiles at me. I smile back. Too bad he's so young. He sure is cute.

The procedure won't take long, but it's getting dark, so we roll the gurney into the emergency room. We've performed this procedure many times and waste no time: cutting a small incision and sticking the tube between the ribs. When it penetrates the chest wall, we stand aside to avoid the gush of blood, then hook the tube up to the suction machine.

The bottle fills immediately, and blood is still pouring! The surgeon clamps the tube to stop the flow, but blood spurts out around it. The corpsman runs for more blood.

The youthful soldier reaches for my hand, terror written on his face. I can't take it, am reaching for dressings to cover the hole as the surgeon yanks out the tube. I put all my weight against it, as we push him into the operating room.

He stops breathing. I listen for a heartbeat; there is none. The surgeon starts cardiac massage, and I bend to breathe for him. Blood cascades from the hole. New blood is hung on the IV. The anesthesiologist arrives to insert a breathing tube. But he's too late.

When I look at the young face again, it's ghostly white. His color has drained all over us, all over the floor, with his life's blood.

Winnie (*left*) at age four and a half, with her cousin Beth in North Carolina

High school graduation, 1961

Just after induction,
Fort Dix, New Jersey

First Lieutenant Winnie Smith,
Camp Zama, Japan, 1966

The main street of Saigon, as seen from the roof of Claymore Tower

Soldiers in Tan Son Nhut attend the Bob Hope Christmas show, 1966.

An MP who loved to play peekaboo with the kids at the Third Field Hospital in Saigon

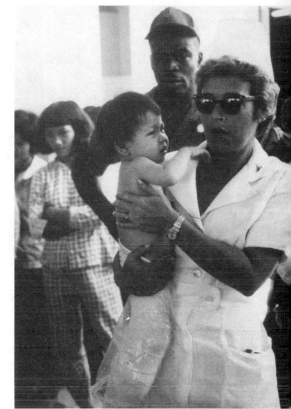

RIGHT: A nurse holds a baby whose legs are covered with napalm burns.

BELOW: The orphans from St. Elizabeth's singing in the triage area on Christmas morning, 1966

ABOVE: Vietnamese children playing around a shell hole outside the Olympic swimming pool used by American military personnel

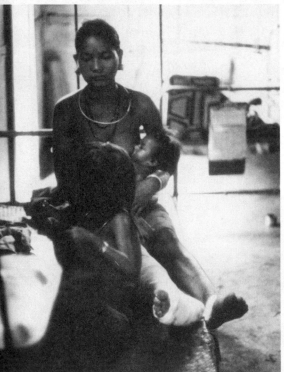

A mother and her children in the Pleiku hospital that was run by foreign civilians for the Montagnard villagers

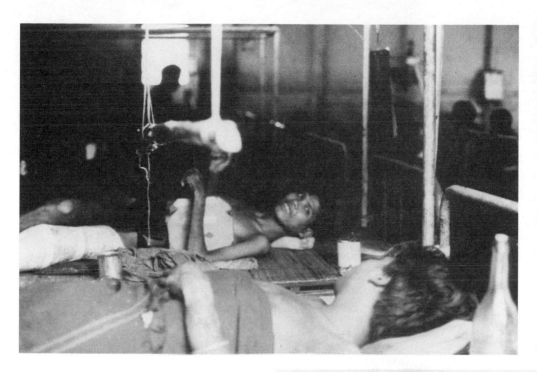

ABOVE: Montagnard patients
at the Pleiku hospital

Promotion to full captain,
1967

Ticker tape in a cemetery
along the route of the
Veterans Parade in New York
City, 1985

LEFT: Winnie with her son,
Ken, at the age of ten months

CHAPTER TWELVE

JULY 1967: The Twenty-fourth Evacuation Hospital, Long Binh

My transfer, requested the day after Good Buddy's death, has come through for the Twenty-fourth Evacuation Hospital in Long Binh.

Army bulldozers worked long and hard to create this place; there's not a blade of grass or hint of a tree anywhere in sight. Though we're not far from the Mekong Delta, once the "rice basket" of French Indonesia, the only clue to its proximity is the flatness of the land.

Long Binh is where I processed in-country. Then it was intriguing, even exciting, despite the heat, dust, and Saigon Revenge. It was the stuff of which movies are made, with tents and Quonset huts, Jeeps and helicopters, concertina wire and guarded gates, warriors in fatigues and weapons of war. Now it's just hot and dirty, smelly and noisy—and *big*. Fifty thousand support troops live here to run the processing center, the big brass headquarters recently relocated from Saigon, the infamous Long Binh Jail not so fondly dubbed "LBJ Ranch" after our Texas President, two evacuation hospitals, and an enormous PX that carries everything from stereos to condoms but next to no personal items for women.

The Twenty-fourth Evacuation Hospital encloses three sides of a big patch of dirt. The helicopter pad, triage and emergency room, operating rooms, and recovery room occupy the closed end of the "courtyard." X ray, laboratories, storage space, and mess hall form the arm of one side. The other is a long string of Quonset hut wards, the officers' club and two "tropical huts" for female officers—long, wooden, peak-roofed buildings akin to barracks but without solid outer walls. These are a boon on sunny days, when we get whatever breeze there might be, but they're a bust in monsoon storms, when rain is blown close to horizontal. Nor do we have shades, so there is no privacy.

Beyond the mess hall there is a twenty-meter portable swimming pool, courtesy of some optimistic officers who are now back in the World; only ordering it has proved easier than filling it. The base's water truck makes a deposit every time it comes to replenish water barrels and shower tanks, but there's still only about a foot of water. Until the pool is full, it's off limits—unguarded and deemed by those in power to be unsafe.

Beach towels or beaded curtains act as doors in our quarters. I have my own room, really a six-by-twelve-foot cubicle with partitions that start two feet up from the floor and end in the open framework of our roof. Furniture includes an Army footlocker and two Army cots made up in Army wool blankets. Wool blankets! Not ritzy accommodations, but there *is* a water cooler in the hallway. No matter that the water tastes like iodine; it's cool and doesn't have to be lugged up six flights of steps.

There's a bathroom in the building that includes a shower but no running water. We trek to facilities across a foot-wide plank thrown across a drainage ditch lined with concertina wire. Negotiating that plank is tricky in a driving rainstorm and downright treacherous on a dark night. We shower in a big room with four heads, where a nurse major in the raw is no less embarrassing now than she was in basic training. But the bigger problem of no privacy is our six-holer that leads to my coming down with that well-documented hazard of the armed forces—piles. Adding insult to injury is a bench seat so high that my toes barely touch ground.

Next to these facilities is our bunker, although one can't even see the base perimeter from it.

The officers' club is two tropical huts down from mine. No potholes to maneuver in the dark, no snipers, no fire fights across the street, no steps to navigate after a drunken evening, and very few scowling Vietnamese. Across the dirt courtyard is the mess hall. Dirt translates into mud at this time of year, but it matters not in combat boots and fatigues. Shit. I should've put in for a transfer my first day in Saigon just to be rid of those fuckin' ridiculous white uniforms, shoes, and nylons.

And there are real American breakfasts! I cram my mess tray with everything offered and ignore everyone else as I eat. Afterward I clomp through the mud and stamp my feet on the cement walkway in front of my new ward, neurosurgery ICU.

Inside the door I stop dead in my tracks. It's like stepping into a cave, air-conditioned to a chilly eighty degrees. The trade-off is that there's only one window on the ward. All things considered, I can live with it.

Twenty-two beds line the walls, looming unnaturally large in the Quonset hut. All are elevated to the same height, holding white turbaned heads in neat rows. Halfway down the left row is a wooden Army desk that serves as a nursing station. Across from it is a stainless steel medicine cabinet, and on the other side of an entry to the medical ICU is the only window. It sits over a sink; only there's no running water and no drainage pipe—just a hole in the floor. We wash our hands in basins of Wescodyne, which turns them an unhealthy-looking orange color. Bath water is dipped from a steel drum outside the back door. There are two outhouses across the street that runs behind the wards. They're labeled "Officer" and "Enlisted." Women aren't allowed in either. We must trek a half mile round trip to those across from our hooches.

Today another nurse manages the ward while the neurosurgeon orients me. It's all old hat, save learning the categories that describe levels of consciousness: "Alert" refers to normal mentality; "awake" to spontaneous eye opening. "Lethargic" is greater than normal sleeping but easy to arouse; "stuporous" is greater than normal sleeping but hard to arouse. "Semicomatose" are those who won't awaken but have purposeful movements. "Decorticates" are those in a coma who curl up to pain; "decerebrates" stretch out to pain. "Flaccid" is one who doesn't respond, even to very deep pain.

"Don't you find this service depressing?" I ask the neurosurgeon as we check the levels of consciousness.

"Not at all. I've only had six months of neurosurgery residency, so it's still exciting to me." To my doubtful look, he adds, "You have to readjust your value system. Someone with a gunshot wound to the head who squeezes your hand on command can process thought. That's better than nothing, even if he'll never recite the multiplication tables."

I search his face for signs of sarcasm but find none. Gazing down the rows of turbaned heads, I wonder what is the purpose in living if your mind is, literally and figuratively, shot to hell. I know I wouldn't want to be kept alive if it were me.

The mess hall closes before our twelve-hour shift ends. I've bought canned foods with built-in heaters at the PX but opt for a drink at the club instead.

It holds the familiar aroma of cigarettes and booze, the sound of laughter and jukebox music, the glazed eyes of drunken officers in fatigues lining the bar and filling the tables. Something, maybe the newness of the place, evokes a sharp awareness of the irony of merrymaking in the midst of so much tragedy.

Barely pausing to catch my bearings, I head for the bar and a Rob Roy.

"I'd like to pay for that, little lady," comes an offer, spoken with a slow southern drawl.

The soldier is a lieutenant, but his insignia is the black camouflage variety, so I can't tell if he's a first or second. On his arm is the Big Red One infantry patch. He's leaning cockily against the bar, flashing a big smile out of a swarthy face.

A forgotten sensation, attraction, brings a flush to my face. "If you want." I shrug, hoping to sound casual.

"That's a hefty drink for a little lady," he observes.

The remark irritates me—the implied judgment and suggestion

that I can't take care of myself. And what concern is it to him anyway? Little lady indeed.

"I can handle it," I reply coolly.

His dark, deep-set eyes turn serious. "You look mighty tired. Just get off duty?" He lifts his glass in way of a toast before taking a sip.

I nod, pointedly staring at my drink.

"Things have been pretty hot lately," he says. "You must be pretty busy."

I shrug. "I wouldn't know. I just got here." For some reason that doesn't seem to matter, I don't feel conversational.

"After three months I sometimes feel like I've been in this hole all my life," he says.

"I can't even remember back that far," I answer. "Just wait'll you've been here for nine months."

"Short-timer! That calls for another drink," he declares, motioning the bartender to refill our glasses. "Where're you working?"

"Neurosurgery." Why am I so reluctant to look at him?

"Do you always talk so much?"

"Does it matter?" I snap. After all, I'm a round-eye. Whether I can talk or not hardly makes any difference.

His eyebrows lift. "Why are you so bitter?"

"What makes you think I'm bitter?" But even I can hear the edge in my voice.

He moves to leave, giving me a small salute. Ashamed that I've chased him away, I do an about-face. After all, he's a line soldier risking his life in this shitty country. The least I can do is give him a few minutes of pleasant company.

"Sorry." I flash my most winning smile. "Reckon I've seen too much of what this war's about."

"No," he says quietly. "What you see is not what the war is about. That's just the price we pay."

"Just? Maybe you'd like to come visit me at work sometime."

"I don't have to," he says. "I've seen it in the field. But brooding over it won't change it, and if I'm not going to see tomorrow, I'm at least going to be happy today."

He's right, of course. What's gotten into me? "Truce?" I hold out my hand.

His dark eyes shine, and he smiles again. "Truce." And we shake on it.

Larry is his name. He's tall and muscular, not a spare ounce of fat on his body. He tells me he's from Georgia, grew up near a military base and decided as a small boy to make the Army his career.

"A lifer?" I ask with unconcealed surprise. "How could anyone make a career out of this?"

"I'm not so sure anymore." He grins. "Where're you from?" And when I tell him North Carolina, he drawls, "A southern belle. No wonder you're so dang pretty."

I bristle. "Where have I heard that before?"

He sighs and shakes his head. "You sure are a hard woman to talk to."

"What do you expect?" I say. "Every man over here says the same goddamned thing. I could be fat and forty, and they'd say I was beautiful!"

He pauses, swirling his drink. "They're a long ways from home."

"And I'm not?" The bitterness just won't stay down.

A long pause. "Look. I find you attractive. I can't change that, so if it bothers you, maybe I should leave."

"No, please. I'm sorry. I like talking to you. I just don't want anybody making a play for me."

He studies me for a long while. "A deal." He smiles and holds out his hand to shake on it. "I won't make a play for you if you don't make a play for me."

I laugh.

"We're all in a world of hurt here," he muses. "You've got to lighten up when you have the chance."

"I know. But it's not as easy as it used to be." I light a cigarette.

"Have you ever visited Georgia?" he asks.

I shake my head.

"North Carolina's not so far away. Maybe you'll let me show you my home state someday."

I laugh. "You won't even remember who I am when we're back in the World."

"You underestimate me."

I can feel myself blushing. "You sound serious."

"That's affirmative. I haven't been gone so long that I don't know a good thing when I see it."

"Oh, no, you don't. No plays, remember?"

His turn to laugh. "I think I'm going to enjoy the next three months more than I thought."

The words scare me. As crazy as it sounds, I want to believe what he's saying and give free rein to the feelings welling inside me. But what about Peter?

Tipping my drink in Larry's direction, I put Peter out of my mind. We toast to good times, to living it up while we can.

Next to the wooden desk, a Stryker frame supports a jet jockey who ejected when his plane was shot out from under him. A broken neck and quadriplegia are the price for his escape. Now a rampant pneumonia threatens to finish him off. A trach helped for a while, but even a respirator can't deliver enough oxygen to keep him going much longer. In a place where the work load is grueling, where too little can be done for too many, he has been largely ignored. He's being allowed to slip away.

Unable to speak with the tracheostomy, unable to write because of his paralysis, he lies gasping for air through the long night. When time permits me to do paper work, I sit by him so he won't be alone. This night I ask if he's married.

He smiles, gasps for air, mouths yes.

"To a beautiful woman no doubt?"

Another smile and gasp for air.

"Do you have children?"

He nods.

"Two?"

No.

"More?"

Yes.

"Three?"

Yes.

Gazing at his swollen, dusky face, I take a deep breath and ask if he wants to see them again.

He nods.

"Do you understand you'll never have use of your arms or legs?"

Tears flood his eyes; a small sob chokes him as he gasps for air. Yes.

"Do you know you have a bad pneumonia?"

Yes, he knows.

"It's killing you."

Yes, he knows.

No going back now. "Do you want to live?"

His tears flow as he stares at the ceiling. Yes.

I had hoped he would say no. "Okay," I say. "There are no guarantees, and it won't be easy, but we can try. It means you'll get very little rest, and you can't change your mind once we get started. It'll mean clapping on your chest and suctioning your lungs every hour and turning you every two hours. Are you still game?"

Yes.

And so, determined that this man will live, I institute a rigorous routine. Since I am the officer, the corpsmen have no choice but to follow my orders. The doctor shakes his head but lets me have my way. Nor am I without doubts. I haven't forgotten the soldier named Guerrero, whom we saved for the trip to Japan only to have him die there.

This man survives to be evacuated. His departure earns a round of congratulations for him, backslaps for us, and something of a reputation for me as a supernurse. But I'll never know if he makes it out of Japan, or if he lives, whether he will be grateful to us one year, two years, ten or twenty years down the road.

Larry comes shouting at our hooch door late one afternoon. With him is his platoon sergeant and buddy, nicknamed Pops because he's nearing the ominous age of thirty. Premature balding and leathery skin make him look even older.

Though I've just met them, I feel as if I've known them for years.

"Keep it down!" "Would you shut up!" come the cries of disgruntled night nurses trying to sleep. Mary Jane, a first lieutenant due to leave this month, is caught in the hallway in bra and panties. She screeches obscenities as she runs to her room.

Pops and Larry exchange grins so ingenuous that I haven't the heart to upbraid them. Besides, they've come bearing gifts—a wardrobe with a light bulb to prevent shoes from mildewing, two camouflage silk poncho liners, and a small "lady's desk" that has a dropleaf and little round mirror at the back.

After they've gone, I sit down at the desk with my mother's last letter:

> . . . I imagine it was wonderful for you to go to Japan and see your friends from Zama. Seems strange that there could be sort of like old home towns over there. Well, you seem to at least have some social life. . . .
>
> I really am not very surprised at the people in Vietnam—it reminds me of the "poor" people in this country. They have no desire to help themselves. . . . It is different there than here in some respects—those people have never had anything or anyone to encourage them, but so many in this country can't be bothered—it's easier on welfare. The borders are really at fault in Korea, Vietnam & the Congo and other areas of the world. They all are good Communist material I imagine—or else how could China have put in such a program—

My concentration is broken by the disquieting sense of someone watching. Unable to shake the feeling, I glance over my shoulder. A huge rat sits on its haunches just four feet away, staring brazenly at me. Stifling a scream, I stand and wave my arms wildly, shouting, "Shoo! Get out of here!"

Slowly, almost sardonically, it slinks into the space between the wall and wall locker.

I chug down a last Rob Roy and hit the sack. The B-52s are hard at work; bombs falling on the Cambodian border shudder the earth beneath my cot. The rat comes back while I sleep, jumping down on me from the partition above. I awaken to its fat body on my chest, its razor-sharp teeth inches from my face.

Terrified, I sit bolt upright and stare dazedly around the empty room.

No rat. Just a bad dream.

The next day I lodge a complaint. They send a Vietnamese engineer who pours a ring of poison around the hooch.

Fat lot of good that'll do! Fuckin' A. I thought I'd be rid of those goddamned useless dinks once I was out of Saigon.

He looks Mediterranean—dark-skinned, massive in frame, and swathed in white Kerlix head dressings—so we call him Turk. A bullet went through the base of his skull and ricocheted inside his helmet until its momentum ran out. It left him flaccid. He doesn't flinch when his nipples are twisted, yet his pupils are equal and briskly reactive. So he stays with us longer than most, a vigil ordained until we know whether he will live or die.

It's another nurse, Grace, who first realizes the terrible truth. She's standing by his side, holding high a syringe with liquid food to pass through a tube into his stomach, when she sees his tears. Guessing but not wanting to believe, she asks him to blink. He does.

Grace tells him to blink twice, and he does. She tells him to shut his eyes, and he does—tears cascading down his cheeks for the joy of someone speaking to him.

He is fully alert but "locked in," paralyzed from the eyes down from a severed brainstem. He is able only to blink, move his eyes up and down, and cry, and there's no hope of his ever doing more than that.

How long can he live this way? Ten years? Twenty years? Thirty or forty? It makes me shudder. What God would permit such a fate? None that I want to believe in.

We print the alphabet on a piece of cardboard, so he can communicate more than yes or no. We run a finger along the letters, and he blinks out a message.

Once in the middle of a quiet night he blinks the message "L-E-T M-E D-I-E."

"That's to be expected so soon after his loss," the neurosurgeon comments. "He'll thank us later, when he realizes he can still lead a productive life."

A letter is sent to his parents with a full explanation of his condition and prognosis. They respond that they want him back no matter what. He's being evacuated this afternoon.

Now, as I shave him for the trip, he's crying—has been ever since I told him that he's going home. I wonder if he'll ever thank us, but I doubt it.

After work I get drunk at the club. Around midnight I sneak past the mess hall and through a dark field, toward the pool. Safe or not, it has become my haven from insanity. It's even better than the Starlit Roof, without disturbance from the stampede on main street or fire fights, and I don't have to share it with anyone else. It's my secret place.

After climbing over its plastic side and slipping into the cool water, I sit down—up to my neck! I float, swirling the water with my arms. It's pitch-black, and all I can hear are the soft ripples. My mind empties; I feel my spirit restored. A chopper passes; then I play the ripples again.

I kick off from the side and bobble toward the other end. When my ears are underwater, the world is at peace, no choppers, no artillery, and no B-52 rumblings—no war. Only the hissing of my breath and the rippling of water.

Something's going on somewhere. Casualties are pouring in so fast that we're taking pre-ops on the ward. Corpsman Johnson and I tread the millstone: vital signs and neuro checks, IVs and dressings, tube feedings and medications. When they push a gunshot wound to the head through the door, Johnson runs for linen to stuff under the head while I cut off the soldier's shirt in preparation for the operating room. I discover a sucking chest wound.

I call to Johnson as I run for Vaseline gauze to stop the leak, gratified he's a former Big Red One field medic on a day like this. He responds with the usual "Yes, ma'am." If only I could break them of that "ma'am."

"O_2," I say, pointing at the chest wound. I'm taping a dressing when Johnson rolls a tank into place. God, I'm tired. Two more hours before the night shift arrives.

"Call triage and tell them what we have. Let them know he's on O₂ and breathing okay for now."

"Yes, ma'am." He bolts for the monster field phone, really a radio, and cranks it up to get the operator.

We don't speak for a while, busy with our respective tasks. Time for medications. One more hour to go.

"Hey, Lieutenant!" The call comes from where the corpsman stands next to the sucking chest wound. "He's blown a pupil!"

A fixed and dilated pupil means pressure on the brain, probably from bleeding. But it's the alarm in the corpsman's voice, not the pronouncement, that causes me concern. The wounded man came to us from the Big Red One, and instinct tells me that he was in Johnson's outfit.

"Tell OR," I order. Hanging Mannitol, I think this isn't the first wounded buddy he has cared for. For corpsmen in the field, it's the norm.

One more hour, and I start report. That takes thirty minutes and then an hour for charting. Johnson reports the neurosurgeon is in the OR. He's barely hung up the phone when the soldier's respirations worsen, so we call triage. A surgeon comes to insert a chest tube, but by the time he's finished, the other pupil has blown. The surgeon elects not to perform a tracheostomy. He returns to wounded in the emergency room who have better chances for survival.

We roll the soldier to the back of the ward, out of our way. No time to waste on an expectant. Not even for a former buddy.

Larry is waiting at the club when I arrive there after work. He's been in the field a long two weeks. My heart beats faster at the sight of him—tall, dark, and handsome with a twinkle in his eye.

Pops is with him; both rise slightly from their chairs. Larry's loyalty to his sergeant supersedes the censure of those officers who disapprove of an enlisted man in our club. To my mind he's got his loyalties straight.

Can they get me a drink?

Thanks, I'll just get it myself since I'm up.

Pops is gone when I get back to the table. "Prefers the enlisted men's tent where folks aren't so stuffy." Larry winks, and we laugh. Everyone here is drunk or headed that way; glasses clutter every table.

The next day is my day off. Larry, Pops, and I are headed for Saigon. Because of regulations against my leaving base, they pick me up early—shortly after the gates open, when there's more traffic and a better chance of sneaking out. Dressed in fatigues, helmet, and flak vest, I rummage for a make-believe article on the Jeep floor as we pass the guard. Flanked by Big Red One patches, I attract no attention.

Larry and Pops commandeered this Jeep from the stockpile at Long Binh, driving into the guarded area with a crippled old beast and driving out with this spirited new one. "She's a good old girl," Larry brags from behind the wheel. "She can do fifty when she has to!" and Pops laughs from behind the machine gun. It promises to be a blistering hot day; the rush of air in the open Jeep evaporates the sweat on my face.

Saigon has lost its appeal for me, but our only other choice is another Army compound. It's not safe to walk through the countryside. Larry's with the infantry, so we have no chopper. And unlike the Montagnard village that Sandy and I visited in Pleiku, Americans are not welcomed by Vietnamese in their villages. So Saigon it is, past miles of scarred landscape with trees bulldozed back to discourage snipers. To judge from the craters that pockmark empty fields, not all are discouraged. But the road is paved, so it can't be mined.

We pass a shrine, a golden structure sitting atop a pyramid of steps, that I've longed to see up close every time I've made this trip. But Larry warns, "That's a no-man's-land. Not even buffalo dare to tread there—a sure sign the fields are mined."

Pops goes his own way in Saigon. No one has to tell me where he's headed, and I note no one has to tell him how to get there. Larry and I do what I've always done here, visit the outdoor café, peruse street stands, lunch on French onion soup, sip cocktails at the rooftop restaurant.

Even paved roads aren't safe to travel after dark, and Larry won't risk it with me in the Jeep, although he and Pops always return to their base camp on VC time. We're back at my quarters by sunset, where Pops leaves us alone to say good-night. Larry's strong arms enfold me. When he lifts my face to kiss, I tingle.

As they pull off in the Jeep, I know what will happen in two weeks when they come back from the field. *If* they come back, I correct myself.

I'm no longer an innocent girl, shy in love, as I was with Tom. No longer a carefree young woman, playing in the sunshine, as I was with Peter. And I'm not an insecure nurse anymore, craving reassurance, as I was with Alex. I'm an old-timer now, and I long for the strength of a man's body under a scorched sun.

This head injury is Cambodian, the first I've ever seen, with rounder eyes in a flatter face than a Vietnamese. He's part of the Civilian Irregular Defense Group.

When he was admitted, I asked Corpsman Johnson why Cambodians are fighting in this war. He told me that like the Montagnards, they are ancient enemies of the Vietnamese.

The obvious next question was why are they helping the Vietnamese now. Johnson's answer was that they're not helping the Vietnamese. They're helping *us*. The difference, he said, is that once we're in control, we can assure them a safe homeland.

It doesn't make any sense to me, since we're here to help the Vietnamese—another riddle. Whoever's side this Cambodian was fighting for, it has cost him his mind.

In the vain hope of catching up on my work before dashing out the door, I've waited until my bladder is about to burst. I *cannot* wait any longer.

Running the quarter mile as fast as I can, I'm stopped by the hospital's commanding officer—a career-type major. He reprimands me for being out in the open without my cap.

I tell him I don't have time to discuss it, salute without waiting for his return salute, and dash off to take care of business.

Predictably he reports me to our chief nurse. I'm pissed. Don't they know there's a war going on? Still, I worry that this nonsense will blow my captain's tracks up in smoke. So I act the good little lieutenant, stand at attention and salute smartly at her desk, wait to be put at rest. She asks if it's true.

"Yes. The ward's busy. I put off going to the latrine until it was an emergency. In fact, the ward needs me now." She must know this is chickenshit. If not, she ought to spend a day on the ward and do some real nursing for a change.

"Just don't let it happen again," she says. "And one more thing, your captain's bars have been approved. Your orders should come through any day."

Would it have made any difference if I hadn't played the game? Probably not. This chief nurse is less sticky about such things than the one at Third Field.

After work I trudge from the ward to the club, from the club to the pool, from the pool to bed, only to be roused by a red alert: The base is under attack.

Donning flak vests and helmets, we head for the bunker. The war sounds closer than usual but is still farther away than Tan Son Nhut was from Third Field—too far away to be of serious concern.

Someone obviously doesn't agree; flares pop everywhere as we cross the plank. I don't see anything I haven't seen many times in daylight, no dark figures lurking in the nearby field where our machine guns have just opened up.

Nervous triggers, I think. And I was so looking forward to a night's sleep.

Those more experienced with these alerts have brought candles and bottles of booze, even a guitar. B-52s are hard at work in the distance, the rumble of their erupting loads are background sound to small-arms fire sputtering like strings of firecrackers. Outside is a surreal world, unrelated to where we drink and sing.

There's enough to worry about without visitors, but these are the parents of a four-year-old Vietnamese boy lying in one of our beds. They ask if I speak French. I bristle. "No."

They ask, "Will our son live?"

"We can't say yet."

"When will you know?"

"I don't know," I tell them. They seem to be doing just fine in English!

"Can we see him?"

"Yes, but only for a short time. We don't allow visitors."

"Will he know us?" the mother asks.

"Probably not."

"Can we see the doctor?"

"No. He's in surgery." It's a lie, but he *is* busy.

"When *can* we see him?"

"I don't know." The part of me that hates the Vietnamese is caving in to the part of me that feels sorry for the parents of a dying child. But I want to scream that their boy is decerebrate, that he's as good as dead, that I don't have time for their questions, that they should go away and leave me alone.

I can feel the fear and animosity of our awake patients as we walk toward the child. In their confused states, do our soldiers think this abject couple is the enemy? Shit. Even if they weren't confused, the presence of Vietnamese would upset them. It's up-setting me.

The turbaned child is dwarfed by the hospital bed, looking especially small on a ward full of men. But his grasp reflex is no different from theirs; his small hand tightens around his father's fingers. Unable or unwilling to understand my explanation, they're certain he knows who they are. Maybe it's better that way.

I busy myself with other patients for a few minutes, then tell them they must leave.

Small and sad, heads bowed and eyes averted, they go.

Would it have hurt to let them stay? Were they really so much in the way?

Fuck it. I don't want them here. If they don't like it, they can transfer him to a Vietnamese hospital.

From deep inside I feel shame rising. I push it back down where I won't have to look at it.

CHAPTER THIRTEEN

AUGUST 1967: The Thousand-Yard Stare

W<small>AVES</small> roar in my ears, drowning out the night nurse's report. Between us on the desk lies an evacuation card for a man admitted during the night with a gunshot wound to the head. It's Pops.

In my mind's eye he flashes a grin at Larry on a Saigon street. Larry winks in return. Where is Larry now? For it's unthinkable that they weren't together.

I push down the question. I have to make rounds and give medications. Pops will have to wait his turn. Along the way I suction a gurgling trach, then reinforce the chest tube dressing that a confused head wound has torn loose despite restraints and bind his hands so it won't happen again. I replace an empty IV bottle, record the bottle absorbed and the bottle hung.

Pops's turn comes. It's not Pops, turbaned and decerebrate, I see but the expressionless face of a head injury, just another casualty of war. When I reach for his hand, I watch his fingers curl around mine.

Good-bye, old friend. Your Freedom Bird is waiting for you.

After work I stop by the emergency room to check the roster of wounded. Larry's name isn't there.

At the club I drink Rob Roys until I can pass out. The next day after work I do the same, and the day after. Twelve-hour shifts six days a week are habit by now; so is exhaustion.

A week passes, and I'm back on nights. My dreamless sleep is broken by the irritating singsong of mama-sans, by rain blowing through the walls, by choppers roaring in and out. When I get up, I'm soaked with sweat, if not rain. I shower, go to the mess hall, work, drink, sleep dreamlessly.

Larry still hasn't appeared. He must be dead or he would have come to see Pops by now.

I'm dragging myself out of my bunk when Mary Jane walks into my room, babbling about Colleen's finding out that her fiancé's plane crashed last night. Two nights ago another nurse's fiancé bought it, so now our entire quarters is in a foul state.

Mary Jane's chatter filters in one ear and out the other. I'm trying to figure out what to write Peter, how honest I should be about what's going on in my life, about Larry—only I don't know what's happened to Larry. I guess I'll put off writing Peter and get a letter off to my folks.

When I sit down at my lady's desk, I'm not trying to chase Mary Jane from my room. I just don't want to hear her story. But she takes offense and leaves, tossing back a remark about my coldheartedness. Part of me feels guilty. A stronger part of me doesn't give a damn.

I pull out my mother's last letter.

> . . . I don't think we have gotten all your mail—no one has heard from you for five weeks now. . . .
>
> It's rather dreary and depressing here with rain, and also Prissy died. . . . Now I really miss her so much and it really has me so upset, I've been rather useless today. Pets are wonderful but it really is heart breaking to lose one. . . .
>
> I understand how you feel about the Vietnamese—so lazy and never doing anything for their own country. But from what I've read they've fallen into the hands of China—warlords, etc.—and it will take time to make soldiers out of the South Vietnamese troops. . . .

I shake my head. The VC certainly do okay. It seems more a matter of their not really believing in what they're fighting for. But that's a long-winded discussion that I don't feel up to writing. In fact, I'm not up to writing much of anything.

Keith is a blast injury who arrived here highly confused from a concussion. Then he contracted meningitis—a result of his brain's being so badly banged that the membrane protecting the brain and spinal cord was torn. The meningitis has brought on high temperatures, further complicating his confusion.

Unlike most of our patients, Keith has complete use of all his extremities. And he's a regular Houdini with an uncanny ability to escape our standard restraints, contrived from padded dressings taped around his wrists and secured to the bed frame with Kerlix gauze.

Once more, working at the tedious task when our backs were turned, he has chewed his way to freedom. Gleefully victorious, he's standing up in bed.

"I'm gonna get those suckers!" he shouts at the top of his lungs.

He ignores my pleas to lie down, and foolishly I climb up on the bed with him. He immediately grabs my throat in a stranglehold, whereupon the corpsman climbs into bed with us and forces Keith to his knees. Keith takes me with him, his grip around my throat tightening, making it hard for me to breathe. I hear the corpsman shouting, "Let go or I'll kill you, you goddamn bastard!" Inches away, I see the confusion and unmitigated fury in the eyes of a madman. Then I start seeing stars, and I know I'm losing it.

Keith lets go. I gasp for air and scramble to climb out of the bed. Keith lunges and clamps his teeth into my shoulder. Pain shoots from my neck through my arm like a bolt of electricity and nearly flattens me.

"Let go, you mother fucker, before I break your neck!" the corpsman warns. He digs into the soldier's jaws to force them open, shoves one knee hard into his back.

Keith's mouth opens with a howl, and I slide to the floor. As we work at restraining him, Keith first threatens to shoot us for what we're doing to him, then entreats us to tell him what he has done wrong. He's a raging beast one minute, a deranged warrior the next, without a clue to where he is or why.

Having tied a sheet restraint over his chest, we're in the process of rendering his hands useless by wrapping gauze between the fingers and then taping them like boxing mitts. The corpsman is being too rough.

"Easy," I warn. "You're liable to break them."

"Serve him right. Goddamn animal should be shot."

Something's wrong. This corpsman has always been gentle with patients no matter how violent they might be.

"He could have killed you!" he says.

"It's not his fault. He's confused."

"Fuck that! I've watched his kind in action. I seen an animal like him strangle an old man who was just trying to stop them from torturing his water buffalo." The corpsman's hands are shaking. Barely audible, he adds, "And I didn't lift a fuckin' finger to stop 'em."

I look back down, continue taping the fingers. I use my best nurse's voice: "That wasn't this guy." It's two in the morning. We have six more hours to go. He can't break down on me now.

He says nothing.

I switch to an officer's command mode. "I want you to take a break. Get a cup of coffee. Smoke a couple of cigarettes. Drink a beer if you have to. But get control of yourself before you come back, or get somebody to take your place."

He snorts. "I can't leave you alone on this ward!"

"I can survive twenty minutes without you. I can't survive all night with you in this state of mind."

Satisfying himself that the restraints will hold, he nods in agreement.

"On your way stop by the ER and have a doc come check out this bite."

"Sure thing, Lieutenant."

"By the way," I call, stopping him at the door, "thanks for saving my neck."

He grins. "My pleasure, Lieutenant."

The grin sets my mind to rest. He'll be okay.

* * *

It's risky in broad daylight in a lightning storm, but I took the chance that these driving rains would cover my tracks and that my number isn't up today. No matter what, I had to get to the pool, to the healing water. The hours have passed in what seems like no time at all. Now I have to hurry or I'll be late for work.

A captain stops me as I cross the mired courtyard in a shift and sandals. He wants to know where I've been. Out for a walk, I answer; I just love a good storm.

Back in my room I jump into my fatigues, wrap my wet hair on top of my head, stick my scissors and clamp into buttonholes and a pack of cigarettes into my sleeve pocket.

I know something's wrong the minute I walk onto the ward. My sixth sense detects it, but I can't put my finger on it. Maybe I'm just nervous about Julie, the night nurse who recently transferred from the malaria ward without prior ICU experience.

"Well," I say to her, and nod to the corpsman behind the desk where she sits, "how was your first night?"

The corpsman shakes his head doubtfully in answer to my question, but she answers, "Not bad, except I still have a lot of charting to do."

She's transferring notes from scraps of paper to the air evacuation cards. She won't be able to keep that up if it gets busy again—and it always gets busy again.

It wouldn't be so bad if I weren't the only nurse on days this week because Grace is on leave. The corpsman and I can manage the fifteen patients we have, but it'll be a bitch if we get new admissions.

"Well, the sooner you can give me the report, the sooner you can finish up," I say, grabbing the cardex. At least I know most of the patients.

We flip through the cardex as she speaks. I'm aware of the rapid breathing of a head wound on the ward, admitted during the night. When we come to him, she says nothing about his breathing.

"What about his lungs?" I inquire.

"Oh, yes, I forgot. They think he has pneumonia."

Forgot! How could she forget! Easy, I tell myself. She's new. "They didn't order oxygen?" I ask.

"They didn't say anything about it."

"Did they get X rays?"

"Not that I'm aware of."

"Antibiotics?"

"No." She fumbles through the air evac cards to double-check.

"When did a doctor last see him?"

"Last evening sometime."

Tempted to tell her just to leave, I watch glumly as she retrieves his card. When she finds it, she stares at it mutely. I reach over and take it from her hands.

"PCN 10mu IV q4h" is clearly written there. "Keep going," I prompt, biting my tongue, while I cross to the medicine cabinet. I'll just get it started and then call for someone to come check him.

"Oxygen," I snap at the night corpsman, and he runs to set it up. He should've known, even if she didn't.

Her notes in her hand, Julie follows me the five feet to the medicine cabinet.

Fuck! The penicillin hasn't been mixed! What the hell did she do all night? She's right behind me as I mix the vials, make up the IV, hang it on the patient, chart it on his card. Maybe it's better this way. Following me around will show her how to organize. Tomorrow we'll do bedside rounds while she gives me the report, so I can point out anything she's missed.

Tomorrow. It sounds so far away. I'm dog-tired, and this day has barely begun.

And then it's over. I'm out of the refrigerated ward and assaulted by the tropical sauna outside. My heart leaps at the sight of Larry's Jeep, parked on one side of our quarters.

He's alive! I want to run to him, but something stops me: the unfamiliar squint in his eyes or maybe the grim set of his lips. As we walk to my room, his arm is heavy on my shoulders. Mama-san's smile evaporates when she sees us, and she leaves quickly, pulling shut the poncho liner that serves as my door.

We hold each other close for a long while, my face buried in his neck. I know we're going to make love, and my heart pounds with the awareness. I'm breathless from desire as he loosens my hair and pulls me onto the bunk bed.

When darkness comes, Larry starts dressing.

"It's better you don't see him," I say, rising from the bed.

He squeezes my arm gently. "You know I have to say good-bye to my sergeant."

We walk to the ward in silence. When the nurse and corpsman on duty read my face, they are silent as well. Larry follows me, his helmet in his hand, stops when I stop.

He looks at Pops and then back to me, as if to say I must be mistaken. His shoulders sag as he rounds the bed and takes his sergeant's hand. I know he has felt Pops's reflexive response by the hopeful look on his face.

Still, I say nothing.

"Hey, Pops." He leans close to the turbaned head, still holding the hand. The body arches stiffly. The face is frozen and expressionless.

"It's me, your lieutenant, come to say good-bye."

A rapid sequence of gasping respirations gurgle through the tracheostomy tube. Tears well up in Larry's eyes.

I feel like an eavesdropper and turn to leave them alone for a few minutes, but the nurse on duty motions that she wants to suction Pops. I turn back, touch Larry lightly on the back.

He whirls on me, instinctively reaching for his weapon. His eyes are wild, like the beast that inhabited Keith. The reflex lasts only an instant. When the instant has flown, Larry has the "thousand-yard stare."

Suddenly I understand that look. It's a retreat from too much pain. It puts a safe distance between the pain and the soldier.

Back in front of my hooch, his first words are "How can you work in that place?"

"It's not as bad as what you do. And I'm safe."

"I wouldn't be so cocky about being safe here," he says. "Somebody ought to be court-martialed for putting a hospital so close to the motor pool and ammo dump."

"Relax, Lieutenant." I squeeze his hand. "We're protected by the Geneva Convention."

"Stop playing the fool, Lieutenant!" he spits back. "This is the goddamn real thing! We blow the bejesus out of their villages, bomb their fuckin' hospitals, shoot the crap out of their women and children. Why the fuck shouldn't they do the same goddamned thing to us?"

"All right." I nod. "I'll try not to play the fool." He's become as bitter as I was when we met. I don't know what to say now that the tables are turned.

He pulls me toward him. I rest my head on his shoulder.

"Before Pops, I figured if a guy made it to the hospital, he would live. He might come up missing an arm or leg, but he would live."

He waits for a response, but I have none. He gives me a long, hard squeeze before he pulls my chin up with his finger, brushes my lips softly with his. He has to leave.

He searches my face as if for an answer. To what? Is he wondering the same thing I am? Whether we'll ever see each other again. "Thanks for taking care of Pops," he says abruptly, letting go of me.

Larry climbs into the prized Jeep, guns the engine, and swings out into the road. I watch as he drives toward the gate. He never looks back.

This soldier sustained gunshot wounds to the head, neck, and shoulder. The shoulder has been repaired, and the spine is intact despite the back of his skull's having been blown away. Eerily his brain is undamaged. All we could do here was suture impregnated gauze over the brain. When he reaches Japan, maybe they'll have a prosthesis—a permanent flap to contain and protect it. For now he's stomach down on a Stryker frame, his brain bulging under the gauze as he waits for the first available slot for air evacuation. Terrified, he cries, "Stay away from my head, man!" whenever anyone comes near.

The decerebrate next to him was blasted high in the sky when his Jeep hit a land mine. His helmet went in one direction, and he went another, landing squarely on his head. Lady Luck did not smile on him that day. A rock in the road caved in the top of his head. When he starts choking, I pull over the suction machine to clear his airway of undigested food. I throw the switch on the machine, pry his clenched mouth open with a padded tongue depressor, and insert the red rubber catheter.

I manage to snag the obstacle with the catheter, then withdraw it carefully so as not to dislodge it on his teeth.

It's not undigested food, but a chunk of brain.

His pupils are working all right, but I wouldn't take bets on his chances.

Damn, it's hot with the air conditioner down. The doors are open, but without windows the ward is a fuckin' oven.

It's the patients who suffer most. Soaring temperatures increase brain swelling; their conditions worsen with every passing hour.

I stop at Johnny's bed to check his level of consciousness. Before the air conditioning went out, he was improving. From semi-comatose two days ago, he had regained consciousness—still confused but with a prognosis that was better than that of most of our patients. Now he's decorticate, stiffly curling his arms and wrists when we twist his nipples or dig our knuckles into his sternum. There's still a chance he'll be okay if the air conditioning isn't out for too long. But the engineers can't fix this one and, so far, haven't come up with another.

On top of everything else, it's malaria pill day, and I've got the runs. I can't possibly reach the women's latrine in time, so I dash for the officers' one-holer and hang on to the door as best I can. My best isn't good enough. Hunched forward with my knees clamped together, I trade horrified looks with a very surprised captain before he slams the door shut.

Fuck it. When I get back, I tell the corpsman to drop everything and get a latch put on the inside of the officers' latrine. Reporting this news at change of shift, I'm cheered. It's actually worth getting caught with my pants down.

But when word gets out that women are using the officers' latrine, holes start popping in the woodwork. I take to chewing gum at work so I can plug them when nature calls. Kids' games. Somebody should transfer those jokers to the field.

After work there's a party at the club. A guy whose name tag reads "Nelson" asks me to dance. Dave is his name. He wears no insignia; he must be a civilian—maybe USO—but I'm not interested enough to ask. I wonder why he's not in the service but don't ask that either. He likes to dance and is free with his money. I'm kept well supplied with Rob Roys as we dance the night away.

Afterward he walks me to our hooch and asks if I'd like to see him tomorrow. I tell him thanks, but I have a boyfriend.

I'm nearly ready for bed when Mary Jane, Colleen, Shirley, and Joyce burst into my room, breathless and wide-eyed. "What was he like?" Mary Jane demands.

"Dave?"

"Of course, Dave! What did you talk about? Are you going to see him again?"

When I ask why this sudden interest in my love life, Colleen turns to the others. "She doesn't know who he is!" she says, disbelieving.

I shrug. "Dave Nelson. So what?"

Dave Nelson! Haven't you ever heard of *Rick* Nelson? That's his brother!

He did say he was from California. "No, I'm not going to see him again," I tell them.

They leave, shaking their heads. I climb into bed.

It's too quiet a night. There's no drone of crickets or geckos as there used to be in the Saigon villa. No roar of motorcycles or rumble of convoys as on main street beneath Claymore Tower. No whine of choppers or jets thundering in and out of Tan Son Nhut. No sound of artillery or rattle of B-52 bombs tonight. Only the disquieting shuffle of rats lumbering along walls and across beams—and the gnawing of a rat we've trapped between two lockers and our hooch's screened wall. By morning there's a hole in the screen and the rat is long gone.

Quiet spells in Saigon meant shorter shifts or more days off. Not so in Long Binh. We're not even allowed to catch up on our sleep. There are two nurses assigned days on our ward; it means one of us just sits around, and that drives me crazy. So, when we're asked for a volunteer to provide lunch relief for the one-nurse wards, I break the cardinal rule in the Army—never volunteer—and raise my hand. I didn't count on the Vietcong prisoner ward. Serves me right for volunteering.

The MP gives me a friendly smile as he opens the screen door for me to pass. The ward is bright and airy, downright cheerful, with screened windows running the length of the Quonset hut. I wonder what happens in a rainstorm. It's strange to see little gook men swimming in Army blue pajamas, sitting on Army cots, and chattering away in singsong. I feel like Alice in Wonderland, unseemingly tall and fair, a stranger in a strange land.

The patients smile broadly, but I can't bring myself to look at them, much less smile back. These are the sneaky vermin responsible for soldiers lying mindless or paralyzed on my ward.

"How can you work here?" I ask. The question rings in my ears. It's the same question I asked when I started on my ward, the same that Larry asked after visiting Pops.

The nurse, a captain, is not surprised by the question. "I don't mind. They're actually a pretty decent lot."

Sounds like a New England accent. I ask what I can do while she's gone, but there's nothing; everything's taken care of. I wish I had something to read, so I could block out the singsong sound.

Even though there are MPs with M-16s at either door, I can't get past an irrational fear that the gooks are planning a break and in the process they'll slit my throat to silence my screams.

It's a relief when the lunch hour ends and an even bigger relief when my shift ends.

Of the twenty women in our hooch, only Margaret is married. That sanctifies her husband's spending the night, no matter how inconvenient it is for the rest of us to have a man in the house or that we have to listen to their lovemaking sounds, which carry over the partitions of our rooms.

I understand their not caring about us; I'd do the same if I dared. What I can't understand is Margaret's saying that she's doing exactly what she wants to do: serving in a war zone with her husband. But then, by the look of his pudgy face, I'd say that Dick is a rear echelon mother fucker who spends his days safe and sound behind some big shot desk.

The occupant of the room next to mine is pretty much a mystery. Nobody even knows where she works, though the grapevine has it that she's a physical therapist. For a long time I thought her room was a storage area, owing to its boarded-up walls and ceiling.

Then I once saw her going in and glimpsed the decor, parachutes draped from the ceiling and over the windows, poncho liners covering the bed and table. These amenities are rumored to be provided by male officers—not friends but customers. She herself is an officer, a first lieutenant. It's said that she's making a fortune off the war as a prostitute.

None of that concerns us this moment. Our concern is that a pit viper has slithered under her door, the only real door in our quarters. There's no answer to our knocks, and the door is locked, so we call the sergeant of the guard, who appears in full combat gear—flak vest, helmet, armed pistol belt, and ax. He's just about to break in when the door opens.

Amassed in the hallway, we goggle at her. There's no need to ask why she didn't answer our knocks. Behind her stand the starched khakis of a very rear echelon mother fucker colonel.

The luckless pit viper is found, and the sergeant delivers the tiny snake a crushing blow.

It's the last time I ever see the woman next door.

I work. I drink Rob Roys at the club in the evenings, then take my secret swim in the pool that's now almost full. My dreamless sleep is broken by rumbles of war in the night. I eat. Go back on nights. Drink gin and tonics at the club in the morning and—fuck the gawkers—sleep out in the cement yard outside the club. It's cooler than the hooch, and I want to go home with a tan. Eat. Work. Sleep.

Today is the pool's grand opening, cause for celebration. Everyone dons a bathing suit to trample my haven. Thank goodness I don't have long to go in my tour. I don't know how I'll survive without it.

But its opening is the signal the Vietcong have waited for. This night they sneak in with knives and slash it beyond repair.

"How could it happen?" everyone wants to know. "The guards were right there!"

So Larry was right. No place is safe. Not even Long Binh.

Papers for me to go on R and R have come through. We get only two weeks out of country, and I've already had my two weeks in Malaysia and Japan, but I don't mention that. Icing on the cake is that my orders are to leave from Cam Ranh Bay. Bien Hoa and Tan Son Nhut are much closer, but I don't mention that either. I'm packed and ready to jump a chopper bound for my departure point, destination Bangkok. My gung ho days are over. No matter how busy the ward may get, I'll take any time I can away from war.

CHAPTER FOURTEEN

SEPTEMBER 1967: The Home Stretch

I T's pitch-black on this lonely stretch of road. Sand dunes loom ominously on either side, making it seem the perfect setup for an ambush. Yet my driver, decked out in an MP's white belt and matching white-banded helmet such as I haven't seen since Saigon, carries only a puny hip pistol. What the fuck good does he think that thing would be should anything happen out here? I've heard Cam Ranh Bay is safe, but this is absurd.

Slouched behind the wheel and heedless of the terrain since we left the airfield, the MP obviously isn't bothered by it. I try to relax, telling myself this is his territory and he should know how safe it is or isn't. Even if he's wrong, the jitters won't change anything. If my number's up, it's up.

Temporary female quarters are on the main part of the base, isolated from the other buildings and unlit except for bare light bulbs on outdoor stairwells. There's no concertina wire in sight, not even along the road ditches; not a single chopper to be heard, not even in the distance; and no guard gate, much less a guard.

Once the MP drives off, there's not another soul in sight. What I've heard must be true: The war has not yet reached this place.

A slight breeze carries the sweet smell of salt water and . . . fresh lumber! These quarters are spanking new. I'm still marveling when I hear high-pitched laughter from the first floor. Fuck. I'm not alone after all. Picking up my suitcase, I climb quietly to the second floor. I don't want to see anyone, don't want the magic of this place disturbed.

There's no one else up here. And should anyone appear, there are real doors, and the rooms have real walls. There's even a real bathroom. I pick a room on the ocean side, cool and dark with the sound of rolling waves, then get ready for bed without a light.

Standing for a long time in front of the window, I stare at a sky crowded with stars, listen to the ocean, breathe the fresh, clean world. When I can't stay awake any longer, I climb into the bed. Even the sheets are sweet-smelling, clean, and dry.

I'm deeply asleep when an explosion jolts me out of bed. Way too close for comfort. Goddamn. There's no flak vest or helmet under the bed. And where the fuck are the flares so I can see where the shit I'm going?

I hear the *whoosh* of another artillery round. Jesus, there's no guard to tell me how the hell to get to the bunker.

Another explosion, then a long silence. How strange. Only one outgoing gun and no flares. Now I distinctly hear women's laughter again. What the fuck's going on?

I open my door to another *whoosh*. There are three women, Korean in appearance, on the stairway balcony. They're giggling and screaming like teenyboppers.

Kaboom!

"What the fuck's going on?" I yell at them.

They giggle. They met some soldiers at the club. Now the soldiers are showing them what real artillery is like.

"But it's a waste of ammunition!"

Whoosh!

"There's a *war* going on!"

I'm screaming, unable to contain my fury. They pretend not to hear me. *Kaboom!*

"Howitzers aren't toys," I scream. "I hope they get thrown in the brig for this!" Another *whoosh* overhead. "You little sluts. Someday I hope you get a taste of what a real attack is like!" *Kaboom!*

When I was a child, an old woman who lived across the street screamed at us kids for making too much noise. We called her the old witch.

Sleep eludes me long after the fun has stopped. When I next awaken, the sun is high. Alarmed that I've overslept for work, I leap out of bed.

And there it is. Beautiful white sands dotted with dune grasses, cerulean blue water that stretches from purple hills to the horizon. Paradise, with a bunker halfway between this building and the beach. Fat lot of good it would have done me if there really had been an attack last night.

I have a whole day here, and I spend it all on the beach, save a trip to the PX for two six-packs of Tiger beer and a small bag of snack foods.

Every hour is a wonder. The morning is cool and fresh, a time to savor the feeling of sand under my feet, the salt water in my mouth and hair. At midday, when it's hot and still, I stand in shoulder-high water warm as a bath and so clear that I can see my feet. In the long, quiet afternoon I stroll the empty beach and take dips to cool off. At sundown I watch coral clouds float overhead. Nighttime I'm tipsy from too many beers and the brilliant starlight.

The next morning at the air terminal, I ask if I can just stay here for my R and R. The soldier behind the counter stares at me as if I were crazy.

Settling into a luxurious padded seat in the bulkhead, I close my eyes to avoid contact with the major in stiff khakis who sits next to me. I know if my eyes open for more than an instant, he'll lean too close for some comment on the scenery below. That's the price to pay for legroom—this game with some rear echelon mother fucker major. Always.

On the other hand, keeping my eyes shut isn't so bad. The plane is wonderfully cool, and for once I'm rid of the sweat that trickles through my hair, under my arms, beneath my bra, and around my waist. But I'm aware of a distinct tickling in my pubic hair. I concentrate on the sensation in alarm. It not only moves down but moves up!

My eyes pop open. The major leans over with a smile and asks if I had a nice nap.

I smile politely, but my attention is definitely elsewhere. There's only one thing it can be. A slight involuntary groan brings a concerned look from the major. Am I all right?

Where could I have gotten the crabs? The latrine? A patient? Larry? Shit. What a way to start a vacation!

Thailand could be Vietnam, blistering hot and humid, a familiar shock as we step off the plane. Single file in Army style, we troop into the waiting Army bus. As the only woman I lead the line of soldiers. A sergeant takes roll call, announces that the bus will deliver us to our respective hotels, and reads off who's going to which hotel. I'm not on the list. The fucking crabs are driving me crazy, and I'm not on the damn list. The sergeant recommends a hotel for officers, especially a woman officer, that's nicer than most.

Once we're under way, the sergeant stands in front of the bus. Unexpectedly he leans toward me to whisper, "Er, sorry, ma'am. I, uh, have to give a little speech." He blushes. "It, uh, could be embarrassing."

He doesn't have to say any more for me to know what's coming. I want to melt into my Army green seat.

The speech is barked. It begins with where to find ladies of the night.

I stare out the window, mildly surprised that there's no protective window grille as on our buses in Vietnam. The sergeant reminds the men to check the ladies' "health cards." From the corner of my eye, I see him holding up a sample.

Bangkok looks a lot like Saigon, but without Army uniforms or Army vehicles in sight. I had hoped for a city more like Singapore, but at least the buildings aren't scarred or strung up with concertina wire.

"By *clean* I mean not diseased," the sergeant stresses. I wonder miserably if crabs count. "If you develop symptoms, this is where you go. . . . " The sergeant reads off a list of places. Do I dare? "The best treatment is prevention. And the best prevention is condoms." Then he tells them how much services should cost, depending on what kind they get.

The lobby of the hotel is packed with officers, all men. Fortunately there is a room for me. As soon as the door shuts, I tear off my clothes. There they are, dozens of crabs crawling all over me.

Oh, God. What should I do? If I were at Long Binh, I could grab a tube of Kwell on the ward. But I don't have the nerve to go to the VD clinic the sergeant mentioned or to a Thai hospital. Shit. I can imagine what they'd think.

Maybe I can burn them out with hot water. I fill the tub, sit down gingerly. The crabs go crazy, crawling up my stomach and onto the sides of the tub.

In the end I decide I'm not going to spend my whole R and R picking crabs out of my pubic hairs. I dry off and get dressed. The hotel pool is right below my window, but I don't want to meet anyone—especially not some lonely soldier starved for a round-eye's company, and this hotel is full of them.

So I go shopping. Hawkers line the sidewalks, promising great bargains inside their shops. If you enter, they serve you tea and parade their wares. If you take something, they toss trinkets into the bargain—an embroidered satin pouch or a silver lighter engraved with an elephant's head.

I should rest and recuperate during these five days; only I can't slow down enough. I rise early and have a hotel breakfast, then hail a pedicab and haggle over the cost—something I hate as much here as I did in Saigon. And the floating market could pass for the Saigon River—the houses on stilts and children swimming naked in a river polluted with the sewage of those living on its shores. The similarities dredge up the anxiety I had in Saigon of danger lurking nearby. I feel safe enough in daylight to roam the streets, browse through shops, and chow down at street stands, but at night I'm uneasy with the shadows. By sundown I'm back in the hotel.

Though nearly empty at breakfast time, the hotel restaurant is crowded with soldiers for supper. Nix supper. Nix the bar. My room is unbearably quiet, but that is where I go. Rob Roys and cigarettes are the company I keep.

I spend my last day on the grounds of the Emerald Buddha, where temple walls are splashed with bright paints and guarded by gigantic wooden soldiers undaunted by the sizzling noonday sun. Soft breezes tinkle bells hanging high on temple eaves to ward away evil spirits. They must work. There is peace here.

This last evening I'm determined to gussy up and enjoy a good meal. All eyes follow me to my table. The band, all Caucasian, strikes up "The Girl from Ipanema," pointedly staring at me. Fuck it. I pay for the meal and leave without eating it. Back in my room I smoke cigarettes and drink Rob Roys.

In my last hour of this escape from the war the morning air is so still that the fronds of palm trees do not stir. I stand at the window in my summer cords, gazing over the pool, whose water is smooth as glass. At the far end of the pool is a "spirit house," a tiny replica of a Thai palace with fresh fruit placed at its door to entice ancestral spirits to smile on this place.

Once in Japan I danced at a festival to call forth ancestral spirits. I wonder if the Vietnamese have a custom to call forth their ancestors. I've lived in their country for almost a year, and I haven't any idea.

The telephone rings twice, signaling that a shuttle has arrived to take me to the airport. My suitcase is much heavier with all the gifts for my family. I think of how eager I was for this week. Now I'm relieved that it's over. I just can't seem to be happy anywhere anymore.

Dry and dusty, treeless for as far as Long Binh reaches, it's home. Not for much longer, I muse, gazing at the big red cross painted on the emergency room's tin roof. No other choppers in the air, no casualties on the ground. If I'm lucky, it'll stay this way until it's time to catch my Freedom Bird.

Home means Kwell shampoo. Dropping my suitcase in front of the ward's door, I brace myself for the inevitable ribbing I'm about to receive and make my way to the medicine cabinet. The lull in the war has not caught up to the ward; everyone is busy.

But not so busy that I escape unnoticed with the tube of miracle shampoo.

"Have a good time, Lieutenant?" a corpsman grins.

I dash for the door.

I'm headed for the showers, Kwell tucked under my towel, when I'm informed that indoor plumbing arrived yesterday. It couldn't have come at a more propitious time; I sure as hell didn't want someone to catch me standing around in Kwell for the prescribed five minutes. The shower stall is Vietnamese size, but the water is hot. I lather up from head to foot and stand for *ten* minutes. For the first time in five days I can stand to touch myself.

Next, I try out our newly plumbed toilet, which is great but unfortunately is stopped up by this evening. The private who comes to check it says he's "happy to be of service to such lovely ladies," but his verdict is not so happy. It needs to be repiped; the dipshit dinks used one-inch pipes for the sewage. Oh, well, we can still use it for our midnight beer runs.

Indoor plumbing is not the only miracle to have occurred during my absence. A tiny refrigerator and two-foot-tall fan I shipped a year ago from Japan await me in the mail room. The mail clerk says they've been on a dock in Hong Kong all this time.

Hot showers, cold beer, and warm breezes for my last two weeks. Things sure are shaping up now that I'm getting ready to ship out. Hardly any reason to leave anymore, I think wryly.

I'm making my rounds, stop to see if the soldier wearing a blood-soaked turban has slipped away yet. Long seconds pass, my deathwatch interrupted when the expectant gasps for air.

"Clean sheet and Chux," I call to the corpsman, nodding toward the expectant as I head for clean dressings.

"Aw, Captain, he'll be gone before our shift ends," he moans from where he's switching an empty oxygen tank to a full one.

"We don't change dressings for the next shift," I say snappishly. "He's earned the right to die in a clean bed."

"Yes, ma'am!" Ever since I made captain, the ma'ams have flowed thick and heavy.

The dying soldier's face is grotesquely discolored and too swollen to pry open his eyelids and check his pupils. Sour-smelling drool from the corner of his mouth has collected in a pool of pinkish slime under his head and shoulders. I suction what I can from his trach tube, mouth and nose, and from that ghastly pool. I wipe the saliva from his face and neck, gulp to stay my stomach when my hand slides into the slime to lift his head. Blood squishes under my fingers when I cut off his drenched turban and dump it onto the dirty Chux.

My hand hits mush on the underside of his skull. I hadn't realized it was so badly squashed. My bloody hands leave stains on the new dressing as I rewrap his head, but it won't be long before it's soaked crimson again anyway. I wrap a Chux over the dressing; the plastic will keep the sheet clean. We can't waste any more clean sheets.

When I wash my hands in the basin of Wescodyne, the blood under my fingernails turns an ugly brown. I have a desperate urge to scrape them clean, but that's impossible here.

My promotion to captain, not to mention my imminent departure from Vietnam, brings expectations of a party. I invite all my friends—infantry officers and corpsmen, as well as doctors and nurses. For the occasion I'll serve an entire country ham, sent by my family upon my request.

The mess hall cook agrees to bake the ham for a few slices off the end. The club sergeant agrees to set an evening aside and order four cases of hard liquor and twelve cases of beer at cost, for a few more slices. Upon my invitation, a corpsman arranges for an enlisted band to play for free—and a slice of ham each.

When the mess sergeant learns enlisted will be there, he lays on a feast to go with the ham. Free feast, free booze, and live music. When the booze runs out, the infantry buys more. When time runs out, the club sergeant stays open on the condition that I dance with every enlisted man. When food runs out, everyone's too drunk to care.

A few nights later the triage nurse calls our ward to warn that there's a chopper on its way with three head wounds—all VC.

When the chopper lands, she calls back to say false alarm. All three are dead, shot point-blank in the forehead.

Fine by me. I've got enough to do without fucking around with goddamned gooks.

I'm sitting on the floor marking chest tube drainage when a gasping cough bolts me to my feet. It's one of our quadriplegics. I run for the portable oxygen tank and ambu bag, yell to the corpsman, "Call ER! Trach!"

My attempt to breathe for the quadriplegic with the ambu bag is futile; he's got laryngeal spasms. His eyes are frantic, belying his motionless body.

"Trach tray," I order when the corpsman hangs up the monster field phone. He lays the tray on the patient's chest. "Suction." I open the tray.

The corpsman grabs a machine. The quadriplegic's eyes roll back in his head. Shit. A cardiac arrest on a Stryker frame—pumping someone's chest on a flimsy frame—is always a flail. I slip on sterile gloves, pick up the surgical blade, and cut his throat.

I've never done a trach before, and the ease with which the blade slices the trachea takes me by surprise. This feat is barely accomplished, the dark red gash trickling blood down the soldier's neck and the edges of his wound sucking at the air, when a hand deftly slides a silver tube into the slit I've made. It belongs to the surgeon of the day.

The predictable cough spatters blood on my face. Swiping my eyes with my arm, a motion perfected from swiping sweat, I attach the trach tube to the man's neck while the surgeon suctions his lungs.

"O_2," I direct the corpsman, taking a pulse while he goes for a tank and trach mask setup. Fast and thready but regular.

When the soldier regains consciousness, his eyes are once again panicky.

"You're doing fine," I assure him, although spending the rest of his life as a quadriplegic doesn't seem so fine.

I'm back down on the floor, marking the chest tube drainage, when combat boots stop nearby. "Good work." The surgeon smiles down at me.

"Thanks." He doesn't leave. I look at him questioningly as I stand and grab the intake and output record to chart the amount of drainage.

"Seriously. You saved his life."

"That's what we're here for." I really don't have time for small talk. I have to finish my charting before the day shift arrives. I hope to get out of this place early for a change.

"Anybody'd think you just gave a back rub."

I laugh shortly. "Now that would be different." He gives me a questioning look, as though he really thinks we give back rubs here. "You must be new in-country" is my answer.

"No," he says flatly. "I've been here a month."

I can't remember who I was, let alone how I felt, after just one month. "In that case, you didn't do so badly yourself."

Now he chuckles. "I've noticed you at the club, but you never seem to have time to speak to me."

"I don't. I'm too short to speak to anyone." Then, in answer to his confused look, I add, "I'm outta here in a week."

"That's too bad. You're a good nurse."

"I've done my part," I return sharply.

He cocks his head at me. "I meant it as a compliment."

"Look," I say, facing him head-on, "I've got work to do. Do you mind?"

He bows slightly. "But of course. Thank you for all your help."

"I didn't do it for you."

He looks genuinely confused. "Of course not. I didn't mean it that way."

"Then how *did* you mean it?"

"Sorry." He shrugs and walks out.

"Kill them goddamned mother-fucking gooks!" one of our casualties screams from his bed.

"Relax, man. We got 'em, for sure," the corpsman says soothingly as he goes about his work.

"Fuckin' no-good cocksuckers. We'll get 'em all right. Ain't no goddamned gooks we can't get! Mother fuckers." The man's voice drones on through the night, calming to the corpsman's assurances but never shutting up.

Lately it seems there's always at least one noisemaker on

the ward. Or maybe it's just that they get to me more than they used to.

"Sure wish I could knock him out with something," I comment to the corpsman as we flip a Stryker frame.

"I might be able to come up with a baseball bat," he answers.

He gets me to smile, not easy to do these days. The shorter I get, the shorter my temper.

Larry is waiting for me when I get off work, bearing a candle and a bottle of Mateus. I didn't want our relationship to end with our last meeting, with the bitterness of Pops's death between us, but these hours are just as painful. We know this is our last time together—Larry won't be back from the field before I leave country—but we avoid talking about it. Nor do we mention Pops or the six months that Larry has left. It's unlucky to speak of those things.

Instead, we speak of the Real World, to which I will soon return, and all the wonderful things in it. Then, falling silent, Larry reaches into his shirt pocket and pulls out a slender silver and blue medal—his Combat Infantry Badge. He holds it toward me. Knowing how proud he is of it, I'm frightened by the significance of such a gift.

"Please, I want you to have it," he says. "I wish it were a ring, but the PX was closed before I could get here."

I gaze at his badge of courage, not knowing what to say. I don't want to worry about what might happen to him before his tour of duty is finished, and somehow it feels as if I won't have to if I don't accept. Besides, there's Peter. I don't know how I'll feel about him when I see him again. I don't even know how I'll feel about Larry.

"I want you to think about me every time you look at it." He smiles. "And when I get back, there's a whole townful of folks I want to show you off to."

If you get back, I think.

"I'm asking you to marry me." Pause. "Well, you think about it," he says to my silence. "Maybe you'll realize what a great catch I am once I'm not around anymore." The words are spoken in jest, but he cannot hide his disappointment as he presses the medal into my hand.

"Please, Larry," I say at last, "we can't know how we'll feel when we get back."

"I know how I'll feel."

"How can you? We're so far away from home, and you've still got a long time to go. You might meet some pretty young nurse who knocks you off your feet."

"I already have. And we're not so far away that I don't know a good thing when I see it."

How can he be so sure? I don't feel sure about anything. Before I can think better of it, I ask, "What if something happens to you?"

His smile vanishes. "Then I don't want some Charlie getting his dirty paws on it."

I hesitate before taking it, then stretch to kiss him.

A little of the old grin lights up his face. "Good. Safe and sound in the hand of my favorite nurse. Maybe she'll even polish it up every once in a while."

Too late I wish I had put aside my prudishness about crabs and we had made love one last time. I wish there were one more tomorrow. I wish there were time to straighten out my feelings.

The candle burns on after he's gone. Long after the flame dies, I fall asleep to the faint rumblings of war, the Combat Infantry Badge clenched in my fist. Sometime in the night it cuts my palm. When I awaken, it's held fast with dried blood.

"Nurse! You gotta do something!" shouts the quadriplegic from a Stryker frame next to the medicine cabinet.

When I rush to where he lies, a quick glance assures me that everything is in order. Probably a nightmare. "It's okay," I reassure him. It's late, and I don't want him setting off the other patients.

"No! No! It's the incoming! They're walkin' 'em in, Captain! I been listening, and they're walkin' 'em in! You gotta do somethin'! You gotta get us outta here! I tell you they got us pegged!"

"It's all right. You're safe here." My voice is calm, but his panic is rubbing off on me. Is he right? There is incoming, and it does sound close. I glance down the ward. What could we do if he's right? All our patients are either comatose, confused and restrained, or on Stryker frames. The standard procedure of laying patients on the floor and covering them with mattresses would never work here. "I'm sure they're not after the hospital," I add, trying to reassure myself as much as him, for they do sound *very* close.

His protests carry an urgency that is upsetting the confused patients. The ward is beginning to sound like a madhouse.

"What am I gonna do?" he cries out. "I can't move!"

"Can it, soldier!" the corpsman snaps. "We got enough on our hands without you starting a stampede."

The paralyzed soldier glares at the corpsman but quiets. I don't want to leave him alone, but I have to get back to work.

"Hey, Captain?" It's the Stryker frame paraplegic.

"What?" I demand irritably. I'm way behind now.

"He's right." He nods at the silenced quadriplegic. "I've been listening, too. They're walkin' 'em in all right." A round falls as though to prove what he's saying.

I've heard hospitals are sometimes attacked when a high-ranking Vietcong is a patient. I haven't heard of any on our VC ward, but that means nothing.

"What you have to listen for is a round falling on the other side of the hospital. Then you'll know they've got us nailed."

"There's still nothing we can do but sit tight," I say.

"There is something you can do."

I look at him expectantly. "When I give you the word," he nods, "you get under that desk. It's the safest place on the ward, and you won't be any use to us if a round gets you."

"Thanks." I smile wanly. Now I'm really nervous. This guy is too composed to be overreacting. But right now I've got to get an IV for that dry bottle on the end of the ward.

There's no way to know what's going on—no windows and no time to ask. I try to catch up on my work. Even if we're not the target, all this action is bound to mean incoming wounded.

When the attack stops, the world is abruptly silent. No matter that there is outgoing artillery and low-flying choppers, the world sounds very quiet.

By morning it's all forgotten.

After my shift, as I'm getting ready for bed, a sound outside jerks my head up.

"Bastard!" I hiss at the eyes staring at me through the wall. Whoever it is disappears.

Why am I shaking so? Surely one Peeping Tom shouldn't bother me, not after a year of being ogled everywhere I go. Yet, wearing only underwear in my own room, I feel vulnerable.

Goddamn son of a bitch!

"You can do it with the pickup, Daddy," Leroy begs. "You just gotta get me outta here. Ain't no swamp that truck can't handle!"

Must be a Clover Leaf Boy, I think. They seem to be the ones who get stuck with most of the delta duty.

Leroy is built like a bull, and his pleas are laced with obscenities for anyone who passes. They began when we covered him with alcohol-soaked towels and blasted him with the fan to bring his temperature under control. While he is miserable and fighting to escape his bed of torture, his cries have agitated another patient, Jules, for whom a swamp is a fish hole and everyone associated with one is an ugly fish. Leroy doesn't like being called an ugly fish. He's gonna get Jules when his daddy gets him out of that swamp.

Meanwhile, the corpsman and I are making our rounds—turning, suctioning, hanging IVs, checking vital signs, changing dressings and oxygen tanks along the way. We work quietly, unwilling to compete with the shouting. Two choppers pass low overhead, headed for the triage helicopter pad. We instinctively pick up the pace to be ready for wounded that might come our way.

Just as a chopper passes low overhead, our cannon cut loose. Leroy and Jules fall silent momentarily, then raise their frightened pleas and angry cries an octave higher. The cries of wounded, the thunder of smoking cannon, and the roar of choppers reach a crescendo.

The field phone rings. The corpsman answers, holds up four fingers. We have twenty-two beds and eighteen wounded. We can handle these four, but there'll be more before the night's over, so we'll have to move some patients now.

We can put the decerebrate in the back. No doubt he'll soon be an expectant. The guy in bed one is stable, ready to be evacuated and will do fine in the back as well. I'd like to stuff Leroy and Jules back there, but they might break through their restraints, so I don't dare. We move the paraplegic to the other side of the nursing station. None of the others is stable enough or close enough to death to be out of constant sight. It'll have to do. Maybe one of the new ones will be an expectant.

The corpsman is ready to move the decerebrate—urine bottle on top of the bed, chest tube clamped, nasogastric tube plugged, and IV on a portable pole. Helping him, I notice pale pink drainage on a head dressing along the way—probably spinal fluid. I must remember to tell the neurosurgeon when he's free.

Leroy is screaming for his daddy to come quick, that these people are trying to kill him. Jules thinks he's drowning in mud. The war intertwines with their delirium.

I can barely hear the phone ring, much less the voice on the other end, but I know before I answer that recovery is swamped and our first of the newly wounded is on the way. Shit, I'm tired.

I've barely hung up when the first admission rolls in. A glimpse through the open door shows the world outside bathed in the eerie glow of flares. Something's going on somewhere close.

"Shut up!" I scream at Leroy before I can stop myself. He does. So does Jules. What's the matter with me? Never mind. They'll start up again soon enough, and the break will do us all good. There're eight hours to go on this shift.

Point counterpoint, the tempo of the ward picks up as the turmoil outside abates. The emergency room, recovery room, and operating rooms are maxed out. Our beds are filled, and three overflows lie on gurneys in the aisle. We give blood for the low blood pressures. When that runs out, we switch to plasma. If that doesn't work, we add Aramine. We hang up more IVs where they're needed, an ampule of Mannitol for the new head wounds, and another for the one with a blown pupil. We check to make sure restraints are secure, insert Foleys to be certain they're making urine.

God, how I wish I could shoot Leroy with Librium to shut him up, but that would complicate his picture of confusion. I check the pressure dressing on this soldier's leg; he's losing too much blood. Jesus, that head wound is digging his fingers into his skull. I snap a tourniquet on this man's leg until I can get back to apply a pressure dressing—better for him to lose a leg than the other man to dig out his brain.

I run a liter of saline into the soldier not putting out urine, then keep looking to make sure it doesn't run dry while I handle this last admission. We cut off the admission's shirt so I can figure out where all the blood is coming from. Is the expectant still with us? Fuck, what's taking him so long? We need that space. Time for four o'clock medications. First, chart this IV. That comatose patient is obstructing; put in an airway. I suction another man's gurgling tracheostomy. God, I'm tired.

I ignore the block letters over their pockets in case there's one I'll recognize. I disregard the blood on my hands; there's no time to wash between patients. I don't look at their faces; it might interfere with what I'm doing. I try not to look at the insignia to see what outfit they're with since it doesn't make any difference, but I already have. The Clover Leaf Boys are catching holy hell again. At least it's not Larry's outfit.

The door opens, and I turn in despair. I see the day nurse carrying two cups of coffee. I've lost track of time.

"You're a sight for sore eyes," I call from where I'm hanging what must be the hundredth liter of IV fluid.

"I guess," she says. "God Almighty. I knew it was going to be busy, but this is insane."

"I think it's known as combat nursing." My voice sounds as tired as I feel. God, this coffee tastes good.

Surveying the damage, she asks, "How long before the ORs are ready for some of these guys?"

I shrug. "My guess is awhile."

I nod to the corpsman, giving him permission to speak before we start report. "Sorry, Captain, but I gotta get. I got sandbag duty this mornin'."

I stare at him in utter disbelief. "Forget it. You don't leave until this ward is under control. You don't even *think* of leaving until I say you can go!" The tension of the night, my tiredness, make my voice almost shake.

"I don't want to, Captain, but the sarge'll get on my case if I don't report."

"You call that sergeant and tell him we need you here. If he gives you any grief, put me on the phone with him."

Sandbags. What the fuck do they mean by having these men fill sandbags? Maybe the sergeant should come over and get a little blood on *his* hands!

I hear the corpsman ask the sergeant if he wants to speak to me. Evidently not. I should have called in the first place to give him a piece of my mind. The corpsman smiles a sheepish thank-you. Anything has to be better than filling sandbags. The stains on his fatigues cause me to look down at mine. We're both smudged with blood and dirt.

After report, I finish my charting, then help the day nurse with pre-ops until all but one have gone to the operating room. It's 1000 hours. I'm falling asleep on my feet when the day nurse nudges me.

"We can take it from here, Captain."

I nod. "I think you'll have to." I stop for the corpsman on my way out, give him permission to leave. I wonder if I look as exhausted as he does.

"Tell that sergeant I ordered you straight to bed, that we're going to be busy tonight." I secretly wish the sergeant will complain. I'm ready for a showdown.

"Yes, ma'am."

"And, Specialist," I say as we walk out the door, "I said straight to bed."

"Yes, ma'am." He heads for the enlisted tents.

Not that bed is where I'm going. I'll never get to sleep without a drink; one Rob Roy should do the trick this day.

Nearing the club, I see Larry's Jeep parked alongside our hooch. A corporal is leaning against it with his arms crossed, waiting. Could he have a message from Larry? No, Larry would have come himself. It must be about Larry.

Before he sees me, I slip around the officers' club and sneak through the back door of our hooch. Whatever he has to say, I don't want to hear it. If Larry's dead, I don't want to know. If he's messed up for life, lying in some hospital bed without arms

236

or legs, I don't want to see him. I want to remember him with a light in his eye and the catlike grace of a warrior.

It's my last shift in Long Binh, in Vietnam.

My replacement is orienting with me, a male nurse, Don. He's older than I am, and that is hard to believe; he's so energetic, so full of life.

The ward is busy but not crazy. Don depends a lot on my help though he'll be on his own after tonight. I decide to see how he'll do if he's left alone for a while. Post-op is busy and can use me.

When I return, I note with satisfaction that the ward seems calm and orderly. Then I notice a decerebrate patient who wasn't decerebrate when I left. I see before I reach his bed what the problem is: The oxygen tank is empty.

I shouldn't have left the ward, but it's too late for shouldn't-haves. We call the neurosurgeon, hang Mannitol, and wait. That's all we can do.

When my last hour of combat nursing is over, one of our corpsmen escorts me to the enlisted men's beer tent to say our farewells. This part of the base brings back the old keenness of being in the Army, of what I expected a war zone to be like—the planks laid over mud and the pervasive smell of canvas. We traipse between tents, the men in this area wearing well-worn fatigues and stripes. I've never been here before, yet it makes me nostalgic.

Though it's early morning, every table visible through the open flaps of the beer tent is taken. I worry my presence will intrude on their good time and decide I won't stay for more than one beer.

"Hip, hip hurray!" erupts as we step through the tent flaps and everyone rises to face us.

Whirling on the corpsman, I demand, "How could you!" whereupon everyone bursts into laughter.

The corpsman grins. "Your reputation precedes you, Captain."

"Get the captain a beer!" someone shouts as I stare numbly at the tentful of faces.

"Right here!" comes another shout, and I locate the table where the rest of our ward's corpsmen sit, with a beer waiting for me in front of an empty seat.

Proudly I make my way to join them. To my mind, these are

the Army's finest, the best corpsmen anywhere. Without them I could never have survived this place.

But we don't speak of such things. In this land we don't need to. We speak our minds to people we don't like and share our time with those we do.

My last night in Vietnam is quiet, an eerie quiet. The B-52s are either taking the night off or dropping their deadly burdens elsewhere. The cannon keep a silent vigil, and no helicopters chop at the sky.

When the war is this quiet, the world sounds dead. There are no frogs, no crickets, no night birds, no yowling cats. There are people. Their shadows pass beyond the range of light in ones or twos or clusters; their voices float our way. When the club door opens and closes, the jukebox is faintly heard, tunes and words indistinguishable. An occasional Jeep whines from somewhere in the dark.

Three infantry officers I know from the club have come to say last farewells before I climb aboard my Freedom Bird. As is often the case here, it feels as though we've known each other much longer than we have. To my immediate left is Jim, a small man with blue eyes and a thin face who wants to become a teacher when this is all over. Next to him, Mike, with hazel eyes and a permanent five o'clock shadow, who plans to be a farmer. David, the first Jewish officer I've met since Japan, whose dream is to be a concert pianist, sits to my right.

We talk quietly in front of my hooch beneath a bare light bulb in line with the other bare light bulbs along the walkway. Our drinks and cigarettes rise and fall to our words.

Now that my time has come, I'm not so sure I want to leave. I feel welded to this war, these warriors, and their wounded. If home is where the heart is, this must be my home.

What's the first thing I'm going to do? Jim asks. Go for a walk in the woods. What about my first meal? Real milk. What will I do while I'm on leave? Sleep in.

It's all part of the going-home ritual, these questions and answers. They cheer up those who are staying as much as those who are going. It's good luck to be so near someone so short.

When I speak of my guilt about leaving, they assure me that I've done my part. When I talk about my fears of returning home, they assure me those will disappear when I get there. When I say I'm not sure life will have any purpose after this, they laugh. What about taking a spin in a real car or chowing down on a real steak? How about getting dressed to kill in a real dress?

We all laugh. Come to think of it, dressed to kill is what we wear here.

When a glass is empty, it is refilled. When a cigarette is finished, it is field-stripped and the butt tucked away in a chest pocket. Periodically one of us swipes at sweat on our noses or chins, unaware of what we do.

I have always been here, belong here. Why am I leaving?

We hear the *whop-whop* of a Huey when it's still far away. All of us fall silent as it grows closer. It's a dustoff. I think about Don on nights, hope there aren't incoming head wounds. Another distant *whop-whop* signals a second chopper before its sound is drowned out by the first, now coming in for a landing. I should go help the new nurse.

The hell you say. You're drunk. Plus he's got to learn sometime and there's no time like the present.

"Somebody's catching shit." There's a distance in David's voice. He's in the field, I think, remembering a dustoff in a different time and place.

There's artillery in the distance, someone else's war tonight that may be his tomorrow. Everybody's war within range of the choppers is our war.

No, I correct myself. Not ours. Theirs. My war is over.

We slug down more drinks, light more cigarettes. It's part of the going-home ritual, this getting drunk. It cheers up those who are going as much as those who are staying behind.

CHAPTER FIFTEEN

SEPTEMBER 19– OCTOBER 19, 1967: My Freedom Bird Home

I T's my last wake-up in Vietnam. No more jungle fatigues or jungle boots for this ex-combat nurse. And, I realize as I don my summer cords, no sweater. In my rush to send things home when I got here, it went along with my winter uniform. I'll freeze my buns off when I get to the World, but all things considered, I'll brave it and go back anyway.

It's my last Jeep ride through this scarred landscape. I stare mindlessly at the bulldozed and defoliated tree line, the mined and pockmarked fields. I try to focus my thoughts, but I can't. My mind is empty. I know I should feel something, but I don't.

I'm the only woman in the temporary female quarters at the Bien Hoa placement center. The quarters are isolated—not a vehicle or person in sight. A wire fence, topped by concertina wire and guarded by a watchtower, stands at a short distance. There are trees on the other side just a stone's throw away, filling me with uneasiness.

I tell myself I've been hanging out with line officers for too long, that trees so close just show how safe it is, how much farther from the war I am. Yet the only source of water is a canvas bag that hangs between the barracks. How odd that the Corps of Engineers hasn't reached this place, this stepping-stone to the World.

The day is quiet, too quiet. I can't get past the notion that it's the quiet before a storm. Nervous as a cat, I pass the day smoking at a picnic table, staring at the canvas bag and the trees beyond the barbed wire and watchtower. It feels like a POW camp. Thank goodness I'm leaving tonight.

The terminal is crowded with warriors, and there's a giddy exhilaration running on the surface of a current of apprehension. We've all heard of attacks on soldiers going home, of soldiers dying on the threshold of their Freedom Birds—a tactic to dishearten newcomers and short-timers alike. Because they are unarmed, with no place to hide, this hour defies the instincts of men who have fought for their lives for a year, men I would like to talk to; only they keep their distance in deference to my being the only woman, and a captain.

Night has fallen when we line up Army style, lady first and then according to rank. When the inevitable major steps behind me and tries to strike up a conversation, I want to spit in his face. A rear echelon mother fucker. I can smell it in his starched khakis.

Roll call. Yes, yes. Do you think we'll run away? Single file, a hushed silence descends as we step onto the tarmac.

Big as life, our Freedom Bird sits before us. She's a Braniff 707 jet, and over her wing is a stewardess, smartly dressed in the miniskirt of the day, to greet us at the door. All eyes are on her as I lead us toward the stairway.

I'm aware of the grated steps, easily felt through the soles of my unaccustomed pumps. At the top I cannot resist turning for one last look, one last whiff, of Vietnam. Single file, the line of soldiers stretches to the terminal.

We enter our Bird, brightly plumaged in orange and yellow. A whispery quietness follows us as we take our seats; we aren't the drunken, happy crowd I had expected.

Of course, the REMF major sits down next to me. Too late I wish I had picked a backseat so I would be with the buddies of casualties that I've cared for this past year. He will *not* spoil this trip. I will *not* speak to him.

When the engines fire up, the whispers silence. There's almost a palpable fear that this dream will not come true, that this trip will not happen.

The stewardess begins her spiel in front of the plane, the words coming from far away. My hands clutch the armrests as our Freedom Bird taxis to the runway, tests its systems. Is Charlie waiting for us? The engines roar, and the Bird lumbers painfully slowly. If only it could shoot into the sky like the Phantoms we watched from the Starlit Roof of Claymore Tower.

Lift-off! I look out the window to watch Vietnam fall out of my life, but it's too dark to see anything. That's good. No anti-aircraft fire. Up, up, and away!

We're safe! The plane erupts into whistles, cheers, and back-slapping shouts of congratulations. We made it! My eyes fill with tears as I press my face against the glass. We're going home.

Home. It's too early for snow. I hope it's not too late for fall colors. I can't remember exactly what month that is anymore.

An announcement over the loudspeaker makes it official: "This is your captain speaking. We have just left Vietnam airspace."

Tumultuous cheers. Then the announcement that a meal will be served, including plenty of fresh milk. More cheers. The milk is guzzled as hungrily as any beer on a sizzling afternoon, the airline meal gobbled as hungrily as a Thanksgiving feast. We are getting closer and closer to the World.

Afterward the lights are turned down. With the drone of engines, quiet conversations taper to silence. When I jerk awake, it's full daylight.

The REMF major sleeps soundly. I stare at the blue sky and darker blue ocean far below, watch white, billowy clouds skim by. I wonder what it will feel like to be home. Peter is now stationed at Fort Belvoir, Virginia, so we'll be able to see each other during my month's leave. What will it be like when we see each other after so long? His face is no longer clear; the times we shared are hard to remember. And what about my family? I've changed so much that I don't know if they'll still love me.

We descend toward Travis Air Force Base, California, in silence. Not until the plane's wheels touch the ground do the cheers erupt again.

"We're home!"

"We made it!"

"The World! The Real World!"

"Please keep your seat belts fastened until the plane comes to a complete stop," intones the stewardess as soldiers clamber to the windows.

When the plane stops, she waves for us to take our seats and listen to announcements about where to go for baggage and how to reach our final destinations. But it's useless. A loud murmur ripples through our Freedom Bird as soldiers crowd toward the windows, hoping to see their loved ones.

"It's been a pleasure to serve you," says the stewardess. "We hope you had a comfortable trip." Then, with tears brimming in her eyes, she chokes, "Welcome home."

No one misses her words. They stun our soldiers into silence, fill us with warmth.

We're really home. It's over.

Those of us met here run to embrace in joyful reunions. The rest of us watch enviously from the sidelines. Standing alone, a woman officer in a sea of enlisted men, I have a sense of not belonging, of not being a part of what's going on around me.

Welcome to the World.

There's some holdup with our baggage. I overhear someone say they're looking for weapons. Someone else says it's drugs. Why would anyone take the chance? Finally past customs, I follow the crowd, teetering in my heels with a duffel bag in tow.

It's freezing outside. Goose bumps come up on my arms, and my teeth are chattering. This must be the place. Soldiers mill around, all waiting for a shuttle to the San Francisco International Airport. The line is long, the sun long gone before it's my turn. My stomach is growling; my body is stiff; my mind is numb. At least the bus is heated.

Pulling out onto the freeway, the bus rapidly gains speed. We must be going a hundred miles an hour! Take it easy, I tell myself.

Light a cigarette and enjoy the trip. Gazing out the side window, I see only pieces of road in car headlights. Just relax, Winnie. There are *no* VC in those long stretches of blackness. I know, I know, but I'm still uneasy.

I concentrate on the front window. It's awesome! Three lanes, all going in the same direction.

Our busload of returning soldiers races through the night in near silence. At the airport a porter asks if he can take my duffel bag. I don't know where I'm going, and even if I did, I wouldn't know how much to tip. I shake my head no.

People rush everywhere, the soldiers disappearing in the crowds. I scan the bewildering array of airline logos stretching the length of the terminal, trying to remember which one goes to the East Coast. No use. I pick one in the middle, get in line, and hope for the best.

Miniskirts are everywhere. I've heard of their popularity, but the only ones I've ever seen were on Nancy Sinatra and my Freedom Bird's stewardess. Both men and women wear jeans—so sloppy in public. And there's a man with long hair and a beaded necklace. What kind of man would wear a necklace?

"Where to?" asks the clerk as I step up to the counter.

"New York or New Jersey."

She gives me a sharp look. "What airport?"

"Just so long as it gets me there." I smile tiredly.

"Look, I can't sell you a ticket unless you tell me where you want to go," she snaps.

Why didn't Daddy ever use the Newark Airport? I can't remember. She's growing impatient, drumming her fingers. "New York," I blurt.

"Kennedy or La Guardia?" she fires back.

Which airport did we use? I can't remember. "Which is closer to New Jersey?"

She glares at me in disbelief. "I thought you wanted to go to New York!"

People are shuffling in the line behind me. I mustn't waste their time.

"Kennedy."

She deftly types out the destination, quotes the flight number, gate number, time of departure. Handing it over, she announces the price.

Fuck! I forgot I had to pay! Shakily pulling out my wallet, I count my cash. I don't have enough! On the verge of tears, I ask what I can do.

Do I have a credit card?

No.

The people behind me roll their eyes, shuffle menacingly.

Do I have a checkbook?

Yes! Oh, thank you. My hands tremble as I write out the amount. Hurry. You're wasting their time.

She needs my ID. I fumble, drop my military card when I pull it out of my pocketbook, retrieve it, and hand it over. My captain's bars must seem like a joke.

She'll take my duffel bag.

Oh, thank you! Now, if only I could get rid of these goddamned useless shoes.

I must call Daddy to let him know that my flight will arrive early tomorrow morning. I try to get change at ticket counters, but nobody wants to part with change. I hope my parents won't mind my calling them collect.

The pay telephone seems so strange, like a relic from some distant past. Dropping the coin, I dial "0."

Daddy's voice, just like that, accepts the charges.

"Where are you?" His voice sounds so familiar. Why does that surprise me?

"San Francisco. My flight arrives at Kennedy tomorrow morning."

"Kennedy! That's way out on the Island!"

He's yelling at me. Kennedy was a big mistake. Long Island is a long way from where we live. Why didn't I remember that?

"I'm sorry. I couldn't remember which airport you like." Tears choke my voice.

"It's nothing to cry about! Just get it changed to Newark."

"Oh, no, please! Don't make me go back to that line!" Jesus, Smith, I say to myself. It's nothing to cry about!

An exasperated sigh, but I can tell he's sorry for yelling. "Don't worry about it. I'll meet you at baggage pickup. What time do you arrive?"

"Oh-six-thirty hours."

"Six-thirty!" He's yelling again. Kennedy is a long way from home. He'll have to get up very early.

"I can wait," I offer. "I don't mind waiting if you want to come later."

"No, no. It's okay. I took the week off so I could spend it with my daughter. I might as well start early."

He's trying to make me feel better, but I feel terrible. I've been back less than a day, and I've already botched everything up.

"Your mother's planning a great dinner for you."

"Thank her for me. I appreciate it."

"She's fixed up your room."

"Yes, she wrote that. That was very nice of her." I'm so tired. I'll feel better after I've had some sleep.

"There's someone waiting for the phone," I lie.

"Good-bye, honey. We'll see you tomorrow."

"Yes, sir. Good-bye."

I should have asked how they're doing. How could I forget?

How long since I left Long Binh? Around thirty hours, I figure. I'd better get some coffee. I could use some food, too. Thank God I'm rid of that fucking duffel bag.

That restaurant smells good, but sitting alone might attract attention to me, and too many people are already giving me funny looks. Some seem downright unfriendly, but from what I can see, nobody is very friendly to anybody here.

Welcome to the Real World.

I wolf down two hot dogs, french fries, and countless cups of coffee at a standup counter. Fuck what anybody thinks, I take off my shoes while I eat.

A man in a suit stands next to me reading a newspaper. The date reads September 19, 1967. Christ, I forgot about the international dateline. It's the same day that I left Vietnam.

I pick a window seat, wishing again that I had a sweater. Why the shit is the plane air-conditioned at this time of year?

The man sitting next to me wants to know what kind of uniform I'm wearing. Then he asks why a woman would join the Army.

"To travel," I say.

"Been anywhere interesting?" he asks.

"I just got back from Vietnam."

He says nothing more, fidgets with a magazine for a short while, then moves to another seat.

Do I smell bad? Or is going to Vietnam some kind of crime?

When another man sits down next to me, I stare out the window. Then I sleep until we touch down at Kennedy.

"Hello, honey," my father greets me, folding me in a big bear hug. "It's good to have you back."

I'm grateful he's here to take care of me, but shouldn't I feel more?

My duffel bag is easy to locate; it's the only one. Daddy flags a porter and tips him at the car, making it look simple. We climb in and close the doors, settle into the seats, and take off.

We fly onto the highway. Clutching at the seat, I try not to say anything but can't help myself. "Do you have to go so fast?"

His eyebrows dart up in surprise. "We're only doing fifty."

I steel myself. We haven't even reached the speed limit, and there's a long way to go.

"How was your trip?" he asks.

"Fine."

"You look like you can use a little fattening up. Can you guess what's for dinner?"

"Anything will be fine."

There's an awkward pause. "What are your plans for your leave?"

"I don't have any."

I can feel him looking at me, trying to figure out what my problem is. "You should take your mother shopping while you're here."

"Yes, I'll do that."

After a while he sighs audibly. "Cat got your tongue?"

"No, I'm just tired."

Another pause. "Well, it's good to have you back."

What's the matter with me? I stare at the countryside whizzing by. I don't want him to think I'm rude, but I don't seem able or willing, I'm not sure which, to make small talk.

Everything looks so different. So built up. So many cars. Look at the people we pass, all pasty white and unsmiling. Why are they so grim?

We pull up in front of my parents' red-shingled house, but everything still seems oddly unfamiliar. Daddy honks to let the neighbors know we've arrived.

I dive forward, hitting my head on the dashboard.

"Are you all right?"

"Yes, I'm fine."

"What happened?"

"Nothing." I shake my head. "The horn just startled me." I resolve never to let that happen again.

I'm shuddering in the cold air, so Daddy tells me to go inside while he gets my bag. I don't want him to carry my duffel bag with his artificial leg, tell him to leave it until later. I know he'll bring it anyway, but I'm too damn cold to wait until he opens the trunk.

Mama's in the kitchen, doesn't hear me come in over the television blaring in the living room.

"Mama?" I say from the kitchen door. She turns in surprise, smiles brightly, and crosses the short distance to give me a hug.

"How was your trip?" she asks.

"Fine."

"Guess what we're having for dinner."

Jesus. Why is everybody so concerned about dinner this early in the morning? "Steak?"

"No."

"Country ham?"

"No. Turkey with all the trimmings. And I've fixed up your room."

"Yes, thanks. I'll go take a look at it and change out of this uniform."

I've made good my escape, but I'm still trapped. The closed

walls, closed windows, stuffy unnatural warmth are suffocating.

What's the matter with me? I slept the whole way on the plane, but I'm still tired.

So, I tell myself, lie down and take a nap.

But I should go talk to Mama and Daddy. They'll be hurt if I don't.

Fuck it. You'll feel better when you wake up.

The first week passes, one day much like the next. I sleep late, throw together a breakfast, then pretend to read a newspaper while I drink coffee and smoke cigarettes. I'd stay at the kitchen table all day, but Daddy took a week off to be with me. So I join my parents in the living room, then pretend to watch TV so they won't bug me with small talk or nag me to get out of the house and have fun while I'm young, go shopping for clothes and visit my friends, none of which interests me.

In the afternoon I force myself to take a walk. There are some woods three blocks away that I long to see, but I'm nervous about going that far. I settle for the sidewalks of our suburban block, hoping I won't meet anyone. I walk down one side of the street and, shivering, run home on the other, then go to my room and pretend to nap while I smoke cigarettes and drink booze. We eat dinner in front of the TV. Afterward I sit in the kitchen to smoke and drink, worried about what my parents think but not caring enough to do anything different. I go to bed before they do, lie awake wondering what's wrong with me.

My parents are right, I know. I should visit friends from high school or take a bus into Manhattan and go see friends from nursing school. But I don't want to talk to anyone, not even on the telephone. It would do me good to take a trip to the ocean and walk on the boardwalk or drive up to the mountains and see the fall colors. But I'm afraid of driving on the highways. I ought to go shopping for clothes; those I brought with me have a musty smell, and those I left behind are two sizes too big. But I don't care about clothes. And I just don't have the energy.

Shit. It's three in the morning, but it's too quiet to sleep. The closed-in walls and windows are stifling, so I open the window and pile blankets on top of myself. Now I feel trapped by the blankets. Fuck it. I get up, shut the window.

I finally drift off, wake up a short time later drenched in sweat, my heart racing from a dream I can't remember.

Not until a faint blue lightens the sky can I sleep, and then I sleep late. The day starts just like yesterday, and the day before that.

The evening before my father returns to work, he takes out the slides I sent from Japan. "That's Sagami-ono," I say, "the town just outside Camp Zama." And I describe the exotic wares in the tiny shops. "That's the Kamiseiya officers' club pool, where there was a sauna." And I tell them what fun we had there. "That's the daibutsu, a giant bronze statue of Buddha, where a class of Japanese students asked me for my autograph."

The slides of Japan are followed by those I sent from Vietnam. "Central marketplace," I say, "in downtown Saigon." And I tell about the rip-off pedicab drivers without mentioning how they sometimes took you where you didn't want to go. "That's the Pied Piper MP guarding our villa, surrounded by the children who played with him." I want to tell them he was shot by a sniper, but there's a knot in my throat, and I'm afraid I'll cry.

"The old French fort in the open field across the street from Claymore Tower, with an old man scrubbing his water buffalo in a mud puddle." I don't mention the fire fights after dark. "And that's another old man we cared for in a small village outside Saigon." And I tell them we took a bullet out of his leg but not that it was an American bullet.

"Us drinking rice wine in a Montagnard village." And we laugh at my description of the roaches crawling out of the jug. I leave out our fear of getting caught in darkness going back to base. "This is the Horse's Head insignia of the First Cavalry on the mountain at An Khe." And I tell them about needing guards when I used the four-holer, but not about getting caught in a rice paddy during a mortar attack.

I don't know why I leave out so much. Maybe it's because I always wrote not to worry, and now I'm afraid they won't believe me. Or maybe it's because it all seems too far away to matter.

The slide show ends with our hooches at Long Binh. "I'm surprised you don't have any shots of your patients," says my father, "to help you remember them."

The neurosurgery ICU fills my mind, occupied by casualties who were there when I left. "I don't need pictures," I answer distantly. "I still remember them."

"Oh?" says my mother. "Tell us about them."

I focus on the remembrance and begin speaking with the monotone I used in nursing report: "On one side of the desk is an expectant; his head dressing is saturated with blood and needs to be changed. Next to him is a decerebrate attached to a respirator, who needs to be suctioned. On the other side of the desk is a gunshot wound to the head, tied to the bed because he's confused. There's a man just like him in the next bed. Across from them is a quadriplegic on a Stryker frame, who was just trached because he had laryngeal spasms. Next to him is a paraplegic—"

"Nobody wants to hear that stuff," my mother interrupts firmly. Then, to my blank silence: "Some things are better left unsaid."

"You can't let those things get you down," my father says. "You have to just forget about it and go on with your life."

"How can I forget?"

"Just don't think about it."

Then shut off the damn TV, I think miserably. Stop the nightly news footage of all those warrior faces, of choppers with red crosses, of wounded with bloodied field bandages and glazed eyes staring out of the screen while we eat steaks and potatoes and fresh salads and drink real milk.

The second week neighbors come to see me. Smiling broadly, they ask what was it like.

To answer the question, I tell them my humorous stories: the rice wine with cockroaches; Captain Cruz and the clogged shower; the Vietnamese scrubbing ice with hot water.

"What's *really* going on over there?" one dares to ask.

"I don't know. I'm here, not there."

"What about when you *were* there?"

"A lot of people were getting blown away," I say bluntly.

"Yes, that is unfortunate."

"Yes," I say, squinting my eyes. It feels as if there were many more things I wanted to say, but I can't focus my thoughts. Then the feeling is gone, I feel nothing.

"How's the war going?" another neighbor asks on another day.

"I don't know," I say. "All I did was care for casualties."

"So, what did they think?"

"I worked in neurosurgery. Most of them couldn't think."

One neighbor wants to know when I think the war will end.

"End?" I grope for an answer but can't find one. "I never think about that."

In light of such visits, any lingering thoughts of calling old friends are put to rest.

When Peter telephones, I'm in the kitchen. Mama calls from the living room to say it's for me, and I know right away who it is; no one else knows I'm here. He's driving up from Virginia for the weekend. This is Tuesday night. His call is the impetus I needed to go shopping.

It's my first time driving on a highway since coming back. My father sits next to me the way he did when he taught me to drive. My mother, too nervous about driving ever to learn how, is in the back. It's not as bad as I feared. Fifty no longer feels like flying, and it's not long before I edge into the middle lane.

"Slow down," my father warns.

"Why?"

"Because we get off at this exit." He points to an exit approaching fast.

"Shit!" I swerve into the slow lane, cutting off the driver to my right. The driver blasts his horn, long and loud.

It's not the horn but the "shit" that reverberates inside the car. No woman in my family ever swears.

Glancing in the rearview mirror, I see my mother's pursed lips. She turns huffily toward the window. Bullshit! Fucking bullshit! I'll be goddamned if I'll apologize!

"Oh, my," my father says with a nervous chuckle. "Guess I don't have to watch my language anymore."

"No, I guess not." My mother agrees with a small laugh. "At least not with your daughter."

I want to let loose with every swearword in the book. Show them what the fuck real swearing is all about. But I know it wouldn't change anything. And my leave won't last forever.

Mama goes off on her own. Daddy and I head for a shoe store. Along with everything else, he has nagged that my pumps from basic training are falling apart and that the shoes I left behind, pointed toes with high heels, are out of style; square toes with stacked heels are in now. It's too cold for sandals, and combat boots are definitely out—no matter how my feet might feel about it.

On the way we pass a music store, and I pick up strings for my guitar. It's my first purchase in the World, and it's not so bad. I'm encouraged.

The shoe store isn't so simple. There's a bewildering array of shoes lining the walls and covering the display stands, too many styles and colors for me to choose from. And I can't get past my sense of guilt for being here. Dying soldiers still lie on the ward where I left them two weeks ago. What possible difference can my shoes make?

"Just pick out a pair you like and try them on," my father prompts me.

I feel so lost and confused that I can't focus my thoughts. "I can't decide," I say at last.

My father picks out a pair of shoes for me. I try them on, say they're fine.

"Are you sure?" Daddy asks. "It looks like they hurt your feet."

"They'll stretch out after I wear them a few times."

"Don't take them if they hurt your feet."

"They're fine. I'm just not used to wearing heels."

The shoe salesman has been eyeing us, clearly astounded to see a father picking out shoes for a woman my age. He's ringing them up when when my father announces out of the clear blue sky that I've just returned from Vietnam.

The salesman stares at me, unsmiling. "That's nice," he says, handing over the shoes in a plastic bag.

Not exactly the response my father had expected, but it doesn't surprise me. Over there I was proud of my role in the war. Here people act as if I should be ashamed.

*   *   *

When Saturday arrives, I spend the morning changing from one outfit to the next, fooling with my unruly hair, and toying with the idea of wearing makeup. I want so much to make the right impression. And what will Peter think about my parents, this red-shingled house? His *mother* is a doctor, for crying out loud. They probably live in some kind of mansion.

Relax, I tell myself. He's already seen me at my best and at my worst. Yes, but I was much younger then, and we were very far away from the Land of Round-eyes.

The blond warrior arrives, braving chill autumn winds in an MG convertible. My heart fairly leaps out the front window when he pulls up.

As I come outside, he vaults over the car door and rushes toward me. The warmth of his body eases my shivers and my fears. It says he still cares, but I try not to let it mean too much. No one knows what tomorrow brings.

My parents are out. Depositing his bag in the spare bedroom, we're confronted by the double bed in an empty house. I blush under his questioning look, say I don't know when my parents will be back. I'm uncertain how I would feel if that weren't the case. We go back downstairs, where he mentions a football game on TV. Snuggled up on the couch to watch it, we're soon necking. I'm about ready to take a chance in the spare bedroom, when he abruptly stands up and suggests we go for a drive.

I assume he means out into the country, where the fall leaves are beginning their brilliant transformation, and I'm grateful he has the strength to stop us. A few miles from my parents' house he turns onto a commercial strip. The scenery is used-car lots and gas stations, shopping malls and fast-food restaurants.

"Do you know what I'm looking for?" he asks.

"No."

A long silence. "Well, can you guess?"

A Roy Roger's restaurant slips by on the left. "Somewhere to eat?"

He shakes his head.

"A gas station?"

He laughs. "No."

"Someplace to buy shoes?"

"No," he practically roars.

Then we pass a motel, and it comes to me in a flash.

"Right. I just didn't want to drive up to one without first finding out how you feel about it."

I don't know how I feel. A motel room sounds smutty, but those are my parents' values. We've gone to bed before, and it never felt smutty. Why should it matter where we do it?

But I sink into the car seat as he signs us in as Mr. and Mrs., certain everyone will notice we don't have any luggage. And I worry about where my folks are shopping; it would be just my luck for them to see us.

Peter draws the drapes, pulls me to bed. My attraction for him is no less than it was in Japan or Vietnam, and I'm hungry for him after our necking on the couch. I put aside my reservations.

Afterward I'd like to cuddle, but Peter never could stay still for long. Leaping out of bed, he announces, "Time for a shower!"

I yank up the sheet to cover myself. "You first."

He has no such inhibitions as mine, picking me up and insisting, "Together!"

I wrap the sheet tightly around myself. "I can't!"

He cocks his head, puts me back on the bed. "Haven't you ever taken a shower with a man?" I shake my head. He stands up authoritatively. "In that case I'll get in first. You're in for a treat."

His retreating figure is so beautiful—broad-shouldered with firm buttocks and strong legs. When I hear the sound of running water, I throw off the sheet and follow him.

Night has fallen when we park in front of my parents' house, embrace awkwardly in bucket seats over the stick shift. "Ode to Billie Joe" comes on the radio. Peter says to listen.

The ballad describes a family eating dinner. As they pass the black-eyed peas and biscuits, the mother and father casually talk about a neighbor's boy who just died jumping from a bridge, a boy who means more to their daughter than they realize.

Yes. That's exactly what it's like eating supper in front of the TV, watching newsreels about the war.

Peter's no better at small talk than I am, and conversation with my parents is awkward, but their verdict is "He's very nice." When they ask how serious our relationship is, I say it's too soon to tell.

Sunday Peter takes me to Brooklyn to visit his sister. The MG's top is down; the chilly wind that whips at my hair seems to infuse me with exhilaration.

The sensation is quickly lost in the presence of his small, bouncy, chirpy sister. I feel like a middle-aged woman next to her. What chance is there of Peter's loving me? My worry seems vindicated when his sister observes that I could be quite pretty if I just wore a little makeup and Peter agrees.

After the visit Peter drops me off at my parents' house and heads back to Virginia. I take a long walk before going inside and try to figure out how I feel. The magic we had in Japan is gone, yet I'm still very attracted to him. Maybe the magic will come back after I get back to work, resume my life.

It's now my third week of leave, and I can no longer put off visiting my family in North Carolina. I wear my uniform to fly down space available.

The plane is nearly empty. We're under way when the stewardess strikes up a conversation, asking, "What kind of uniform is that?"

"Army," I answer warily.

"Are you really a captain?" she asks, nodding at my bars.

"Yes."

"Have you been overseas?"

"Yes. Japan."

"Oh, I hear that's a beautiful country!"

"Yes, it is," I say. I'm not in the mood to talk, but she makes one more stab.

"What are your medals for?"

"They're nothing," I answer. "They give them to everyone who serves overseas." Then I turn pointedly toward the window, fearful I will give away where else I have been.

The hillsides of North Carolina are brushed in reds and yellows. I think of Tom, fondly remember how we reminisced in Japan about this part of the country. I try, but I can't remember what happened to him after that. Nor can I remember what city he came from. I walk toward the terminal.

Two aunts, an uncle, and my cousin Beth are waving with big smiles as I cross the tarmac.

"It's so good to have you home," says my aunt Jenny with a warm hug and pats on the back. "I was worried sick that something might happen to you."

"My goodness! You look so impressive in your uniform," says my aunt Sarah with a big squeeze.

"We've missed you," Beth says, hugging me next. "I thought you'd never come home."

"We're all glad to have you back safe." Uncle Edward beams.

In my honor my favorite dinner is served—country ham with grits and red-eye gravy, not to mention fresh milk and homemade angel food cake. It's southern hospitality at its finest. No one seems to notice that I don't have much to say, but the meal ends with the inevitable question: "What was it like?"

Their warmth and the special meal have broken down my barriers. "Sometimes there were so many casualties that we didn't even have enough space for them," I say, careful to keep my emotions under control. "A lot of them lost their arms and legs." I take a deep breath to hold back the tears. "The last place I worked, most had been shot in the head."

My aunt Sarah shakes her head. "You can't think about that," she says assuredly. "You have to put all that in the past."

I want to scream, "Why did you ask?" But I say nothing, looking down at my plate.

"I know that's hard to do," she adds. "But people don't want to hear about sorrows. They have enough of their own."

So I tell my funny stories—rice wine, Captain Cruz, the block of ice—and everyone laughs. I want to say that it's not funny over there, that soldiers are getting blown away while we sit around laughing. But I don't. Nobody wants to hear that stuff. And there's no booze in this house to help me forget.

I can't even speak my heart to Beth, who is my own age and more like a twin sister than a cousin when we were growing up. I don't belong here anymore either.

The next morning I rise before anyone else to take a walk. It's warmer here than in New Jersey, and I don't have to worry about running into someone I know. There's a stream in a wooded corner lot, where I sit for a long while.

In spring there'll be the light green of new growth here, blossoms in the trees, birds singing, and sun-warmed grass. By then I'll be out of the Army. Where should I go? Somewhere away from my family, I think, but I don't know where. What should I do? Something besides nursing, I hope, but I don't know what that might be. Never mind, I've still got five months. A lot can happen in five months.

My last week of leave is spent agonizing over what kind of car to buy.

"What a hard life you lead," my father teases, "with such difficult decisions to make."

I point to one we pass on the road—a Pontiac Firebird.

Even more than shopping, I hate bargaining. Daddy comes with me to deal with the salesman. When we walk into the dealership, I know what I want. "I'll take that red convertible with the black top and four on the floor."

"Just like that?" the salesman asks.

"Yes. I'll pay in full with a check." He looks at the check doubtfully. My father offers to cosign.

Fuckin' A! I'm a captain in the Army, and he doesn't trust my check!

My father can't understand why I'm so upset. "Not many people pay cash for a car," he explains. "Not many people *can*. Especially someone so young. You have to be reasonable, Winnie."

All I want is to be shown the respect I've earned. Is that so unreasonable? But I hold my temper. Thank goodness leave is almost over.

The next day the Firebird's inspection and getting an approval sticker take much of the afternoon. By the time I get home and pack, it's getting dark. A storm is brewing, and my parents are anxious about my driving a new car in bad conditions. I'm nervous, too, but I'm impatient to get on the road.

By the time I reach the Pennsylvania Turnpike, it's pitch-black and pouring rain. No matter the driving conditions, it's a relief to be alone.

CHAPTER SIXTEEN

OCTOBER 20, 1967– MARCH 8, 1968: Fort Leonard Wood, Missouri

Fort Leonard Wood, not so fondly dubbed Fort Lost in the Woods, nestles in the undulating Ozark Mountains. A lonely stretch of road, lined by straw-colored fields and trees in autumn foliage, leads to the officers' quarters. When I catch sight of them, two-story brick buildings with spacious lawns in front and forested hillsides in back, the sun is sinking behind a mountain.

I've dreamed of a walk in the woods since Japan. A short plunge down a hillside of trees, and I lose sight of any sign of people. It's better than the portable pool in Long Binh, the Starlit Roof in Saigon, even the barbecue pit in Japan.

Perched on a boulder, I hug my knees against the wind and wait for signs of life. I see none. No rabbits or deer, no birds or squirrels. So I listen to leaves rustle in the trees, watch them flutter down and skip along the ground. I stay until failing light and frozen feet force me to leave. Never mind. I can return tomorrow, the day after tomorrow, and the day after that.

Captain's bars rate my own apartment, and Lady Luck has

granted that it be upstairs in a corner. The front faces other quarters with forested hills beyond; the side overlooks the plunging hillside from which I've just come. I'm eager to unpack and make it feel like home, but I'm even hungrier than I am eager.

The officers' club is fashioned from a studio apartment on the first floor. It has a bar, a short-order grill, and coral-colored booths that leave barely enough room for an aisle. The menu suits me fine—sandwiches, chili, hamburgers, and french fries—but it's too stuffy, too noisy, and, as everywhere in the Army, crowded with too many men and too few women. The odds no longer intimidate me, but I don't want to meet any men. All I want is to eat.

The tables are filled. Three officers, infantry types dressed in stateside fatigues that look foreign after a year of jungle fatigues, flag me over to their booth. To deflect unwanted advances, I tell them I'm engaged.

It works. Now, so far as I'm concerned, we can talk without playing games.

The Army's conviction that any Army nurse can do any job anywhere no longer surprises me. Nor does my being made an assistant head nurse now that I'm a captain. But I'm disappointed that it's a medical floor.

The head nurse is kept busy with time schedules and staff evaluations, meetings, and administrative duties. On an hour-to-hour basis, I run the show on two upper respiratory infection wards, a general medical ward, and a four-bed medical ICU. The hard part is learning the ins and outs of scheduling and preparing patients for special procedures. The easy part is relieving in ICU for breaks, a cinch after Vietnam and a welcome relief from directing traffic. Twice a day I round on the respiratory wards to catch up on doctors' orders, be certain that temperatures are under control, and check patients for such things as rashes, stiff necks, or swollen glands—potential signs of the rare case of meningitis, encephalitis, or mononucleosis. The wardmaster huffily assures me that he can handle this, but I'm compulsive about my work. "Better safe than sorry," I smile, then break for lunch.

I smooth the skirt of my starched white uniform to prevent

wrinkles and sit down at a long, empty table. My head nurse major joins me, whereupon other nurse majors join her; gold leaves drift and fall weightily around me. I'd rather eat with lieutenants, but they wouldn't dare come near this table now. Not that the majors are so bad, but lieutenants are closer to my age.

Enter a captain doctor whose thin brown hair is prematurely balding and whose light brown eyes have the persistent squint of someone wearing contact lenses. He asks if a seat across from mine is taken. Everyone shakes her head no, smiles "have a seat," and tries to include him in the conversation. Only he's not much for talking, just sits staring at me so brazenly that no one misses it. Glares I throw his way do not dissuade him, so I try to ignore him. The conversation lags; the majors are clearly as uncomfortable with his staring as I am. Enough of this bullshit.

"Do you always stare at people you've just met?"

His eyes widen in surprise. "No," he admits slowly with an accent I can't place.

"Then I would appreciate your not staring at me." He acts embarrassed. Serves him right. Even a child knows staring is rude.

"Sorry," he says. "I just thought I might know you."

French. What's he doing in the Army?

"I'm sure you don't." I meet his stare head-on. "I would remember you if you did."

Dumbfounded, he says nothing more, but he continues to stare. Turning back to the nurse majors, I find them looking at me with disapproval written all over their faces.

I don't give a damn. He's the one out of line, not me.

Working only forty hours a week leaves too much free time. I try filling it the way I did before I went overseas—knitting, drawing, reading books, and writing letters—but I can't sit still for long. Walks in the woods help but not enough.

There's a stable on base, and I find that the bridled power of a horse under me seems to release more energy than walking. I ride a mottled gray with black mane and tail; they are colors that suit the approach of winter with overcast skies and dying autumn leaves. We race headlong over meadows until we're breathless

with the effort, then roam wooded trails and listen to the whispering trees. The horse snorts at the sights, perks his ears to the
sounds, whinnies understandingly when I speak.

I tell him my deepest secrets. My guilt at leading such an easy
life. My fear of something wrong with me for being discontent
with this world after dreaming of it for so long. My despair of
feeling old—too old for Peter despite our being only a month
apart in age.

When weather does not permit the mottled gray to leave his
stable, I put the Firebird through its paces, pitting us against empty
winding roads. We spin out more than once, almost but never
quite getting mired in muddy shoulders alongside the road. Like
the horse, my car becomes an outlet for my pent-up energy.

When darkness falls, I sit with my guitar, my old friend from
the Starlit Roof in Saigon, in my living room. When I get hungry,
I join the infantry officers I met my first night here. Only they
talk about going to Vietnam and how many VC they'll "waste"
once they get there—a topic that I once found intriguing but that
now makes me uncomfortable.

Back in my room, hospital types who live in this building
come to visit. My cupboards are bare of pots and pans, but
there's never a shortage of booze; Johnnie Walker Black is only
four dollars a bottle at the PX. My most frequent visitors are
John, my next-door neighbor, a first lieutenant and the pediatric
head nurse, Howard, a major and operating room head nurse
whom I met through John; and Claude, the French doctor from
the cafeteria, whom I've told about Peter but who still pursues
me. I figure I've done my part by being honest. If he gets hurt,
that's too bad.

Halloween night is marked by a round of parties, but I'm not
in a party mood. I skip supper to carve jack-o'-lanterns with
Claude. Carving pumpkins brings back some measure of holiday
spirit, but at six o'clock sharp Claude turns on the TV for the
day's news. The broadcast begins with an appeal by Hanoi for all
nations to help stop the United States from bombing their city.
There's a follow-up story on an antiwar demonstration by fifty
thousand people in Washington one week ago. It ends with a

newsreel of soldiers with the Big Red One patch on their arms, fighting the Vietcong.

Ghosts of war haunt my room, dance with ghouls and goblins and jack-o'-lantern spirits.

My status as a Vietnam returnee evidently outweighs the consternation of our chief nurse over my waist-length hair. I am one of two nurses to be interviewed on local TV about the Army Nurse Corps. The other is John, who is also a Vietnam vet, although I didn't know that until now.

Armed with my slides, requested to "show where we were and what we did," we climb into a sedan to go to the TV station. Our interviewer sits in front, probing for information as we whisk in comfort through the drizzly, cold countryside.

"How old is the Army Nurse Corps?" he asks.

I have no idea, but John provides the answer. "Nurses were enlisted in the Army as far back as the Civil War, under Dorothea Dix in the North and Captain Sally Tompkins in the South—the only woman to hold a commission in the Confederacy. But it wasn't until 1901 that Congress officially founded the ANC as a permanent corps for peacetime as well as wartime."

"How many Army nurses are there now?"

Again, I shake my head, and John answers. "About thirty-one hundred on active duty."

How does he know all this stuff? Did we learn it in basic training? Gazing at the dreary landscape, I think that I'm obviously the wrong person for this mission.

"Did you bring pictures?"

"I have slides."

"Good. John can speak about the Nurse Corps, and you can explain the slides." He holds them up, nodding approvingly of those showing hospitals, putting aside those of Saigon and the Vietnamese.

"Do you have any of the wounded men?"

"No, but I do have one of a Vietnamese boy in an evacuation hospital."

He holds it up to the window. "What happened to him?"

"He got shot in the head."

"By the VC?"

"No. His village was VC. We shot him."

The reporter hesitates. "I don't think you should mention that," he says finally. "Too political. People might not understand. Besides, he's nude. We can't show nudity. Now, here's one of a nurse holding a child all bandaged up. What happened to her?"

"Napalm."

"VC?"

"No, ours."

"I see. Well, we'll skip this one, too."

My mind is swimming, trying to understand why I shouldn't mention these things. There's a war going on. Civilians get wounded just like soldiers. Just like London, Dresden, and Tokyo during World War II, only in Vietnam. But I won't mention it if he doesn't want me to.

On the air he asks what kinds of wounds I saw there, and a sharp vision of a ward full of maimed and dying soldiers fills my head. I blink down the image, shut down the part of me that wants to cry how awful it was. The interviewer would think it too political. Families might not be ready to hear it. Besides, no one wants to hear about that stuff.

I say gunshot wounds, burn wounds, head wounds, blast wounds. I don't say bellies full of pus, or crispy critters, or blown-off arms and legs, or fixed and dilated pupils left to die alone.

When the program airs on Saturday, I'm at home with a bad hangover and ignore the insistent knocks at my door. Later I learn it was John to remind me of the show. The opportunity of a lifetime to see myself on TV, and I forgot all about it.

Shortly afterward John moves on to another duty station. I replace him as head nurse on pediatrics.

Peter, now a general's aide in Kansas City, is coming for the weekend. When Friday night arrives, I turn merrymakers away. Claude demands to know why, and when I explain, he accuses me of leading him on.

"I told you about Peter from the start," I snap, "just as I told everyone else. If you read more into our friendship than is really there, it's not my problem."

Am I making a mistake? Claude doesn't care how old I am. He thought I was twenty-eight when we met and was still interested.

Yes, but I don't love him. And Peter must be interested, too, or why would he drive all this way to see me? Unless, I think, he has met someone else and is coming to break the news.

Sipping on a Rob Roy to calm my nerves, I double-check the mirror. I look old and plain. Maybe I should wear makeup. No, makeup won't change anything. It's like falsies. If he wants a woman with big breasts, he'll have to go elsewhere. Same if he wants a beautiful young girl.

I hear the MG from a long distance, growing louder until it downshifts into the parking lot and the engine is silenced. I freeze, not daring to look out the window, afraid he might see me. He mustn't know that I've been listening for his arrival like some silly teenybopper.

My mind's eye sees him vault out of the car, run up the steps, and start to knock. I stare at the door with my heart pounding, but there is no knock. It must have been someone else. I sit down to finish my drink.

Three sharp raps make me jump. I gulp down the Rob Roy before answering. I must be careful not to show how upset I'll be if he has come to end our relationship.

"I ran into an acquaintance from West Point downstairs," Peter says with a curious cock of his head. "He asked if I'm the guy you're engaged to."

Oh, God. "I say I'm engaged to keep them from chasing after me."

He says nothing, still looking at me curiously.

"What did you say?"

"That I didn't know you were engaged." A pause. "He said I'm a dead ringer for your fiancé's description."

"I had to use someone. Do you mind?"

He shrugs. "I hardly know the guy." He grins crookedly, then pulls me to him and kisses me hello.

There's not much to do at Fort Lost in the Woods, so we go

for dinner at the Pig and Whistle off base. No matter how much I try to relax and enjoy the meal, my edginess will not go away. Peter is no help, and dinner is strained as we search for topics of conversation.

As we drive back to my quarters in the convertible, the cold wind in my face lifts my spirits, and my laughter rises in the night air. We're both laughing when he keeps the wheel in a tight turn, going around and around in the parking lot in faster and faster circles, getting closer and closer to parked cars.

I don't have to ask why. I understand the restless craving for the fine edge between control and the loss of it.

The weekend ends early Monday morning, when he must drive back. Sunday night we lie in my single bed with my body pressed tightly against his.

"How do you feel about this?" he asks with a squeeze.

"I like it." I squeeze back. "Why?"

"No real reason. Just that most women like a soul-searching talk after making love."

I don't dare be like most women. There would be no reason for him to come back if I were like most women.

"I think you're like me," he says. "You enjoy it without worrying about what it means."

Long after he's asleep, I lie awake. I'm twenty-three. I want to settle down and have children, but he's still not ready for that. What if a few years down the line he decides he wants a younger woman after all? Though I dread the thought of losing him now, just think how much harder it will be to lose him then. On top of which he's a career officer; he's bound to go back to Vietnam. Could I face wondering from one day to the next if he was still alive? Still in one piece? I don't know.

Winter is just around the corner; this Friday's sun hides behind mustering black clouds as I leave work at 1600 hours. Today a corpsman mentioned a nearby graveyard that dates back to the seventeenth century. I'm drawn to the idea of wandering among the old headstones.

Thirty minutes later a small guard station in the middle of

nowhere marks my exit from the base, and the paved road turns to gravel. I pat the Firebird on the dashboard as encouragement and accelerate.

It begins to drizzle, and the sky turns so dark that it could be sundown. The gravel gives way to a slippery clay soil; the road becomes deeply rutted and narrows till it's barely wide enough for a car. The Firebird's fat tires track poorly on slick surfaces; I feel the car slide skittishly down the steep flank of the mountain.

I pat the dashboard again. Sorry, my friend, but the road is too narrow to turn around. Hugging the mountain, I clutch the steering wheel and gingerly inch us down. Halfway there the clouds burst, pouring sheets of rain over the windshield and into the rutted road.

I'm skidding! I remember to stay off the brakes. When I've conquered the steep part, I remember not to let my guard down. That gets soldiers killed. My grip eases when I feel level ground under the Firebird's wheels. But I still can't turn around; there are runoff ditches on either side of the road. I come to a stop just short of a stream running right across my path.

I get out of the car to see how deep it is. Only four inches, but pure mud at the bottom. Fuck, it's cold. I get back into the car and turn on the heat. Well, Firebird, it's do or die, I say silently. Backing up to give us a head start, we go for it. And die.

Better check damages. I put one foot out the door and sink ankle-deep in freezing cold mud. So much for my white duty shoes. Might as well take them off.

Shit. The Firebird is stuck up to the hubcaps. Rocks under the tires might help, but there are few in this meadow, and it's hard to see in this light. It's so dark I can't make out trees on the hillsides, only their black silhouettes against the darkening gray sky. When even the silhouettes dissolve, I try coaxing the car out with what rocks I've found.

It's no use. Goddamn. What the fuck was so important about seeing an old graveyard?

That doesn't matter now. The way I see it, there are two choices. I can spend the night and walk out in the morning, or I can walk out now. I'm supposed to drive to Kansas City tomorrow to visit

Peter, and he's expecting me before noon. Besides, walking in rain in the cold dark might be bad, but shivering all night in the Firebird has to be worse. I grab my shoes.

My Army raincoat is unworthy of this pouring rain; I'm already drenched. The road is barely visible as I start the long climb back, and the world turns pitch-black soon after. I walk by braille, caring no longer about my shoes, but about my ankles.

Walking keeps me from shivering with the cold, but I'm stiff and totally exhausted. I stumble through the blackness, closing my eyes as I walk, and then snap back. Numb from head to foot, I slip and almost fall, crying out loud in the night.

Startled, a cat screams from the side of the road. Panic pounds in my heart. It sounded small—maybe a bobcat. I know they aren't dangerous, but what about bears? I pick up my pace, but my weariness soon overtakes me, and I falter, then stumble again.

After two or three miles the storm quiets to a drizzle, but the temperature drops. A thin layer of ice seals the mud puddles, cracking when I step into them. My feet are so cold that I no longer feel them. But my eyes pop open when they hit unfamiliar gravel and, a little later, pavement. There's the guard station!

The guard is clearly amazed when he opens the door to my knock. He peers past me into the night.

"I'm alone. Can I use your phone?" My lips are so stiff I can hardly speak.

It takes awhile to convince him I'm real and awhile longer to find anyone at home on a Friday night. In the end I dial Claude.

"It's miserable out there!" he says, but he'll come. Only he takes his own good time; more than an hour passes before he pulls up and honks. When I climb into the car, he moans that my wet raincoat will ruin his upholstered seats. Under way he tells me how grateful I should be—that not just anybody would come to the rescue on a night like this.

I cannot hide my vexation over his petulance. Conversation grinds to a halt before we reach the quarters.

At home I warm up with a quick shower, jump into dry clothes, and head for the club. I haven't eaten since noon, and it's after eight o'clock.

My infantry officer friends crowd a booth in a far corner, waving me over when I enter. My story over supper elicits offers of help. They scrounge up picks, shovels, crowbars, and boards. Then we scramble into a four-wheel-drive pickup. By the time we reach the Firebird, the mud has frozen solid around the wheels, and we must rock the car mercilessly to yank it free.

I have to have the Firebird's wheels aligned before I drive to Kansas City. I'm late, but thanks to the infantry, I make it.

Thanksgiving falls under cloudless blue skies. There are football games broadcast out of apartment windows, passing cars, the hand-held radios of pedestrians. Peter has written that he loves me. It is what I've wanted, yet it does not change my ambivalence. It does not make me happy.

A houseful of us gather at Michael Martin's home to watch the Army-Navy game on color TV. He is a captain—the company commander of my infantry friends at the club—and another Vietnam returnee. In true Army tradition, our merrymaking goes from beer in the morning to hard booze in the afternoon. In true American tradition, Meg, his wife, lays out a feast of turkey with all the trimmings. We stay late into the night, sitting on the floor with drinks and cigarettes, singing and playing guitars.

Once the conversation turns to Vietnam. This past month fierce fighting in the Central Highlands has seen more than a thousand dead and wounded. Michael's old outfit is in the thick of it. He's worried about those who were under his command before he left. And though he loves the Army anywhere, he misses the closeness he had with his men over there.

Meg breaks into his reminiscing to denounce the Army bitterly for passing him up for promotion to major on grounds that he fraternizes with his enlisted men. Guilty, says Michael. Nor will he change his ways, so she'll just have to settle for being a captain's wife.

Faces form in the far back of my mind. Tom and his crew chief in Japan. Chris and Good Buddy in An Khe. Larry and Pops in Long Binh. But my mind saves me. Their faces are unclear, and the memory of what happened to them never surfaces.

* * *

AMERICAN DAUGHTER GONE TO WAR

I try not to hurt Jennifer as I comb through the tangles in her thin blond hair. I wonder what will become of her. Her parents visit daily, showering her with love that no one doubts is genuine, yet she's emaciated; her ribs stick out of her thorax, and she's half the weight she should be for her five years of age.

She came to us when her parents brought her infant brother to the emergency room—dead on arrival. A social worker found their home so filthy that it was deemed a health hazard and discovered that five children slept haphazardly on the floor, the kitchen held no food, and the house was freezing cold. A review of records revealed the father's IQ to be forty-four, though he is clearly more intelligent than the mother. The death of the infant was judged unintentional. It's obvious these parents love their children, but they are incapable of coping with basic survival needs: shopping, cooking meals, bathing and dressing their children, paying the bills.

Turning Jennifer's face toward me to check the part in her hair, I think how somber she is. Wordlessly she wraps her thin arms around my neck and clings to me. For a moment she is Le Ly at the orphanage in Saigon.

I push away the reminder, remove the child's arms to pull up the crib's side rail, and escape to my charts.

Casualties from the war increase in number as the number of shopping days until Christmas declines. Both are gloomily tallied at the end of news broadcasts. I put off shopping until the date to send packages home in time for the holiday has come and gone.

Peter calls. Our telephone conversations over the past two weeks have been stilted; he is clearly waiting for a response. What is my problem? He's a career officer, I answer myself. I don't want to be an officer's wife, wearing my husband's rank to hail-farewell parties, never settling down in one place, living on Army bases with nothing to do but take classes in Japanese flower arrangement with other officers' wives. But I know that's not the real problem. The real problem is that he's a line officer and there's a war going on. And I'm too much of a coward to face his returning to Vietnam.

Washing down too many cigarettes with too many Rob Roys,

I draft a Dear John letter. Better now than later, when he's closer to going back and it might cloud his mind, endanger his life. I've tried telling him in person. I've tried on the telephone. But the words choke in my throat. Even as I write, tears stream down my face, falling too fast to catch and smudging the ink. I crumple the page and start again.

I write that I don't want to be an officer's wife. I don't write about my fear of one day losing him to a younger woman. Or about my dread of MPs knocking on our door one day to say he'll never return, our baby crying in the background. I do not write about my visions of him paralyzed, our child watching with somber eyes as I wash his lifeless body.

Claude assumes my breaking up with Peter means my heart belongs to him. I say nothing. I care little for Claude, but he serves the same function Alex did. He keeps me from loneliness. He keeps the other wolves at bay.

The price to pay is his possessiveness. He now feels free to chase friends out of my apartment, to tell me I smoke too much and drink too much, to tell me what I should wear and shouldn't. When I ignore his advice and his demands, he accuses me of being stubborn. When I say he's trying to make me into someone else, he claims his criticisms are for my own good. When I say I can decide for myself what's good for me, he tells me if that were the case, he wouldn't need to criticize.

As miserable as I am in our relationship, I do not end it. I'm afraid of never marrying, and as he does not hesitate to remind me, I'm getting older and running out of time to find someone else. And as he points out, a doctor outside the Army can give me nice things—a nice house, a nice car, nice clothes, nice vacations.

I hate his kisses, his slimy, writhing tongue ramming down my throat. But to keep him longer—until I can decide what to do—I let him in my bed.

I turn my head so he won't see the revulsion in my face. My tears choke me. I can't breathe. Oh, Peter! It's you I want. Please, oh, please, forgive me!

Claude ascribes my breathlessness to excitement, sends his slimy tongue to my nipples. He climbs on top of me.

Oh, God. I should never have written that letter. I was wrong.

"Oh, it's so good!" Claude groans, thrusting greedily inside me.

I tell myself it will be over soon. But it takes an eternity. Afterward I cry. Claude believes this to be an expression of my ecstasy.

I rise, clutching my robe to me. At the window I empty my mind into the black night and wipe away my tears with a mindless gesture. I wish I were dead.

I have left my Christmas shopping to be accomplished in this single trip to the city with Claude and Howard. Any Christmas spirit I had when we started was destroyed when Claude hinted to Howard that we are to be engaged, something I've told him I'm not ready for. I won't make a scene in front of a friend, but my anger sits on the tip of my tongue. Sullen, staring gloomily at the black countryside, I wish I had not come.

At the shopping center the pushing and shoving of shoppers make me irritable. And the lines for paying are too long, so I wind up spending too much on gifts I don't like for the sake of shorter lines. My mood grows blacker by the minute.

The only solace in this holiday season is my Christmas tree. It is sweet-smelling, its branches are full of twinkling lights and bright baubles, and it stretches to the ceiling with an angel at the top. I spend my evenings staring at the tiny flickering lights, sipping on drinks and smoking, ignoring the telephone and knocks at the door. I'm glad to be alone. This evening is no different until time for bed, when the first snowfall comes. The next morning the world is a wonderland, white and glittering with icicles that hang from tree branches. It's beautiful, yet my spirit does not respond. I'm staring dully out the window when the phone rings.

Stunned, I hear Peter's voice say that he's got my letter, that I can't end our relationship just like that, that he must see me. He'll be here for the weekend.

The roaring MG sets my heart to pounding, but I'm determined not to weaken. I'm too ashamed to tell him about sleeping with

Claude, and not telling him would be a lie. And nothing else has changed since I wrote the Dear John letter.

When the awaited knock comes, my heart skips a beat, but I stay calm.

His eyes look at me with such pain. Oh, how I want to jump into his arms! Instead, I play hostess and offer him a drink.

"Do you still love me?" he asks.

"Yes," I admit.

"Then what happened? Is there someone else?"

"Yes," I answer, hiding my eyes.

"Do you love him?"

I shake my head.

"Would it help if I got out of the Army?"

My heart leaps at the hope. "Could you be happy?"

"I don't know, but I'll give it a try."

"No." I shake my head. "That would just be the reverse of my staying with you in the Army."

His voice cracks. "I'm terrified of losing you!"

My mind careens wildly. I grope frantically for the controls. I can't let that happen again. I say good-night.

Slumped on the couch, he watches me retreat to the bedroom and shut the door between us.

I sink to the floor, my breaths coming in strangled gasps to silence my sobs.

In the morning my sheets are soaked though it's freezing cold in the room. Another of those dreams I can't remember.

Early light filters through the curtains; it's the first clear day in a long time. It reminds me of that sunny autumn day when Peter visited me in New Jersey.

My heart races. Providence has brought us such a day. We love each other. What difference does anything else make?

Jumping out of bed, I quickly wash my face and run a brush through my hair before opening the bedroom door. If he's asleep, I'll wake him with kisses.

But I'm too late. The couch is empty, the blanket neatly folded on one end.

I spend several days staring at the phone, but I never call him.

I spend countless hours with a pen in hand, ready to write of my change of heart. But I never do.

When I schedule myself to work two weeks without a day off during the holidays, Claude accuses me of hiding in my work to avoid facing our relationship. For once, I think, he's right. Major Buss, my nursing supervisor, warns me that no one can work without time off. I assure her that I not only can but want to, that it's my Christmas present to my staff. Besides, Christmas should be spent with children.

Our wardmaster, Jackson, has the day off and a family at home. Yet he makes a special trip to see these children, dressed as Santa Claus—the first black Santa I've seen. He carries a duffel bag of gifts. The corpsman and I go with him to each bedside, where we sing a Christmas carol and Jackson hands over a present. At one bed we sing "Away in a Manger," and the song dies in my throat. An infant lies here. His intestines protrude from his abdomen, protected from the outside world by a mere layer of mucous membrane, bluish and sickeningly soft. He has an umbilical hernia—a gap in his abdominal muscle wall. He is here in case of regurgitation and aspiration if his feedings don't pass through his strangled intestines.

There are no guarantees, not even at birth, for a good life.

The world goes on day by day. Peter gets farther and farther away. Claude is more and more demanding.

In the past year, the newspaper reports, 9,353 American servicemen have died in Vietnam, and 99,742 were wounded. Since New Year's Day 1961, a total of 15,997 have been killed, and 137,480 wounded.

This New Year brings nothing new, not even hope. I'll be out of the Army in two months, but I have no idea what I'll do then. I can't even think about it.

Claude continues to nag. I wish he would leave me and find someone else. Instead, he proposes again. When I tell him I'm still not ready to marry, he replies that if I'm not ready now, I never will be, that having children is what a twenty-three-year-old woman should be doing. I put him off.

The last week of January my father calls to say my mother is very sick with congestive heart failure and needs me to take care of her. To my way of thinking, she can't be all that sick if she's not in the hospital, but I agree to come. Howard drives me to the airport.

Nothing has changed at home except that it's colder outside and stuffier inside. And the Tet offensive has begun.

My father is in his reclining chair, and my mother and I sit on the couch, watching the news. "That's Claymore Tower!" I exclaim.

To their blank stares I add: "Where I lived in Saigon."

"You must be mistaken," my mother says flatly.

I bristle, knowing I am not, but I say nothing more. The three of us stare at American troops firing on my old quarters, recapturing it from the enemy.

So, I think with a perverse satisfaction, the Vietcong finally took it, just as we always said they would. Only we figured they would blow the place apart in the process.

Two weeks later my mother's condition is unchanged. Satisfied that she doesn't require skilled nursing care, I return to base. I have problems of my own.

It's Valentine's Day. Standing motionless at my bedroom window, I stare out at the Missouri hillside. The landscape looks and feels dead, the trees are skeletons, and it's a gray, drizzly afternoon.

For weeks I have been denying what I have known to be the truth. Finally I must admit that I'm pregnant.

Claude believes it to be his child and has offered to pay half the cost of an abortion. I've refused the offer, but I didn't tell him why: that my dates say it is Peter's child. I'm grateful for that, but I now must decide whether to tell Peter.

If I do not carry his child, will he ever have another? Do I have the right to deny a life that might be his only heir? If I keep the child, is it better for him to know, or would the knowledge someday destroy him, distracting him in a time of danger? I know he would never forgive me if I had an abortion. But would he feel trapped into marrying me because he had to, not because he wanted to?

I turn away from the window. I can't tell him. What would I do with a baby? My family would never forgive my having a child out of wedlock. Could I endure raising a child without family or friends? Could I make it a happy home? Without a father? And what man would want me enough to be willing to take both of us?

I sit in the dark with my Rob Roys and my cigarettes. Three weeks left in the Army. If I could only wait until I'm away from here, away from Claude, but it can't wait. The Army requires a discharge examination, and being pregnant could earn me the lifetime sentence of a dishonorable discharge. With so little time left, there's no possibility of taking leave or I'd do what other women do and fly to Puerto Rico to circumvent the antiabortion law. Instead, the deed will have to be done on time off.

A friend from nursing school who still lives in Manhattan arranges it for the following Saturday, with a doctor in a small town two hours north of the city. When I step off the bus, a gust of cold wind nearly blows me off my feet. The sidewalk is icy; the sun is buried under clouds. I'm frozen and shivering by the time I find the place.

The doctor's office is in a semiresidential neighborhood with a treatment room in the back. The doctor is a stern-looking middle-aged man whose expression reads strictly business.

"I want payment in advance," he says. When I pull out my checkbook, he shakes his head. "Cash only."

"But I didn't know that!"

"I'll take what you have and a check for the balance."

"I have to keep enough cash to catch a bus back to Manhattan."

He shakes his head. "I'll finish in time for you to go to the bank."

The room is cold, so I wear my coat onto the treatment table. The only light is the spotlight he uses to perform the procedure.

He doesn't bother to drape a sheet over me. I feel like a stone as he draws up the local anesthetic.

The speculum is freezing cold, but I don't flinch, turning my eyes to the green-tiled walls, watching the shadows of trees swaying outside the window. I jump slightly at the stab of the needle, and he snaps at me not to move. The local anesthetic isn't complete, and the pain as he dilates my cervix seems unbearable.

But I don't move, and I don't cry out. I feel him scraping the inside of my uterus, and I grip the table to keep from curling up from the cramps.

A thunk in the silver basin wrenches a small sob out of me. I search the ceiling for something else to think about. Only I can't think of anything but how I've just killed my child. With it I've killed a piece of myself.

Once I'm fully dressed, I ask if it was a boy or girl.

"A boy," snaps the doctor. "Something I couldn't tell if you had been the eight weeks you said you were."

The bank won't cash an out-of-state check, not even with Army identification.

I wait an hour until my nursing school friend is home from work, then call to tell her I don't have money for the bus.

"I can't believe she didn't know she needed cash!" I hear her boyfriend say in the background.

It takes two hours for them to get to me. I'm too ashamed to wait in the bank and have perched myself on a stone wall, hugging my knees in the freezing cold, until they arrive.

I am back to work on Monday. It takes all the energy I possess. Two days later I pass my discharge physical. If the doctor suspects anything, he says nothing.

A week later, my last day as an Army nurse, I go through the motions of saying good-bye and wishing luck to those I leave behind. But I feel nothing.

The next day I pack up the Firebird and head back to my parents' red-shingled house. I do not look back as I leave my last Army post.

I leave the past on the wooded hillside beyond the bedroom window of a corner apartment. I care nothing about the future, I don't even think about it. In two weeks I turn twenty-four. I'm old, I know, and very tired.

CHAPTER SEVENTEEN

MARCH 1968– JUNE 1983: From Sea to Shining Sea

THIS is America, the land of peace that we dreamed about in Vietnam, but there is no peace in my parents' red-shingled house. My spirit is as restive in New Jersey as it was in Missouri. I still don't belong here, no longer think, feel, or believe as they do, and acting the way they want me to act, saying the things they want me to say take more energy than I possess.

During the day I take long walks alone in the woods. In the evening I get drunk alone at the kitchen table. At night I toss and turn for hours, wondering what Peter is doing or if I should accept Claude's marriage proposal. Even sleep fails to bring me peace; some dream I can never remember wakes me in a pool of sweat, sometimes with a terrified cry.

If my parents stir, I pretend to sleep. When I'm certain they're sleeping, I cry.

Peace escapes not only this house but this nation. Though our homes are safe from mortars and our countryside from snipers, controversy rages over the war. It's the warmongers against the peaceniks. Caught in the middle are the returning warriors. Everyone is too busy taking sides or going on with his or her life as if there were no war to pay attention to them.

When attention does focus on the soldiers, it's the wrong kind. A week after my discharge, March 16, the My Lai incident takes place. When the news breaks, I sit dazedly in front of the TV, reeling from the conflict within me. One part is sickened by the slaughter, but another part understands what happened: that collective hatred can explode in such an atrocity.

While I avoid discussing it, inside I scream at those who condemn the lieutenant in charge at My Lai. I'd like them to get off their self-righteous asses and learn about war firsthand. I want them to be terrified for their lives day in and day out, to watch a couple of buddies get blown to pieces and *then* see how long they can hang on to their high-and-mighty ideals.

My second week out of the Army a dozen long-stemmed roses arrive from Claude—who is moving to Dallas when he gets out—for my twenty-fourth birthday. At home eyebrows rise, and questions fly. Does he want to marry you? Why don't you want to marry him?

When I answer that I don't love him, my mother advises that it is better to be the one more loved than the one who loves more. And, she nods significantly, a doctor could buy me many nice things. Of course, I know that, and there was a time when I dreamed about those things—the big white wedding and trousseau, the sets of sterling silverware and fine bone china, the beautiful house and big yard—but they no longer seem important to me.

March closes with President Johnson's announcement "I shall not seek, and will not accept, the nomination of my party for another term as your President."

His presidency, newscasters say sagely, has become another casualty of the Vietnam War. To my way of thinking, he got off lightly.

On April 4 Martin Luther King, Jr., is assassinated. It isn't so much the violence of his death that surprises me as the shock wave that follows. I stare in bewilderment at the ever-present TV in my parents' house, watching people cry hysterically. Why does one man's death mean more to our people than the deaths of so many in Vietnam?

Easter week I visit my family in North Carolina, where spring is bursting in a rainbow of lilac and soft blue crocuses, bright yellow daffodils and lacy white dogwoods, pink azaleas and the darker redbuds. There may be little peace, but I am grateful for the beauty in this world.

After church on Sunday my grandmother, my aunt Jenny, aunt Sarah, and uncle Edward, and my cousin Beth and I go to Duke Gardens. When my grandmother tires, we sit in a gazebo where purple wisteria tumbles in sweet profusion over our heads. It takes me back to Japan, where I laughed with Tom about how the prettiest wisteria always grows around outhouses.

Early this evening we relax on the back porch of Aunt Sarah and Uncle Edward's house, sipping from tall glasses of iced tea. Beyond, lightning bugs twinkle in the falling light.

I think back to when I was a child and Beth and I impatiently excused ourselves after supper to run and play. As we grew older, we felt proud to sit with our elders and sip iced tea. We weren't supposed to say much, just to behave ourselves. Now we're expected to take part in conversations; only I can't think of anything to say—or what I have to say is not what they would want to hear. Like my parents, they still believe in God and Country, still consider nice possessions and polite manners very important.

Another month passes in New Jersey. I'm still miserable, but I seem incapable of changing anything. I have fantasies about Peter—about surprising him in Kansas City and confessing my love, then resuming our lives as if nothing had ever happened. I've turned down Claude's marriage proposal but have put off deciding whether or not to join him in Texas. I never call, much less visit, friends from high school or nursing school. I think about calling Retta—she is also out of the Army and living in Denver— but I never quite get around to it.

One evening my mother confronts me in the kitchen, where I'm on my fifth Rob Roy. "You can't spend the rest of your life moping around," she says. "Honestly, anyone would think you had just lost your best friend."

Even the alcohol doesn't take away the sting of her words. "But I don't know what I want to do," I answer, almost in tears.

"You could start by going back to work. You can't expect us to support you for the rest of your life."

One part of me hates her for saying it. Another part hates myself because I know she's right.

My father is in the living room. My back is to him, but I hear the hollow thud of his artificial leg as he approaches.

"Your mother doesn't mean it exactly that way," he says. "She's just worried about you. We both are."

I don't answer, light a cigarette to fill the awkward silence. Why can't they just leave me alone?

"It's time for you to get on with your life," my father adds. "You're too young to be sitting around the house day in and day out. You should be going to parties and dating."

I flick my cigarette, absently push the ashes around in the ashtray. I feel cold and empty inside.

"Look at your father when he speaks to you!"

Stamping out my cigarette, I rise unsteadily from my chair, unaware until this moment how drunk I am. But I'm not too drunk to give my mother a cold glare before turning to face my father. His face wears a look that says he can't figure out what's wrong with me. Somehow I don't care.

The next morning my father goes to work before I rise. When I go downstairs, my mother isn't talking, doesn't even look at me. It's the silent treatment that I hated so much when I was a child. I still hate it.

I won't stay where I'm not welcome. I pack in the morning and hit the road in the afternoon. Even though I don't know where I'm going, I push the Firebird west for three days. I cry at the drop of a hat, once for want of a tree within eyeshot.

At the crossroads between Dallas and Denver I pull off the interstate and park in the lot of a shopping center. Not by chance,

282

the roads intersect not far from Kansas City, where Peter is. Which way should I go?

My heart pulls me toward Peter, but my mind asks: To what purpose? Nothing has changed except that I miss him more than I thought possible. Reason pushes me toward Claude in Dallas; I'm more fearful of growing old alone than I thought possible. The safe road would be Denver and Retta, but that would mean starting all over again, and I don't think I have the energy for that.

It's June 6, an uncomfortably hot day with little movement of air through the car windows. Music on the radio is interrupted by a news broadcast: Robert Kennedy was shot last night.

My eyes fix hypnotically on light glinting from the chrome of a car bumper. The triage area at Third Field Hospital fills my mind, and I can feel my starched white uniform sticking to me from sweat. I stand in the background staring at the casualties, too overwhelmed by a sense of hopelessness to do anything. The war is not far away, not even here.

When I snap out of it, I can't think. I drive to a nearby motel and stay there several days, not even leaving the room to eat. Over and over I review my options and try to decide which way to go. I finally choose Dallas.

The day I arrive, I tell Claude I'm not ready to live with him, and I move into the first apartment I see—a dark one-bedroom that does nothing to improve my disposition. I'm so unsure I want to be here that I don't even unpack my belongings.

On the basis of my experience in Vietnam, the surgical ICU at Baylor Hospital hires me the day I walk through the door. It handles open-heart surgery, which sounds challenging, but the work proves to be tedious, almost boring. Most patients undergo single operative procedures, such as removal of a gallbladder or thyroid gland, and even the care of open-heart patients is very straightforward—more a matter of following doctors' orders than managing life-and-death situations. Within a week I astound the staff by starting an IV in someone for whom no one else has been able to find a vein. Within a month, to the chagrin of older nurses who have been here longer, I'm put in charge on evening or night shifts.

My disappointment in the work is matched by my unhappiness with Claude. He's generous—buys me nice things and takes me to expensive restaurants—but in return he insists that I date only him. Within a month I stop accepting his gifts and start making excuses not to go out with him. My mother's idea that it's better to be the one more loved just doesn't work for me.

The weekend before Thanksgiving, five months after coming to this city, I'm so nauseated that I'm unable to eat and so tired that I can hardly get out of bed. When I arrive at work on Monday morning, my fellow workers shrink from me in horror: I'm badly jaundiced. As it turns out, I have hepatitis.

My last two months in Dallas are spent as a patient at the Veterans Administration hospital. All I want to do is sleep, and I now learn to appreciate how hard it is to sleep in a hospital. They wake you up before sunrise to draw blood. They wake you up for meals, even though you've told them that the smell of food makes you vomit. They wake you up to give you shots, and they wake you up for visitors you're too tired to talk to.

It takes a month to feel halfway normal and regain my appetite and another month for my bloodwork to be close enough to normal to be discharged—on the condition that someone take care of me. I don't tell the doctor that I have to go to North Carolina for that to be possible.

The day of my discharge I pack and start driving east to Aunt Sarah and Uncle Edward's. I'm so tired that I pull off the road where I sleep for three hours, before I reach Oklahoma. It takes me five days to reach North Carolina.

For a month I do little more than eat and sleep. By March I'm awake more hours than asleep, but I still don't want company. I shut the door to the bedroom and pretend to sleep. Instead, I cry. Mostly I cry for Peter. More than anything I wish I could bring back the times we shared in Japan.

At the beginning of April my bloodwork is back to normal, and I feel almost well. I've decided to move to San Francisco, a city that I admired when I shipped out to Japan and that is close to Palo Alto, where my cousin Christine now lives. First, though,

I'll visit my parents in New Jersey. Beth comes with me.

We're on the outskirts of Washington, D.C., when the radio warns motorists to skirt the city. Antiwar demonstrations have turned into riots. From the interstate we can see the city's skyline belching dark smoke.

That night, watching TV in a hotel room, we see national guardsmen with M-60 machine guns mounted on the White House steps. And, the news anchor says, there were also demonstrations today in Manhattan, San Francisco, and Los Angeles. The images fill me with a certainty that it is only a matter of time before America erupts into civil war—which strikes Beth as unlikely. For her it's just eerie to see our capital burning.

We spend three days with my parents, and I envy how easily Beth relates with them. My parents say the demonstrations are Communist-inspired, and Beth thinks it's possible. My mother says protesters should leave the country if they don't like it, and Beth agrees.

As the demonstrations subside, I'm less fearful of a civil war, but I'm no less confused about the issue. It bothers me to watch college students burning the flag and Vietnam veterans tossing away their medals, but I agree the war is misguided, and there seems to be no other way to end it. But I don't dare say such things in front of my family because I'm too afraid they will think I am a Communist.

I stay with Christine while I look for a job in San Francisco. That doesn't take long; I start work in the surgical ICU at San Francisco General Hospital my second week here. The position has had a long list of applicants, but once again my Vietnam experience wins me the job. The same week I move into an apartment with a nurse and a medical resident who are looking for a third roommate.

San Francisco General's ICU is staffed with at least two and usually three nurses for six beds. I finish my work too quickly, and I know my constant offers to help exasperate other nurses. I end up pacing the floor, and I have developed the habit of pounding a fist into my palm as I pace.

On top of that I'm terribly frustrated by the restrictions on my authority. If someone needs blood, I have to get a doctor's order. If a fresh post-op dressing needs changing, I have to call a doctor. If someone is ready to get out of bed, I have to check with a doctor. And the doctors are interns, less experienced than I am, so they frequently have to check with their residents before they can grant me permission. All this leaves me pacing the floor, my right hand punching my left in a restless staccato.

It's even worse when I'm at odds with an intern or a resident over patient management. Once, in response to an irregular atrial heartbeat, the patient's intern orders me to push lidocaine into the IV—in this case an inappropriate treatment. I say so to the intern and refuse to give the lidocaine, so he orders another nurse to draw up the medication. When Karen sticks by me, he goes to the medicine cabinet himself, whereupon I call his resident. It's a real showdown. The resident agrees with my assessment, and the intern never forgives me.

Hardest of all for me is accepting my fellow workers' system of values. The other nurses complain about needing more help; the residents complain about their long working hours. I have no sympathy. Then a ninety-year-old man with complications from an appendectomy is admitted to the ICU. I think of the soldiers in Vietnam—those who are still being put aside to die because of lack of space or staff even to try to save them—and it infuriates me. Shortly after that a nineteen-year-old with a traumatic amputation from a motorcycle accident is admitted, and the staff showers him with pity—but I can't feel sorry. It's only one leg and below the knee at that, a small loss compared with what nineteen-year-olds in Vietnam are losing every day. If the unit is quiet, everyone sits around shooting the breeze without giving it a thought. But I pace the floor, full of guilt at how easy I have it here.

Outside the hospital I go to a lot of parties and I date a lot of doctors. I'm comfortable with this, having mastered the art of dating without entanglements in Japan. The biggest difference is that these men are not warriors. The men I go out with here value money very highly; warriors treasured just being alive and in one piece. Men here are concerned with the future; warriors cared more for the present. I adopted the warrior values, but now I want to fit in again, to be who I was before the Army. So I shop for nice clothes and try to believe these things mean as much to me as to everyone else.

The attentiveness of the men I meet restores my confidence. Things are different now that I'm out of the Army, and the odds are slim that a man I care for will be killed. It's finally time to find that special someone.

My twenty-fifth birthday is a month away when I go to Jackson Hole, Wyoming, on my first ski trip, a sport introduced to me by my roommates. I've called Retta to come along, and she flies up from Denver to join us. She's just as I remember, flamboyant and forever cracking jokes, despite limping from pain that she attributes to her "ski knee."

While on this trip, I meet a man named Brad whom I find attractive. I'm older than he, but he says it doesn't matter, and we start dating. The relationship lasts a year and gives me hope that I can have a future with a man, and then one day, while I'm at work, he reads my diary and discovers there's been more than one man in my life before him. And that's the end of our great romance.

I burn the diary and bury the past. I know how: just don't think about it. As I learned to do in Japan, I live one day at a time.

The following spring the head nurse at San Francisco General's ICU leaves with the recommendation that I fill her position. Instead, I quit. I'm now twenty-six. If I'm never to marry, there has to be something in my life to keep me going, and nursing isn't it. The GI Bill will provide me with an education. I enroll at San Francisco State University and move into my own apartment before I begin classes in the fall of 1970.

Around Thanksgiving Retta writes that she has bone cancer in her right knee, and her leg is to be amputated. During the winter-semester break I visit her in Denver and find a very different Retta from the woman I saw in Jackson Hole. Her moods swing wildly from a fury that flings her crutches across the room to a despair that breaks my heart to see.

By spring of 1971, my sophomore year, I've settled into the

geography department. I know there is limited professional opportunity for a geographer, but I do love the subject—especially physical geography, which teaches why things in the natural world are where they are, why they look the way they do, and how people affect that world.

My social life now revolves around school. I avoid dating to avoid entanglements and not just to avoid a broken heart: I'm uncomfortable with my classmates' politics about the war. I agree with them that the war is a mistake, but I can't agree that the warriors are somehow to blame. I'm antiwar but prowarrior.

They argue that if no one fought, there would be no war, that if doctors and nurses refused to go, that would put an end to it, that anyone who dies over there gets what he or she deserves for going. In time I refuse to discuss Vietnam.

Will is the exception among these friends. He's medium tall, has long blond hair and a mustache, and likes to think he looks like Wild Bill Hickok. We develop a special friendship before we discover each other's history. He was a marine in the north country, in and around the DMZ.

The day we make this discovery, we skip classes and spend the afternoon talking. For the first time I laugh at my funny stories—like the one about the Vietnamese moving the block of ice—without concern that he mistakes war for fun and games. Will tells me about being pinned down in a trenchful of water for three days, confident that I don't believe his story is a plea for pity. We discuss how ineptly the war is being fought, knowing we do not disparage those who fight it. We never mention the tragedies; we know the other sees them as backdrop to everything we talk about.

Our friendship grows, and our conversations over countless cups of coffee are the highlight of my school days. We meet frequently outside school, but we don't "date." We smoke marijuana together. I pretend this is something I've done a lot; the leftover schoolgirl in me wants him to think I'm a worldly woman. At the beginning of summer vacation he invites me on a backpacking trip to Kings Canyon National Park in the Sierra Nevada.

Although I've always liked to walk in the woods, I've never been so challenged by it. Countless switchbacks climb mercilessly upward. My neck hurts, my back hurts, my legs hurt, my lungs hurt, and, most of all, my feet hurt. My jungle boots burn blisters into my heels. Halfway up the mountain we stop.

Below and beyond, the glacially carved valley is drenched in midafternoon sun, and all around are the soft sounds of whispering trees and songbirds. So there really is a God—though not the kind I believed in before Vietnam.

After the climb the trail follows a stream through a redwood forest. Streaks of sunlight pierce the treetops, but the trail is shaded and smells of damp evergreen needles. As we walk, the pressures of city life fall away, and I feel as if no place else existed, as though my only worry were taking the next step.

This night, sharing the warmth of his parka around both our shoulders, Will and I sit in front of a campfire, watching make-believe worlds in the burning logs tumble and form new ones. Part of me thrills to his closeness, but a bigger part feels very cautious. I am silently thankful for the smoke that will not be waved away and keeps forcing us to shift positions.

We sleep without a tent, and it's the best sleep I can remember. The raucous squawking of Steller's jays wakes us, and we lie in our sleeping bags, watching them swoop from tree to tree. I feel pure joy to be alive. There is nothing contrived in the wilderness; everything acts according to its true nature and takes only what it needs to survive. This, I think, is the way life should be.

It was to have been a five-day hike, but the blisters on my heels make it impossible to go on, and we head back on the third day. Driving across central California, we stop for a beer. Will sits across the table from me.

"There's something I have to tell you," he says, and sighs. "I live with a woman."

Serves me right, I think. Why should he be any different from the rest? I shrug and say it doesn't matter in light of this being a friendship, not a relationship; but I drink too many beers, and I feel dizzy and nauseated the rest of the way home.

Back at my apartment I sit in the middle of my living-room floor unable to shake the strange sensation of not belonging here, of being unable to do anything, of nothing's being important. I haven't bathed in three days; I should take a shower. I should read the mail that has accumulated. I should call someone, go somewhere, do something. I do nothing. I sit.

My mind is drawn through the open windows, instinctively following the *whop-whop* of a Huey helicopter. When it disappears into the distance, I come back to the city—to street sounds, to the ringing telephone in a dusty apartment.

Back to the world. The Real World.

I still see Will at school, and when we go drinking after classes with other friends, I pretend nothing is different, but it is. It will be four years before I date another man.

During these years I visit Retta during semester breaks. The first year she regains much of her exuberance. We go day hiking together in the Rocky Mountains during the summer, and this winter we go downhill skiing; she has runners on her ski poles. Her biggest complaint is the weirdo men she meets, who want to sleep with her just to find out what it's like with a one-legged woman.

The second year, 1973, Retta's cancer metastasizes to her lungs. Radiotherapy fails. After an experimental treatment in Los Angeles she spends Christmas with me in San Francisco.

By then the American public has been in an uproar over secret bombing raids in Cambodia since last summer. It's not the news but the uproar that amazes me. It was no secret that we were bombing the Ho Chi Minh Trail and no secret that the trail goes through Cambodia. What did people expect?

This amazement is followed in May by one of even greater proportions—over the impeachment proceedings against President Nixon for covering up the break-in at the Democratic National Committee offices at the Watergate Hotel. For the life of me I can't understand why the cover-up is regarded as so much more horrific than the bombings.

I never discuss these subjects and seldom read a newspaper. I concentrate on studying and graduate summa cum laude with a bachelor of arts, in May 1974. It never occurs to me to take part in the graduation ceremony.

AMERICAN DAUGHTER GONE TO WAR

My GI Bill support ends with the commencement of my master's program. I survive on the salary of a technical assistant in cartography at San Francisco State University, supplemented by my working as a special-duty nurse a few days a month. Advanced studies in physical geography turn more and more to ecological problems; my classes now focus on endangered species and human destruction of natural habitats. My classroom hours, once a source of joy, sadden me.

Meanwhile, my desire to recapture who I was before the Army has slipped by the wayside; silk dresses and high heels never have regained their appeal, nor have the people for whom those things are important. Whenever possible, I escape to the mountains, where life feels simple and pure, where just eating and sleeping make me content. Most of my trailmates are men, partly because few women care for the physical hardships of hiking but mostly because I feel more comfortable with men. I'm a buddy, not a sweetheart.

I know I want more, but I've put romance on hold. For now I'm happy to just go drinking or backpacking with the guys.

Thousands of Vietnamese clamber at the Saigon embassy gates, and American sailors pitch helicopters into the ocean like so many cans of garbage. It is the end of April 1975, and the war is over. President Ford says we have finally achieved "peace with honor."

On television I watch America cheer and clap as our POWs (they're much older than when I knew them) disembark from their Freedom Bird. I wonder what their lives will be like now— how many of their marriages have survived their absences and how long before their patriotism is squelched by an ungrateful nation.

It doesn't take long for the returned veterans to be banished from the public eye. And like everyone else, I just go on with my life. And life doesn't seem so bad. I'm dating again, and we do a lot of fun things.

I visit Retta over the summer and find her in a great deal of pain and needing oxygen to get through the nights. She wavers between acceptance and bitterness, and for the first time she speaks about Vietnam. It's something I don't think about anymore, but she seems desperate to find some meaning to it all.

In the fall my course work ends, and that means an end to my cartography job. I return to nursing to support myself while I write my thesis—an exposé of the state's poisoning of California ground squirrels and the secondary killings of untargeted wildlife in the process, a war against nature that has been going on for decades.

My nursing position is in the ICU at San Francisco General— twelve-hour shifts three days a week, which allow me to take backpacking trips to more distant places from the Cascades in Oregon to the Wasatch Mountains in Utah. It's not easy to find trailmates for these longer excursions because most of my hiking companions are now married or live with women who invariably object to our camping overnight together. When I can find no one to go with me, I go alone.

This winter I receive a package from Retta—slides of us with warrior buddies in Japan and of me by the swimming pool in Saigon and in her hooch in Qui Nhon.

Two weeks later her family writes to say she has died.

I knew it was coming, yet her death affects me deeply. I don't want to see anyone or go anywhere, and I start spending my evenings alone, except for the friends I have known the longest— cigarettes and booze. Once, drunk by ten in the morning, I miss the noontime wedding of friends.

When summer comes and goes and I still can't shake my depression, I think about suicide for the first time in my life: I could take a trip to the mountains alone, hike for a few days, and then shoot up potassium chloride on the banks of a stream.

On September 5, 1977, I'm working in the San Francisco general ICU when there's an appeal for help with mass casualties in the emergency room. The Golden Dragon restaurant has just been fired upon with automatic weapons. Victims are in ambulances and en route.

It's been years since I worked in triage, but I'm confident my reflexes are still intact. When I get to the emergency room, staff members nod gratefully. "We can use all the help we can get," the head nurse says.

Doctors and nurses are all over the place, moving excitedly from room to room to check and recheck that everything is properly set up. I figure a whole building must have been blown up. "How many casualties are you expecting?" I ask.

There are eleven wounded. Most have single gunshot wounds that would have waited in the wings for hours during a push in Vietnam.

This is *the* trauma hospital for San Francisco. God help us if there's ever a major earthquake.

When the shooting occurs I've started dating again, but my feelings of unworthiness soon sabotage our relationship. I break up with him a year later, and then start the cycle all over again with another man. Life goes on, time passes, but nothing changes for me.

In January 1981 the Iranian embassy hostages come home to a hero's welcome. I want to scream, "What did they do?" But I avoid going anywhere rather than be confrontational and I start spending a lot of time alone again. During the day I work on my thesis. In the evening I get drunk with or without my current boyfriend.

In May 1981 my thesis is accepted, and some of my old classmates convince me to join this year's graduation.

It's warm and sunny day, perfect for the outdoor ceremony. Our postgraduate robes are white with wide hoods that drape over the shoulder and long, flowing sleeves. We are the first to march onto the field, filing into front-row seats from which we watch the ceremonial passing of thousands of undergraduates in black robes and caps. Because I came with no thought of solemnity for this event, the emotions welling up take me by surprise. I'm envious of those around me who stand on their seats to wave excitedly at family and friends in the bleachers.

When it ends, I feel sad and lonely—out of step with the joviality all around me as my classmates share this day with families and friends. It's my fault that no one I care for is here. I didn't tell anyone about the ceremony—not my boyfriend or any of my family—much less invite any of them to come. But that doesn't make me feel any less lonely.

Later, when I tell my father about the graduation, he's hurt. He can't understand how I could not know that they would want to be there. Indeed, why I keep shutting them out of my life.

I can't explain what I don't understand myself.

A master's degree proves I can do research and earns me a job in neurosurgery research. The job gets me out of critical care, where I've grown restless, but the research is on severe head injuries. Although I'm aware of using knowledge gained during my year in Vietnam, I'm unaware of emotions from that year rising with it.

I do know I'm depressed by the work, and it's a full-time job that pins me down to the city. I spend more and more evenings alone, drinking and smoking. I break up with my boyfriend and become even more deeply depressed. It becomes increasingly difficult to do my work and I quit before the two years I promised to the position are completed.

Thinking to find some of my old vitality, I plan a three-month trip around the world. My traveling companions are two men, one a nonromantic friend and a friend of his from the East Coast.

First stop Hong Kong. The three of us share a room at the Chungking Palace, where you feed the air conditioner quarters to keep cool. These days are fun—hopping the ferries and local buses, traipsing through the "Thieves Market" on Cat and Ladder streets, and dining outdoors at the night market.

But then we go to Bangkok, which is awful with its sputtering tut-tuts, rip-off pedicab drivers, narrow, crowded streets, and dust in the air that settles on my sweaty skin. It reminds me more of Saigon than of the Bangkok I remember from nearly fifteen years ago. Even the Emerald Buddha has become a popular tourist attraction, with no magic.

Chiang Mai is the jumping-off point for a week's trek through mountain villages. The tropical forest and the flat faces of people remind me of the Montagnard village I visited with Sandy and

Pamela so long ago. I remember laughing as we got drunk on rice wine, but somehow the memory doesn't make me happy.

Back in Chiang Mai, we stay a few days in a Buddhist monastery, but I find no comfort in the peaceful surroundings. Then we hit the beaches at Penang—another place I remember as wonderful when Sandy and I came here together, yet the memory only makes me feel miserable.

Everything seems to make me miserable. I cut the trip short and come home.

In the spring of 1983 I turn thirty-nine. I've been old for a very long time. I keep looking for happiness, dating one man and then another, but I can't find it. I know that happiness comes to those who deserve it, and I can't figure out what I've done wrong.

In late June I bring home a syringe and vial of potassium chloride from the hospital. I have drafted a letter to my parents and obtained a wilderness permit for August. I have no doubts about what I plan to do. It's a relief to know I will soon be done with this life.

CHAPTER EIGHTEEN

JULY 1983–
OCTOBER 1984:
Spirits of the Past

I${}_{\text{T'S}}$ a warm, sunny morning in July 1983, a rare summery day in a month usually distinguished by cold fog in San Francisco. I've taken a cup of coffee to the porch steps, where I sit with a book my cousin Christine has sent. It's called *Home Before Morning: The Story of an Army Nurse in Vietnam,* by Lynda Van Devanter.

The first page does not impress me. Twelve years later she's blaming Vietnam for not being able to sleep at night. What nonsense, I think, taking a sip of my coffee. At the bottom of the page I read: "They flew him in by chopper and there were streaks of dirt along his face."

Without warning, my eyes fill with tears and overflow. Wiping away tears, I swallow hard and continue: "His sandy brown hair was uneven, with patches pressed down where the sweat-soaked straps of his helmet had been."

A vise grips my chest, and I begin to gasp, unable to fill my lungs. Still, I read: "With his eyes closed, he might have been just another tired soldier resting. However, the bloody mess that was once his body told a different story."

I can smell the blood now, the stench of Vietnam in its humid tropical air. I see the dazed stare in the haggard face of a young soldier. I hear the choppers, the sound of more wounded on their way; taste the dust, my mouth dry as from a great thirst; feel the fear, the sick dread of death in the air all around me. She writes: "Maybe, if there were time, he could be saved. But there were too many others."

My tears fall in a torrent. From deep within me, from a lake of sorrow that I have long since forgotten existed, a desolate spirit breaks loose like a great sea serpent. I feel it rise to the surface, and I clutch my sides in a desperate hug as if I could hold it in. Unbidden, unwanted, its moaning wail escapes my lips and unfurls above the sunny backyards of my neighbors.

I flee inside, sink helplessly to the floor with my back against the door, overcome by visions of specters that are tragic to behold. Their war-torn forms stagger out of my broken heart, pour out of my eyes, tear my breath away as they spill from my open mouth. I struggle for air, rocking on my knees and bowing in their presence.

I hear myself begging over and over, "Why, oh, why, oh, *why? Why so much? Why so many? Why? Why? Why?*"

For the next week these ghosts of my past are my constant companions, and the past is more real than the present. Somehow my mind has crystallized them, brought their tortured faces and tormented voices back to life. Events from my year in Vietnam play through my mind's eye like reels of a movie. Only the tone of the movie changes: sometimes tragic, sometimes poignant, sometimes terrifying. I am powerless to stop it. I am the captive audience, a prisoner.

When they come, they bring everything with them: the sights, the smells, the sounds, the tastes, the very essence of that time and place. Sweat trickles under my arms and scalp; adrenaline surges through me. When they go, I am drained; I have been as much a participant in their coming as a spectator.

These are flashbacks, though I do not yet know the word. I am reliving, not just remembering, the past.

At night I drink enough alcohol and smoke enough marijuana to pass out. Then I have nightmares and for the first time since leaving Vietnam, I remember them.

It's midday in the delta. The air is hot and sticky, and there's not a breath of wind or the slightest sound to relieve the oppressiveness. I'm watching from outside my body, see myself squatting Vietnamese style on the raised porch of a Vietnamese hut. A Vietcong—head shaved, wearing black pajamas—squats to my left. He has an automatic weapon loosely propped between his legs. I can't see if it's American or Chinese.

Following his gaze over the rice paddies, I see myself approaching from far away. I'm wearing the light blue pajamas our patients wear, which are commonly worn by Vietnamese as well. My long hair is blowing back from my face.

The VC is nervous about my being out there; he sets his rifle on lock and load when I draw within a hundred feet. I smile at him to say not to worry, that I'm just out for a walk. When I'm within thirty feet, he aims. Still smiling, I hold out my empty hands to show I'm unarmed. When I draw within twenty feet, he shoots me in the chest.

The impact of the bullet feels more like a dull thud than an explosion; the slight cavity under my pajama top shows no trace of blood. When I step to within three feet, I can see a little surprise on my face but no fear. He shoots three more rounds into my chest in rapid succession, but there's still no blood, though the impact throws me back several feet. My face begs for an explanation as I regain my footing and reach to steady myself on the porch edge.

He shoots again. I can feel the bullet exploding from my back, but there's still no pain or blood. Hanging on to the porch, my eyes ask, "Why do you want to kill me?"

Unable to understand how I can still be alive, the VC rises in terror. Just before he fires again, I collapse to the ground.

My only emotion is bewilderment over someone's shooting me for taking a walk through the rice paddies.

* * *

The second week I'm still unable to regain touch with the present for more than minutes at a time. And I still can't stop weeping, not even to break plans with friends. When they knock at my door, I cower in a corner where they can't see me. I ignore my phone when it rings. I have no appetite, force myself to eat.

I keep thinking this will soon end, but there is no sign it ever will. I begin to believe that I'm crazy.

I discover writing helps me regain control of my mind. The reels won't stop, but I can slow them enough to record portions, and once they're put to paper, they fade back into the past, change from experience to memory. Only there are too many of these scenes, no end of new ones to replace those that writing puts to rest.

At the end of the second week I vaguely remember a Sunday news story published a few weeks ago on the subject of women Vietnam vets. I rummage through my stack of old newspapers and find it—and the name of someone to call. But it's too frightening to admit I need this kind of help—psychological help. I wait another week, hoping it will pass.

It does not. Nor do my tears. I weep constantly. When I finally do reach for the phone, I'm unable to speak through the breath-wrenching sobs that overwhelm me when someone answers. I have to hang up.

Several days later I'm able to control the sobs.

"Concord Vet Center. This is Rose."

I'm crying again, but I don't hang up. I clutch the phone with all my might.

"Hello?" I hear from the other end.

I take a deep breath, swallow to choke back the tears, and manage a barely audible "hello."

There's only the slightest hesitation before she says, "Can you tell me your name?"

"Winnie," I whisper.

"Are you a Vietnam vet?" she asks.

"Yes," I choke into the phone.

"Where are you?"

But I can't answer. She takes over in a clear, firm voice, telling me when to come and how to get there, not requiring any answers, and repeating everything so I can write it down.

"Don't miss the appointment, Winnie," she says. "Even if you're feeling better by then, it'll do you a lot of good to talk to someone who has been there. And," she warns, "if you don't have anyone to bring you, take public transportation. The sessions can be very emotional, and it might not be good to drive yourself home."

I drive. I can't stand for anyone to see my tear-swollen face. More than that, I'm terrified of making a fool of myself in public. It's bad enough to do it in private.

The door reads "Vet Center," but it might as well read "Help for the Insane." Nervously checking to be certain no one sees me, I slip inside. A girl behind the desk smiles. She knows I'm one of the crazies. Fighting back the urge to turn and run, I say my name.

Rose will be with me in a minute, please take a seat. But I'm too skittish to sit. I pretend to read bulletin boards as I pace the floor and wait.

Rose is the director, rates a corner office with big windows. She's about five feet five with short brown hair and clear blue eyes and traces of crow's-feet. We sit next to a coffee table, where a box of tissues fills me with fierce determination not to cry. I want to learn how to control myself, not blubber like a baby.

Rose calls what is happening to me posttraumatic stress disorder. The word "disorder" echoes through my mind. So, I think, I am crazy.

"I remember my first day there," she says, "when they put us in buses that had grates on the windows. Remember those?"

I remember, but I say nothing.

"Until then I assumed I wouldn't be in any danger. I didn't have any idea what it was going to be like over there."

She pauses, but I don't respond. I clutch the arms of the chair, stare at the floor.

"I was twenty-six, a captain. They made me head nurse of the ICU in Cu Chi, even though I didn't have any ICU experience. I didn't know which end was up, but the nurses there had just come through the Tet offensive so they really knew their stuff."

I visualize casualties from the Twenty-fifth Division—covered in red dust. Then I see Peter's face in the Redbull Inn.

"What I saw on that ward shocked me," Rose continues. "All those boys torn apart and all those we couldn't save because we didn't have enough time or staff. After six months I hated the Vietnamese. When there was a push, I ignored them even though I had taken an oath to do my best for anyone who needed my help." She takes a deep breath. "That made me feel guilty."

Her words sink deep within me, and I must reach for the box of tissues. Only these tears are not so much for grief as for relief that here is someone who has been where I've been, seen what I've seen, done what I've done, who gives credence to my relentless sobbing, who does not think I'm weak or crazy after all.

But I will not fall apart, will not free the wails that echo inside me. Not with a witness. Not yet. At the end of our meeting Rose shows me a videotape of other women vets breaking down in tears. It strikes me as degrading. I stare stone-faced at the TV screen, not wanting to be one of them and ashamed that I am. Rose makes an appointment for me to return in a week, but I don't know if I will.

On the drive home I have an urge to scream down the freeway at a hundred miles an hour, to careen through the railing of the Bay Bridge, once and for all to put these ghosts of war to rest.

In my dream I've reupped in the Army. My first assignment is the Third Field Hospital. I'm surprised; I didn't know the Army still had troops in Vietnam.

My first day off I go to the central marketplace in downtown Saigon. The outside is the same as I remember, but the inside now has a narrow cobblestone corridor leading to the shops. The cement walls are damp, as in a dungeon. I'm ill at ease, but the three corpsmen with me are confident that we're okay.

The corridor opens onto a large room in the center of which is a circular staircase with an iron railing. Vietnamese in black pajamas crowd in on us as we climb to shops on an upper floor.

There's an American girl on the steps above us, with her face pressed against the railing. She's very pale and sinking on the steps.

At first I think she's just hung over. Looking more closely, I see blood dripping off the step, and the girl passes out.

"We've got to get her to fresh air," I cry.

The corpsmen pick her up, and we start down the steps. As we fight our way through the crowd, I remember all the wounded in the hospital. I thought the war was over. But it must not be.

I awaken to the continuous ringing of my telephone. My clock says 10:00 P.M. It takes a few more rings for me to remember coming home from the vet center and then drinking a whole bottle of wine. I must have passed out.

The only person I know who would be so persistent is my father, worried because he hasn't been able to reach me.

When I answer the phone, I'm determined to set his mind at ease by telling him that I'm fine, that I've been away on a trip.

"Where in the hell have you been?" he opens. "I've called day and night for the past two weeks. When I called your work number, nobody had seen you for three weeks. Your mother and I have been worried sick that something happened to you!"

My tears erupt. "I'm sorry, Daddy. I kept thinking I'd be okay and I'd call you then."

"What do you mean? What's the matter with you?"

"It's Vietnam. I can't stop thinking about it. All I can do is cry. I went to the vet center today to get help. Only I still can't stop crying."

There is a stunned silence. Finally he says, "Vietnam? What brought up Vietnam?"

"A book. I've been crying ever since I read it. I'm scared, Daddy," I sob into the phone. "I'm scared I'm going crazy!"

Another long pause, followed by a deep sigh. "I'm sorry, honey. We never talked about it because we thought you would want to forget."

But my father is a combat vet of World War II. The wars were fought differently, I know, but I can't believe that the effect was so different. Could our homecomings be the reason? The fact that he was never told that he deserved losing his leg for being fool enough to go to war in the first place?

302

Whatever it is, he can't understand why that year in Vietnam has come back to haunt me so long after. But he doesn't tell me to forget it. He says, "You're a good person, Winnie. And you're strong. You'll come out of it all right."

My mother not only can't understand but accuses me of using Vietnam as an excuse for my failures. The real problem, she maintains, is that I'm lazy, or I would have done better with my nursing career. And I'm boring, or I would have a man by now. My attempt to explain how that year changed me launches our first discussion about the war.

"If the leftists and the doves had let us bomb Hanoi the way we should have," she says, "we wouldn't have lost."

"I can't believe that, Mama," I say. "We dropped four times more bombs in Vietnam than in all of World War Two. There were nights when my bunk shook from loads dropped by B-fifty-twos, and that was just to keep *South* Vietnam under control."

"If what you say is true," she says, "then we lost because our soldiers were dope addicts and cowards—and those kinds of men aren't worthy of wearing the American uniform."

Her words cut deep into my heart. What about the arms and legs left behind? About those paralyzed or mindless? About humping the boonies, never knowing if you'd come out in one piece and seeing your buddies who didn't? But tears smother my protests.

"As far as I'm concerned," she says, "Vietnam vets who blame that war for their problems are just shiftless good-for-nothings. They're too lazy to pull themselves up and work for a living like everybody else. It makes me ashamed to hear the bad things they say about our country."

"Then," I lash out, "you're ashamed of me."

It's as if she suddenly realized that I, too, am a Vietnam vet. "I didn't mean that, exactly," she says, quieter. "It's just that they should be proud of this country. They shouldn't work against it."

Does she think we don't want to be proud of our country? That I want to spend all my time crying? And can't she see how I've tried for all these years to be the way I used to be?

No, I answer myself. She can't understand what it was like,

that somewhere along the line we must stop and cry for what we saw and did there.

The word gets out, and my family in North Carolina calls to see how I'm doing. My aunt Jenny is surprised at what's happening to me. "But," she says, "war is a terrible thing and couldn't help but affect you." Aunt Sarah says she knew I was deeply affected while I was recuperating from hepatitis. "I heard you crying when you were alone," she says, "although I never mentioned it."

I'm a passenger in a Jeep, traveling with a friend who is not a vet, headed for a vineyard in the country to pick grapes.

As we round a bend, soldiers in jungle fatigues block our way, leveling their M-16 rifles on us. There are soldiers lounging among trees and along the road, and I realize there must be an entire company in the area. They have an air of readiness that fills me with dread. A soldier asks our business here, and we chat for a while about homemade wine before he allows us to proceed. As we drive off, he warns us it's a secured area and not to stay long.

The vineyard's caretakers are a Norman Rockwell-like husband and wife, who help us load the grapes. We talk about the harvest this year and hope that good weather will hold out. Suddenly a rifle shot rings out from not far away. I look at the caretakers in alarm.

"Best you leave now," the husband says calmly.

"What's going on?" my companion asks.

The caretaker shakes his head. "Best just take the little lady out of here. Then keep on going."

There are several shots in rapid-exchange fire, slightly closer. "Come with us," I say to the couple.

The husband smiles ironically. My partner is tugging at my arm, climbing into the driver's seat. "Let's go," he prods.

"But something's wrong!"

"Time's apassin', little lady," the caretaker warns. "Get out of here while you can and do your job. We'll be okay."

Larry spoke those words, long ago in Vietnam. "Do your job" means it's time to leave. I jump into the Jeep. There are more shots as we round the bend, and I know the caretakers have taken up weapons and disappeared into the woods; I wonder how long they'll be able to hold out. In any case I do know what my job is: to tell everyone that the Army is taking over our country. They are starting in the foothills and farmlands, and then they will overrun the cities.

By late summer I'm working part-time in the recovery room at San Francisco General Hospital. I have no energy to go anywhere else—the flashbacks and nightmares persist, and they exhaust me—but my sobbing has given way to quiet weeping, the reels of memory play slightly less often, and I'm no longer disgraced by my breakdown—a priceless gift from Rose. I speak openly of this posttraumatic stress disorder.

Friends of more than twelve years who knew me before I became a "closet vet" aren't surprised that the war has come back to haunt me. Barbara reminds me that she tried to get me to talk about Vietnam when she first met me, but I'd do so only when I was drinking—and even then I didn't say much. Steve remembers that he asked if Vietnam had changed me, and I said, "No, except for making me a better nurse." He didn't believe me but couldn't get me to talk about it any more than that. Jamie tells me that I'd get "a faraway look" in my eyes when the war was discussed— what she knows now is called the thousand-yard stare.

Friends I've met within the past ten years never knew I went to Vietnam, say they never would have guessed it. They did wonder about my moodiness and were sometimes hurt by something I did—or didn't do, as when I missed Marlene and Ken's wedding. When I ask why they put up with me, they say that despite those times, they knew they could open up to me, could trust me with their feelings.

In war lives depend on trust. Grunts in the boonies trust everyone in a fire fight to take his fair share of risk and look after one another. In a hospital we trusted each other to take a fair share of work and give the best care possible. Where trust is so vital, distrust is a source of loathing. We didn't trust the Vietnamese. Nor did we trust our own big brass; we felt they cared more about their careers and what fat cats in Washington thought than about what was happening to their men in the boonies.

I now see that when I came home, I brought with me the sense of fair play that was a big part of our trust and a loathing for the rich and powerful who care only for themselves.

But none of my friends was in the war, and none can truly understand what is happening to me. Nor do they really want to talk about it; for them, it's history. So with them I talk of other times, and I'm free for a while from the horror films. Yet oddly it's more of a strain than a relief to live in the present and speak of anything but that war. No sooner do my friends leave than the ghosts return, having waited for me all evening.

I should balance my checkbook, pay my bills, return phone calls, or answer letters that go back two months. Or go to bed so I won't be so irritable and tired at work tomorrow. But I just can't get the Nam out of my blood.

I'm on a jumbo jet where everyone, including the stewardess, has yarn hair, big eyes painted on cloth skin, trouble bending his or her arms and legs, and all wear funny clothing with big basting stitches along hemlines and cuffs. They stare at me strangely, and I wonder if I'm on the wrong plane: I can't remember where I'm going.

My meal is served, and the milk won't pour. I'm about to ask for another glass when there's an explosion and everyone goes up in flames.

The next thing I know, I'm on the ground, on an airfield somewhere in the Midwest. All around me are parts of the plane but no bodies. That strikes me as odd. There's a telephone booth about a half mile away, and it's a long walk in my high-heel shoes. I call an old boyfriend.

He arrives dressed in a suit and driving a big convertible. Neither he nor his car looks familiar. He greets me warmly, as if nothing out of the ordinary had happened.

I'm at work in the recovery room when, out of the clear blue sky, a patient claims to have served in Vietnam.

He looks so young! "Who were you with?" I ask, pulling the stethoscope out of my ears.

"Special Forces."

"When were you there?"

"My first tour was in 1964. I did three more after that."

When I return to the nursing station, his chart tells me that he's thirty-five years old. He was fourteen in 1964.

I'm furious. I want to expose this asshole, humiliate him. But I hold my temper; I say nothing.

Though daytime flashbacks are quieter, my mind still conjures up tortured tales during sleep. Night after night, month after month, they come. Sometimes with tears of remorse, sometimes crying out in terror, I awaken confused or panic-stricken, drenched in perspiration.

In autumn the vet center forms a women's group. There are eight of us. We could be middle-aged women anywhere, some in jeans and some in dresses. One woman in particular, blond with dimples, quite slim and smartly dressed, draws my attention. She seems friendly, but something about her makes me uneasy. I sit apart, envious of their ease in conversing.

Rose opens the meeting by having us tell our names, when and where we were stationed, and in what area we worked.

As I recite, the woman I've noticed gasps. "I can't believe it," she says, staring at me.

Turning to face her, I realize who she is. "Sheila Murphy," I say as we stare at each other in wonder.

So many years later, on the opposite coast from where we both entered the Army, fate has brought us together again. She's married, she tells me, to a doctor. They live in Napa, and they have two sons in high school. After all these years I'm still envious of her.

Our group learns about those things we have in common. Most of us are Catholic. Most of us are unmarried. Most are childless. Most worked with fresh casualties in critical care, the emergency or operating room.

One notable exception to this last is Linda, who served as a communications sergeant and whose contact with casualties was through a computer. Day after day she read their names, ranks, branch of service, hometowns of record, next of kin, and the descriptions of their injuries ranging from sprained ankles to "pieces of remains not positively identified." The messages came alive when she passed the triage area of the Twenty-fourth Evacuation Hospital in Long Binh.

It's not the statistically accountable common threads that have brought us here but the fact that those threads long ago transmuted into cages; layers of forgetfulness have welded into steel bars that lock out emotions. We're here to dismantle the cages, to free our emotions in a "safe place," but this can be accomplished only layer by layer. It's a scary process, worsened by an underlying sentiment among us that we have to be strong and the fear that we'll be considered weak. I resist speaking from my heart, too fearful of crying.

We push down the past with one hand while raising it with the other. Painful as it is, the group is the only place for us finally to learn about ourselves and about how the war affected us. Within these walls we talk about Vietnam.

For us the subject is not history; it's a condition of our lives. In a country where youth is adored, we lost ours before we were out of our twenties. We learned to accept death there, and it erased our sense of immortality. We met our human frailties, the dark side of ourselves, face-to-face, and learned that brutality, mutilation, and hatred all are forgivable. At the same time we learned guilt for all those things. The war destroyed our faith, betrayed our trust, and dropped us outside the mainstream of our society. We still don't fully belong. I wonder if we ever will.

We meet every week for three months. Then our sessions are canceled for a month during the holiday season, and I miss them.

The annual rush of Christmas shoppers reinforces my disdain for Americans' obsession with material goods. Apparently it doesn't matter what we do as a nation to maintain our high standard of living. Buying gifts is an ordeal. I find no spirit of peace on earth or goodwill toward men in the unsmiling crowds. I hate the frantic pushing and shoving.

To escape the frenzy, I retreat to the mountains for a ski trip with Brad, the old boyfriend who read my diary twelve years ago.

It's wonderful to be back in the mountains. They still weave a spell on me, instill a confidence that there is a beauty and purpose in life. And although I have some bad dreams here, I have no flashbacks.

Sunday we leave the slopes early to miss the traffic. We're halfway down the mountain, and I'm acutely aware that a Huey helicopter has been following us since we began our descent.

Finally I ask Brad, "Why do you think that chopper's following us?"

"What chopper?" he asks.

I look at him in alarm. "Listen," I say. "Don't you hear that *whop-whop?*"

"That's not a helicopter," he says, his brow furrowing. "It's the sound of our tires on the road.

Night has fallen by the time we reach the Sacramento Delta. It's my turn to drive while Brad takes a nap. I peer into the pitch-black landscape, unable to shake the sense of an unseen enemy bearing down with mortars. Goose bumps stand my hairs on end even as my sweaty hands slip on the steering wheel. A flash in the distance startles me, and I half expect the roar of war to follow.

They're headlights briefly visible behind a hillock, I tell myself, but I wait anxiously for them to reappear. The part of me that dreads dying in the rice paddies of the Mekong Delta flees from the darkness at breakneck speeds. I cling to the part of me that knows this is the Sacramento Delta.

Our women vets' group comes to a natural end in the spring of 1984, but I still have personal issues to understand. For one thing, I want to learn how being in the Army during those years when I should have learned how to interact with the world as a woman has affected my relationships with men.

In search of answers, Linda and I have joined another vets' group, these all men. Like us, they have examined the past and want to get on to the present—all save one, who quit the group when he heard a nurse was joining, afraid that my stories would recall a buddy of his who died on a hospital ward.

The men are mostly unmarried or separated from their spouses, childless or separated from their children, and have problems relating at work. Like our women vets, they are intense about everything, too intense for most people. Like us, they are unsympathetic toward such things as burned fingers and sprained ankles, too much so for most people. Like us, they are prone to unreasonable anger when someone doesn't do his or her fair share of work or when the "system" fails them. Having been taught that a temper is unbecoming to a lady, I've always put a lid on it. But these men have put fists through walls as well as to faces.

They know, as we do, that they are out of line, sometimes out of control. Most use alcohol to numb anger and forget their sense of isolation, to escape the world and themselves. Some use drugs when alcohol won't do the trick. Yet, unlike us women, they're not afraid of being wimpish, and they seem much more at ease when we meet. I feel safer with them than I did in the women's group.

Although November is still eight months away, politics is very much on our minds. We talk about the upcoming elections; there is little doubt that Reagan will win again. Americans want to believe their country is the champion of freedom fighters for oppressed peoples, that we are the last hope for a free world against communism and the "Evil Empire." I can't blame them for believing such things—I wish I did—and it's easy to point to our good life as proof that God is on our side. Provided you still believe that there is a God. But our group doesn't believe. We share a fear that Reagan will get us into a war in Central America, a war too much like the one we knew. One of our members has sixteen-year-old son and vows he will take his son to Canada or New Zealand if it ever comes to that.

Getting to know these men brings back an old buddy in my dream.

I've regrouped on the Gulf of Mexico with Chris. We're sharing a hotel room as friends, not lovers, on the twentieth floor. There's a flagpole extending from our balcony over the water, but no flag.

Sipping gin and tonics, we sit on the balcony to watch the sun set over the water. We stay long after nightfall, and the world turns pitch-black with no moon. We talk about Japan, Vietnam, the Real World, about how old and tired we feel though we're still young. As we talk, we try to make sense out of it all.

When we can no longer stay awake, we climb into our twin beds. I awaken with a sense of dread shortly after sunrise.

Chris is gone.

I find him sitting at the top of the flagpole. He's shirtless, and for the first time I see his scars from the war.

"I'm sorry," he says, "I was hoping you wouldn't wake up."

I'm trembling. "Please come back."

"I can't. It's too late to change any of it."

I know I won't change his mind. I want to run away, but I can't desert him.

He lets go of the pole, and a gust of wind blows him off. I shut my eyes. For an instant it's me falling, and I'm terrified.

When I open my eyes again, there's no sign of Chris, only the pole and water twenty stories below. The pain in my chest feels like a heart attack.

On June 21 pops shatter the still night air.

They are not rifles, I tell myself; they're firecrackers. But I can't get past the fear of a fire fight on the perimeter and mortars to follow.

Something rumbles in the distance. Those are not bombs, I say to myself, only fireworks. But I keep waiting for the B-52 bombers to come closer, to shake the earth with payloads dropping on the Cambodian border.

Frozen at my kitchen table, stonily staring through the windows into the night, I fight my terror of turning on the lights. Do it, I tell myself. Prove to yourself that there's no enemy out there, that these sounds do not carry the threat of death. Open the door.

The sounds grow louder. People are shouting in the streets, and I can't shake the terror that it is some fanatical group making a valiant last stand.

Don't be silly. It's just a bunch of teenagers, whooping it up with firecrackers. But what are those deep rumbles? The Fourth of July is still two weeks away. Whatever they are, they are *not*

311

bombs. Walk outside and you'll see— The phone rings. I startle like a scared rabbit. I don't answer. I don't want anyone to know how frightened I am. More than that, I don't want to know what's going on. If it's bad, I'll know soon enough.

In the dark I cower at my kitchen table until the scattered pops and deep rumbles stop. When my shaking subsides, I turn on the lights. But I can't shake 1968, no matter how many times I tell myself it's 1984.

When the phone rings again, I answer.

It's my father, wanting to know how I'm doing.

"Fine," I say, not wanting to worry him.

Afterward I drink myself into a stupor so I can get some sleep.

I dream I'm with another nurse, standing on the roof of Claymore Tower in Saigon, looking down on the old French fort in the open field and, beyond that, Tan Son Nhut Air force Base. Only in the dream the base is Cu Chi, where Peter was stationed.

The base camp looks like a three-ring circus with flimsy red-and-white-striped tents, enclosed by a corrallike fence. The whole area is empty, the soldiers gone out on a mission.

The other nurse has a boyfriend based here. She's crying, shivering in a chilly night wind on the roof. I hold her in my arms, rocking and swaying to comfort her. "Sometimes," I say, "I think it's better if we don't know what's going on while we're here." Then, staring at the empty camp: "Maybe it'll be easier when we get back to the States."

When I awaken, I understand that both nurses were myself, the woman I am today comforting the girl I used to be.

All day last night's disturbance haunts me. I wonder if I've reached some new level of posttraumatic stress disorder. Or if I am losing my mind after all. By sundown, taking courage from a bottle of wine and pack of cigarettes, I telephone Linda. I'm careful to keep a casual tone. "Did you hear fireworks last night?"

"Yes, for the opening of the cable cars," she says, and after a long pause she chuckles. "Did you think you were going crazy?"

I make an attempt to chuckle back. "A little."

"Don't worry. It happens to the best of us." She pauses again, then says, "You know the firecrackers I hate the most?"

"The whistlers?"

"Right. They sound too much like..."

"Incoming," we say together, and this time I laugh.

It's the Fourth of July, and the smell of wounded fills my kitchen. I'm feverishly at work on a casualty whose bright blood oozes from his chest. I break into a sweat in spite of a chill that passes through me from the shadow of his upcoming death.

When the firecrackers stop outside, I snap out of it. Neighborhood celebrations, a string of explosions followed by scattered pops from the hillside behind, sound too much like small-arms fire. My decision not to go out to watch the fireworks was a mistake. From my apartment the sound of cracks and pops punch holes in the night air.

The rhythm of that burst was all wrong, too erratic. That set was a dead ringer for semiautomatic fire from two rifles. That one got cut off in the middle of a burst. That one was too close for comfort but was a dud. That whistler lasted too long, fizzled in the end. But not this one—and I tense for an explosion that never comes, that I knew would never come even as my muscles contracted.

Rumbling in the distance! But no lightning. Must be the big fireworks. Or is it the big guns? Something's going on somewhere. Choppers! Where did they come from? I fight the urge to run for the triage area.

Get hold of yourself, Smith. This is the States. There is no triage, no M-16s, no artillery. But I can't shake the sounds of war.

Deeper and deeper I flounder. From my back porch I monitor muffled sounds in the fog and sporadic flashes in the misty darkness. I'm in Saigon, watching a fire fight from the roof of Claymore Tower.

I must get out of here, I think, and turn away from the porch railing, go down the steps, and run toward the street. Just as I open the gate, there is a string of shattering pops, and I instinctively fall to a crouch. Trembling in what I know is irrational terror, I run back to the safety of my home. But I can't stop shivering; an unnatural cold clutches the very core of me.

I need to talk to someone—something I've learned from the vet outreach center—but there is no answer when I dial Linda or Jamie or Steve. The only one in my family who might understand such a call is my father, but I don't want to worry him. I ask the operator for the number of my father's close friend, Lin, whom I've known since shortly after my return from Vietnam.

"I feel like I'm going crazy," I choke into the mouthpiece, and start to cry.

"I know," Lin says, not surprised by my call. "And I think it's healthy. Once you get the crying out of your system, you can put Vietnam to rest."

We talk for an hour, mostly about how Vietnam vets were treated when they returned—and how good it is that they're speaking out now. When we hang up, I'm back in the present and my fears are quieted.

The lights are still out, and I stare through my kitchen window at the thick fog blanketing the city. For a long time I listen to the staccato bursts. When the big fireworks boom overhead, I open my door to hear them better.

Now that I'm free of the fear, the sounds of war blend with strains of nostalgia. Part of me longs to be back in that place—to have purpose in my life as I did then, to regain the sense of belonging and share the camaraderie that was so unlike anything I have found since.

CHAPTER NINETEEN

VETERANS DAY WEEKEND, 1984: Washington, D.C.

Several of us from the Concord Vet Center are going for this year's Veterans Day ceremonies in Washington. I fly there on Friday afternoon with Sheila, Margo, Rose, and her roommate, Pam, also a nurse from those days. Linda and Bonnie, another member of our old women's group, will fly in tonight. On Sunday we seven plan to stand with other women vets and "declare" ourselves as part of the dedication ceremony for the "Three Fighting Men," the statue added across the lawn from the National Vietnam Veterans Memorial—better known as the Wall. I'm uncomfortable about the public display, but it means a lot to Rose, and I owe her too much to refuse.

The taxi ride from the airport to our hotel is through softly rolling hills, covered with maple, birch, and dogwood trees that have turned the deep reds, golds, and browns of late autumn. It is even more beautiful than I remembered.

After checking in, Rose and Pam offer to take me to the Wall, which I've never seen. It's a crisp night that hints of winter, and we pass few other strollers on the sidewalk. Hardwood trees line the way, swaying fitfully over our heads and in the halos of street-lights.

Rose and Pam converse as we walk, but I'm lost in my thoughts. I'm thinking about how my mind has protected me for such a long time, locking away conscious memory of the war while my unconscious mind lived by its dictates for a quarter of my life. My mind still protects me, opens my eyes only a little at a time. The example at hand is that this Wall was erected more than two years ago, but I never heard of it until last month.

I breathe deeply. We never have nights as sharp and spicy as this in San Francisco; it revives my five senses in the same way such nights did when I was a child. I can almost feel myself emerging from the sense of hopelessness I've experienced for more than a year.

We turn onto a paved path that leads to the Wall. Rose and Pam say little, whisper when they do talk. At night, lit only by footlights along a narrow path in front of it, the Wall is difficult to see. I can make out the closest panels of polished black granite, but the Wall seems to slip off into the earth after a short distance, and much of it dissolves in darkness.

When my eyes adjust, tears well up at the sight. For as far as the Wall reaches, there is a cheerful profusion of flowers and tiny American flags, wreaths and old combat boots, yellowing photographs of the names, and notes from the living.

Family and friends are here. A cluster of gold star mothers, distinguished by their white suits and gold-trimmed hats, and fathers and sisters and brothers and wives, and sons and daughters who barely remember or never knew their fathers.

And there are many veterans, buddies now middle-aged—some potbellied, many with gray or thinning hair. Men finally proud to have served in that war, they wear bits and pieces of old warrior uniforms: worn combat boots, jungle pants with pocketed legs, fatigue jackets with unit patches I still remember well—the Horse's Head of the 1st Cavalry, Tom and Chris and Good Buddy's outfit; the Big Red One of the 1st Division, Larry and Pops's outfit; the Lightning Bolt of the 25th; the Screaming Eagle of the 101st; the Clover Leaf of the 9th. . . . I regret not having packed some piece of my own uniform to wear.

Everyone searches for names and tearfully adds a token of remembrance to the colorful carpet bequeathed to the Wall; there are even bottles of beer propped up against it.

The Wall rises higher as the path sinks deeper into the chevron of the Wall's heart. My emotions range from despair at so many graven names to gratitude that they are so lovingly remembered. Having come empty-handed, I stand at a respectful distance from where men and women kneel and whisper to the names, praying that they rest in peace. I realize I've become separated from Rose and Pam and move closer to the Wall to search for them. I linger near a wheelchair veteran who gazes long and hard at names too high for him to touch.

And then, suddenly, rising behind the names and swimming out of the obsidian black into a blinding tropical sun, casualties form, warriors from so long ago careening through my mind. I crumble to the ground, gasping through my sobs for air, still crying for these names who suffered so much, still asking why, oh, why.

When my crying subsides, I rise shakily. I have no idea how long I've been here. Have I made a total fool of myself?

Sheepishly I sneak glances at nearby faces. No. No one is staring at me. It's all right. It's all right.

In some kind of gesture, maybe good-night, I place my hand against the Wall, my palm against the names.

The Wall is warm!

I press my face to the stone, gaining a measure of peace in knowing that these names rest in warmth on a chill night.

The next day is one of those perfect autumn days with a not quite summery sun and not quite wintry winds. Bonnie is sharing my hotel room, and we rise early and set out together.

The two of us are very different on the outside—she has dark hair and eyes and a rich Mediterranean complexion—but we're much alike on the inside. We carry the same sorrows and show the same scars for having gone to war.

The Wall lists the names of warriors in the order that they fell, and we want to find the section memorializing those we cared for but could not save. Bonnie served in Vietnam a year after I did, so her panels should be close to mine. We stop a park ranger with a directory and discover that panels covering just my years in Japan and Vietnam stretch from 2E to 27E.

Thousands of names! And so many faces with names I can't remember. However will I find them? But it's worse for Bonnie. She can't remember even one name—only an emergency room filled with casualties and repeating to herself: "I can't think about any of this. If I do, I'll go crazy."

Today the crowd is so thick we can't get close to the Wall without disrupting the flow of people. Gone is the quiet reverence of last night; many here have no connection to the war and jabber nonstop along the way. I resent them as I would a tour bus stopping at the graveyard of a loved one.

But even they respond to some magic in the Wall. Their chatter quiets and then ceases as we follow the path downward. As we walk, the polished black stone reflects billowy clouds racing across the sky, the colorful edging of flowers and flags and a mirror image of ourselves, much older now than we were then, reunited with those who never came home. Some people are on their knees, and others sit on shoulders to trace names onto paper as a keepsake. Our quiet weeping and whispers sanctify the names, warmed by the sun and the love of those who have not forgotten.

"We didn't lose that war! They wouldn't let us win it!"

The cry slashes angrily at the air and then chokes on the speaker's tears. He's an ex-marine, leaning heavily on crutches with braces detectable under jungle fatigues. Anguish is plain on his face.

An older couple, obviously embarrassed, hush and prod him out of the arena through a path of curious onlookers.

I want to shake them. Why can't he stay? I want to tell him it's okay, to put my arms around him and soothe his pain. When I start to move toward them, Bonnie puts her hand on my arm. "No," she says. "It's his time of mourning, not our place to interfere."

Is she right? My uncertainty keeps me silent. The crowd still stares. I imagine what they're thinking: another deranged Vietnam vet; all a bunch of crybabies. A woman rushes after the departing marine, pushes a camera in his face as she snaps away. I'm ready to gouge out her eyes, but Bonnie hangs on tightly to keep me out of it.

I press my hand against the Wall for its solid warmth to reassure me. Let the outsiders be damned. We have this place, and we are finding one another. We will grow strong again together.

Bonnie and I turn away and cross the green, manicured lawn toward the "Three Fighting Men"—positioned opposite the Wall to observe the names for eternity. We do not speak. They are three unimposing figures, lifelike with their fatigues and weapons and their familiar stance. They are troopers coming in from the boonies at some base camp where we've gone for a party. They are haggard, and their expressions are bewildered, wistful. They have old eyes in young faces. They seem to ask why of the Wall.

At noon there's a band playing on the Mall near the Capitol building, so we meander in that direction and stop for hot dogs at a concessioner's stand along the way.

We are standing in line when the sound of choppers breaks our ranks.

Electric shouts of "Here they come!" bombard the Mall as veterans race for hilltops, waving, whooping, and hollering. Blade tip to blade tip, a gaggle of ten Hueys passes over treetops to the green, chopping air with a haunting familiarity, silence falling in their wake. All eyes follow their swoop over the Wall as they dip to salute our fallen. Thousands of us stand in hushed attention as the honor is rendered. Our tears fall unabashedly. Close behind, five Phantom jets thunder past in close formation.

As quickly as they came, they are gone. Clusters of veterans stare where they disappeared into the sky, shouting, "Come back! Come back!" But they don't. We turn away in disappointment.

"Sometimes," I say to Bonnie, "I wish I could bring back that year." She nods. She feels the same way.

The two of us join Rose and other women vets, sitting on the grass near the bandstand. Many around us are teary-eyed. Cans of beer are popping. Nostalgia is rampant. We search the crowd for faces we remember, but we all are so changed. Even so, I feel as though I am among long-lost friends.

Chris Noel sings "America the Beautiful." Her voice drifts

across the lawn and creates a kind of backwash, a ripple of murmurous voices. At first singly, then in clusters, we stand. Many come to attention with a military salute. We all join in singing the words, thousands of voices ringing true and clear.

When the song ends, shouts of "Welcome home!" reverberate through our ranks as we hug and salute one another. "Thank you for going," we say, "and congratulations for making it back."

Rose, tirelessly trumpeting the cause of women vets, has arranged for us to go onstage. We take turns at the microphone, giving our names, telling where and when we were stationed. Then, linked at our waists, we sway to a refrain of "America the Beautiful" once more floating across the sea of thousands, our voices joining those lifted toward us. When the song ends, thumbs-up are everywhere, granting us the same status shown the men.

"Hey. Remember me?"

Offstage I'm confronted by a Special Forces first sergeant in dress greens. Still, I marvel, in the Army.

Behind him stand friends similarly dressed, but without his impressive rows of medals and stripes and considerably younger than us, maybe our age when we went to war.

His face is not familiar. I shake my head.

"Ewings! Jim Ewings! Don't you remember me?"

I don't.

"You patched me up, lady!" Turning to the younger men, he says, "Hey! This was my nurse! She patched me up!"

His eyes squint with a faraway look. "I was wounded three more times after that, once for each tour I served over there," he says. "I kept going back because I never felt quite right being back in the States."

I nod understandingly.

He sighs deeply. "The Army's different now. The Special Forces fell out of favor after the war."

My heart aches for him. I can imagine how many buddies he must have seen killed, maimed, and otherwise destroyed—all to fall out of favor after the war. I give Jim Ewings a big hug. "Welcome home," I say from the bottom of my heart.

He wipes away tears as he says, "Thank you." Then, catching

me by surprise, he bends me way over and plants a big kiss on my mouth. I suspect the gesture is more for his friends than for me, but I'm delighted anyway. It's the flamboyance of a warrior coming home from the fields of glory, a ritual we who grew up on World War II movies once expected.

This night thousands of candles illuminate a hill in the Mall to commemorate those missing in action, some of whom may still be prisoners of war. I don't want to believe that any of our warriors are still suffering in the name of a war that no one but families and fellow veterans care to remember. But if they are, I have no faith our government will get them out unless it's pressured to.

That's just what the crowd tonight hopes to do. Program speakers are constantly interrupted with angry cries of "Bring them home!" Though the protest echoes my sentiments, my conservative upbringing recoils at interrupting speakers. I'm embarrassed by the rudeness but, at the same time, grateful for the audacity that refuses placating words in place of actions.

When the ceremony ends, we form a procession to pass the Wall.

I love this place at night, love the thousands of fluttering candles that narrow to a single file as processioners patiently await their turns to present each tiny flame to the Wall.

The candles drip like waxen tears. A park ranger begins to remove them to keep them from streaking the Wall.

"Hey! Don't do that! Leave them alone!" someone shouts.

The ranger apologizes, explains there won't be time to clean the Wall before the statue's dedication ceremony tomorrow. He is absolved; he's here to rescue the Wall.

"Don't worry about it," a long-haired veteran assures him. "We'll take care of it. Just don't take them away."

The candles stay. When we reach the top of the Wall, there are so many candles that photographs are being taken of the names on the polished black stone.

Several of us share a cab back to the hotel. As we climb out, we're met by Vietnam vets on the prowl. "Hey! Look at this! Women!" one of them says enthusiastically.

"Not just women," I call back. "Vietnam vets!"

We join ranks in a nearby bar for drinks. It's a night for making rounds and getting drunk in the old Army days way, playing homecoming warriors no matter how many years have passed.

When the others move on, two men remain, content to share a conversation with a middle-aged woman vet. One served in the 1st Cavalry, and the other was a marine, the three of us an impossible mix when we were there. They talk about humping the boonies, and I say I couldn't have endured such dangers day after day. I talk about the casualties, and they say they couldn't have stood the bloodbath day after day.

Their words bring back a face, the swarthy face of an infantry lieutenant. "How can you work in that place?" he asked, grieved by the sight of his dying sergeant.

We agree that the emotions we experienced that year were much the same. And we all survived the same way, by numbing ourselves to what was asked of us. They swallowed their fear in order to face the enemy. I buried compassion to face the wounded. Back in the World with hearts desensitized and minds numb, we shut out the horrors of the war zone and turmoil on the home front, and our self-administered anesthesia has been wearing off in variable times.

Veterans Day is overcast and wintry. Bonnie and I stand before the Tomb of the Unknown Soldier for their tribute, but my patriotic spirit—renewed just yesterday—has nose-dived. Bonnie has just told me that there was no Unknown Soldier from the Vietnam War until this year, a long wait. The Korean War honored its unknown men in 1958.

We have been excluded in many ways from the homage paid to warriors of other wars, but I can't change it. And what really matters is that our warriors finally have a place to be honored, even if we have had to pay for it ourselves. So I tell myself I may as well enjoy the pomp and circumstance: the clicking precision of young servicemen in impressive uniforms; the rigid faces for presentation of arms; the resounding of rifles in solemn salute.

Afterward there are speeches in the rostrum. Even though I

know the speakers have lied before and will again, I embrace their words. I cheer with everyone else when General Westmoreland praises us for a job well done, for having done what our country asked of us when many would not.

And then Secretary of Defense Weinberger announces that this week is dedicated to the women who have served in the armed forces, and the audience explodes with an exuberant standing ovation.

Bonnie and I throw our arms around each other. Not until this moment did I know how much I craved this recognition.

The plan is for us women vets to stand together for the three o'clock dedication of the statue. Knowing there will be hordes of people, Margo, Bonnie, and I arrive at the Mall with offerings of flowers an hour beforehand. We find check gates with guards at the entrance, searching for weapons and explosives. The three of us can't believe it. Weapons? Explosives? Here?

The flowers will have to wait until after the ceremony. With these lines we'll be hard pressed to reach the veterans outreach trailer in time to meet the other women vets. Once we're finally past the check gate, we find the entire area of the trailer cordoned off.

Exiting the gate against the incoming masses, we ask a guard how to get to the trailer. He directs us to a check gate on the far end of the Wall. At this gate we can't get through without special passes. We're directed to a check gate on the other side of the Lincoln Monument.

Time is short now. We break into a run, climbing over a fence constructed to keep us from taking a shortcut around the Lincoln Monument. Bonnie and Margo are worried we'll be arrested, but I don't give a damn. Out of breath when we reach the third check gate, we're once again turned away for lack of special passes. We race back to the check gate near the trailer.

"We're women vets," I tell the guard. "Please have someone tell Rose Sandecki that three of us are at the gate."

"Sorry," he says. "We don't have anyone to run messages."

"Then please let one of us through to tell her."

"Sorry, lady." He nods impatiently toward the growing crowd behind us.

"What do you mean, 'sorry'? Why do we need special passes? We have every right to be here! We're vets!"

Bonnie and Margo are tugging at my arms. "Don't make waves," says Bonnie. "He's just doing his job."

"Please, Winnie," Margo says. "Let's get out of here."

But something is happening inside me. An anger, as beyond my control as my tears, is taking over.

"The President is coming," the guard says in an effort to explain why we can't pass through.

"What does *he* have to do with this? Why the fuck is *he* coming?"

The guard stares at me speechlessly. Bonnie pulls more firmly on my arm to leave, saying, "It's not his fault. He doesn't have the authority to let us pass." But I'm out of control, beyond soothing words or reason.

"He's got nothing to do with this place!" I shout at the guard. "He hasn't done anything for us in fifteen years! He wouldn't have anything to do with us *now* if it didn't look good to the voters!"

The still-speechless guard's worried glance shifts from me to the growing crowd.

"This is *our* memorial! What right does *he* have to keep us from getting in when *we're* the ones who were there?"

The guard's face hardens. "Look, lady," he finally responds, "if you don't leave, I'm going to have to throw you in jail."

"Go ahead!" I threaten. "I dare you! I *want* the newspapers to hear how you're keeping the women vets out!"

Distantly I hear Margo say that she's leaving, that she has children and can't afford to be arrested. Bonnie is on the verge of tears, unwilling to abandon me but begging me to leave.

"You go," I say, "but I'm staying." The crowd behind silently watches another freak show by a deranged Vietnam vet. Let them stare.

Two new guards converge at the check gate. "Hey, lady, it can't be that important," one of them says sardonically.

The bastard! "You can say that because you didn't watch them die!" I scream. For the first time in my life I'm shaking with rage.

Unable to meet my gaze, he shrugs at one of the other guards. Bonnie has given up trying to reason with me, no longer tugs at my arm.

Now an older woman, somebody's mother, appears on the other side of the gate. "Don't make a scene," she says to me. "This kind of behavior is what earns the veterans a bad reputation. It won't do anything but hurt the chances of getting help for all of you."

The disapproving mother scolding the naughty child. I turn toward her with loathing. "How much less help could they give us than they have for the past fifteen years?"

The woman retreats. I whirl back toward the guard. I'm shivering from an unnatural chill. And suddenly I'm ready to leave. "If there's ever a war, I hope you're the first to go," I choke at the guard. I can feel tears coming up.

Then, taking us by surprise, he lets us pass—just like that. But when we get to where it should be, the trailer isn't there. I turn away, drained and discouraged. We are in a crowd of a few hundred, facing a stage constructed against the back of the Wall. My heart sinks. And just look at the people in this privileged area. Not vets distinguished in piecemeal fatigues but outsiders spruced up in fancy suits and dresses. We've come to the circus.

"This is not where I want to be." I start to stomp out.

"But where else can we go?" Bonnie asks.

She's right. There are hundreds of thousands of people outside this protected area, and we don't know where our group is or how to find it.

Two more women vets join us, laughing heartily. Having witnessed our mode of entry, they approached the gate prepared to do the same. Only when they said they were vets, the guard didn't even try to stop them. "One crazed woman vet must be all he can handle," one of the new women says, and we laugh.

In the grand scheme of things, much more important personages have come to speak than Jan Scruggs. But he's our inspiration, the ex-marine whose single-minded determination got our memorial built. Without him, there would be no Wall.

A thunderous reception greets his introduction from the other side of the stage. The program is being broadcast in front of the Wall. Tumultuous cheers are raised as well for designer Maya Lin. When Jan Scruggs comments on the irony of Vietnam vets who built the Wall giving it to the government today, laughter booms.

Enter the President and Nancy, tightly guarded by men in dark suits who look like Mafia thugs. They ring the stage, glowering at the crowd during the boss's speech.

The President says how we all have suffered. He says the nation is healing. And he says how grateful the country is to all the men who served in Vietnam.

My anger rises out of me in a shout before I know it's coming. "What about the women?"

And the cry is taken up by our small band. *"What about the women?"*

The President looks at us in confusion. The thugs, I note with satisfaction, have turned their glowers on us.

"The women! What about the women?" We're jumping up and down, pointing to our buttons and badges as if he could read them from fifteen feet away.

He looks around to see if anyone knows what we're talking about. I wonder if he's aware that women served in Vietnam, much less that there are women's names on the Wall.

Our cries are heard over the loudspeaker, though we aren't aware of it at the time. The hundreds of thousands on the other side of the stage hear, firsthand, how the service of women to their country is so carelessly forgotten. Though we miss being with the women vets who carry a wreath to the Wall, miss tearful reunions with others of us who join from the sidelines, and miss being cheered by the thousands upon thousands in our honor, we are heard—and we figure it's worth it.

After the dedication, still among the privileged with special passes, a gold star mother comes up to me with tears in her eyes.

"Were you a nurse there?"

I nod yes. She falls into my arms, her body shuddering with sobs. I feel my heart breaking.

Her husband comes to pull her gently away from me.

"I'm so sorry we couldn't save him," I say through my tears.

I want to say how very hard we tried, but I can't. Her son may have been an expectant who died alone in a corner or behind a yellow-curtain screen.

Tears stream down her face. "Thank you for trying."

Her husband takes her, protecting her sagging figure as they disappear into the crowd.

Not until we walk around the stage do I see how close we are to the statue. A few dozen people duck the rope on the other end of the Wall to come directly here. The rest wait their turns in a procession that wends past the Wall and emerges in a thin stream at this end.

Some bear gifts for the "Three Fighting Men"—colorful bandannas and neck scarves, old boots and bottles of beer.

The next day Bonnie and I make our last visit to the Mall with thousands of other veterans.

Every two hours taps are played from where the black and white MIA/POW flag stands on top of the Wall, and everyone stops to salute. The long, slow notes flood me with memories: taps played at Army bases as the American flag was lowered for the night; taps played at the funeral of my uncle who served during World War II; taps at events for disabled veterans that I attended with my father.

I press my hand against the Wall one last time. Others follow, and I smile when they marvel aloud, "It's warm!"

CHAPTER TWENTY

DECEMBER 1984–
APRIL 1985:
Back in San Francisco

I⊤ has been eighteen months since the ghosts first rose in my life. I now understand why nice clothes and a big house don't mean as much to me as to my family and friends, but I don't know that it makes any difference. Near or far away my past sets me apart.

When a Huey chops at the sky, I'm transported back, gazing through an open door at a tropical landscape. When a jet drones overhead, I instinctively appraise its size and speed. Is it a Phantom hurtling toward a war mission or a Freedom Bird bound for home?

You *are* home, I remind myself.

But I miss the warriors.

On Christmas morning I awaken on the Long Binh helicopter pad. We're under attack, and yellow flares light the night sky. A chopper has just delivered us casualties, and upon lifting off, it drips bright red blood that saturates my hair and runs down my face and arms. Seeing it on my hands makes me want to cry.

Every spring I take the required annual recertification in cardiopulmonary resuscitation. This year another recovery room nurse, Warren, comes with me. It's a rare summery day for San Francisco, and someone has opened the tall windows in the old hospital building to take advantage of breezes.

The large room is crowded, and the only "station" without a line for certification is that for resuscitation of an infant. Step right up, puff air through its nose and mouth, watch the baby chest rise and fall.

The image of Chopper's napalmed body pops up. I see his dressings, know the heart-sickening truth of his wounds. I wince as I pump on the tiny chest, knowing how painful the slightest touch is. And I know that he is going to die.

Shake it off, I tell myself. That was Vietnam, 1967. This is San Francisco, 1985. But my hand shakes as I sign off here and move on to the next station—the two-man resuscitation of an adult. Warren bends over the mannequin and breathes into its mouth as I pump on its chest.

The smell of wounded is all around me. I sense the impending death of the soldier under my hands, and a small panic rises inside me. I focus my mind's eye to try to see who he is, but I make out only the dim shadows of a ghost from the past. When I stand, I'm sweating.

One more station to go—to assess whether the "victim" is breathing and has a pulse. A cinch. I instinctively check both at the same time, as I have learned to do while working so many years in critical care.

"No," barks the certifier. She uses her foot to point to where I'm taking the pulse, and her shoe brushes my hand. "You can't check for the pulse until you've watched for respirations for a full five seconds."

I transfer my glare from her foot to her face. She assures me that she had not intended to kick me.

I know she didn't mean it, and I try to ignore it. I can't. She's too military, somehow "holier than thou" just because she's in the superior position. "Why waste time?" I challenge.

Astonished, she stares at me.

"It's a waste of time," I repeat, looking her straight in the eye from where I kneel on the floor.

"The Red Cross requires that we do it one step at a time," she says. "Otherwise you might miss the pulse or lose track of how long you've waited for a breath."

"Five seconds is a long time just to *watch!*" I'm trembling with the effort to control my anger. I know I'm way out of line, but I just can't drop it.

In the corner of my eye I see Warren making his escape. I don't blame him. I probably would, too, if I were in his shoes.

The certifier argues that there have to be rules. I reply that rules that hinder should be changed. She says these don't hinder, that you *have* to wait the five seconds to be sure.

I'm standing now, glowering over her shorter figure. "That's fine before *pounding!* But why not check the pulse at the same time if you've been doing it for years?"

Her eyes dart to the others waiting their turns to be certified. They discreetly look elsewhere.

"Just how many *real* resuscitations have you done anyway?" I demand.

No answer.

None! A paper nurse! Enraged, I step closer. "You've got a lot of nerve! Acting all high-and-mighty when you haven't ever even done one yourself!"

We're saved when the woman who runs the show, a nurse with whom I worked for many years in the intensive care unit, comes to investigate the commotion. She's never seen me angry before, and surprise registers on her face. Vouching for my competence, she okays my certification.

I find Warren in the outside hallway, his nose stuck in a bulletin board.

"Remind me never to get your goat, Smith," he says, grinning. "How about breakfast?"

We stop at an outdoor café to take advantage of the beautiful day. But I can't shake the ghost soldier I glimpsed during the two-man resuscitation. He's still a shadow, but I now see the place and time clearly: the intensive care unit in Saigon, nearing the midnight hour.

"Hey, Smith!" Warren calls from San Francisco. "Where are you?"

I smile with a shake of the head. "Just daydreaming." He's not a vet and wouldn't want this sunny day marred with talk about a casualty from so long ago. I apologize to him and head home.

Painters are working on an apartment next door. When I get home, their van is blocking my driveway.

I parallel park in front of the van, not noticing two buckets of paint in my path. Not until I climb out of my car do I see them, now spilled all over my driveway.

My irritation implodes. What the fuck is the paint doing here? Where the shit is that jerk painter? I'm ready to go after him and give him a piece of my mind, but I manage to contain myself. What purpose would it serve? Besides, one blowout a day is enough.

I leave the buckets where they lie and go inside.

There I see the ghost soldier more clearly. He was younger than most, an eighteen-year-old private with multiple gunshot wounds to the abdomen. He had had a splenectomy, pancreatectomy, repair of the liver, and partial colectomy with temporary colostomy. But he should have lived.

"Hey!" comes an angry shout from my front door, the shout of a sergeant to a private.

The painter! Furious, I race toward the confrontation.

"What the hell do you mean by knocking over my paint buckets?" he yells.

"I didn't see them! And what the hell were they doing in my driveway?" I yell back.

"You'd have to be blind not to see them!"

"Take off your glasses and we'll see who's blind!"

That stops him. "What's that got to do with it?" he asks.

"I don't even wear glasses, so who's blind!" It's a ridiculous argument, but I don't care.

"What the hell are you doing home anyway? I thought women these days worked for a living!"

"I do! And it's more than just pushing a paintbrush all day long!"

Again he pauses. "Look, I have permission to park my van here. I parked here all last week, and you were never home. How the hell was I supposed to know you'd be here today?"

"I don't care about the van! You left room for me to park my car, and that's what I did! How the fuck was I supposed to know your goddamn buckets were in the way?"

"You didn't even have the guts to come tell me what you'd done!"

"Why should I? You fuckin' should have put the buckets where I could see them!"

"You goddamned should've looked!" He steps toward me. I take a measured step to separate us.

"Keep your filthy body away from me." I look him straight in the eye. I half hope he'll lunge for me so I can throw him with a judo kick. But he keeps his distance.

There's nothing more to say, so he leaves. I pour a glass of wine, grab a pack of cigarettes, and retreat to my backyard—to escape the telephone, the city, the people, the World.

The ghost soldier returns. Not until his death cry do we know anything is wrong. We rush to his bed, move swiftly with the resuscitation. He's not trached, so we pump air into him with a mask and ambu bag. Slippery green vomitus pours out of his mouth and over his chin, making a seal with the mask impossible. We wipe off the secretions, but when we pump on his chest, more spews out, spilling over his face and filling the mask. His face turns the purple color of death.

Alex and Luke arrive. Luke tries to insert a tube into the soldier's lungs, but he can't see the path with so much green slime in the way. No matter how much I suction, more wells up to hide the lifesaving route. It overflows the darkening lips, pours down his chin and neck, and spreads over his bed. Counterpoint to our whirl of motion is his deathly stillness.

I attach the gastric tube to continuous suction on the machine we use for pulmonary secretions. There's so much! The suction bottle is already full! A corpsman relieves Alex on the breathing bag. Alex administers drugs while I withdraw secretions by hand. The syringe I use is warm and slimy with the nauseating smell of vomitus. I breathe through my mouth, so I won't gag. My hands ache from pulling and pushing on the syringe.

It takes too long. When a path is finally cleared and the tube inserted into his lungs, the young soldier's heart will not start up again.

The ghost soldier's eyes are frozen in a terrified fight for air. His face is swollen and purple and streaked with green. His hair is matted with more green, and his head rests in a puddle of it.

Cleaning up afterward, we notice the empty water bottle on the portable suction machine—water used for rinsing the suction catheter after use. The young soldier had drunk the water to quench his thirst.

"Now that's what I call dying of thirst!" says our corpsman. But I don't laugh.

He should have lived, but he died.

Unable to weep for him then, I weep for him now.

One of the men in our veterans group asks me how many casualties I cared for. It's a question I have not asked myself.

At Fort Dix I estimate somewhere between twenty-five and forty, which seemed like a lot then. In Japan I figure there were between five and seven hundred, these weren't devastating injuries by later standards, but they seemed so at the time. In Saigon it was one or two hundred, many with devastating injuries, and in Long Binh between fifty and seventy-five, most with devastating injuries.

The grand total is six hundred to a thousand men, but I can't even decide if that's a conservative or generous estimate. In the end it doesn't matter. However many there were, it was too many.

They will never leave my heart, but they are loosening their grip on my mind. Flashbacks are rarer, and I seldom weep, unless I'm looking at photographs or reading about Vietnam—something I do obsessively when I come across anything on the topic. Nightmares are still common, sometimes two or three a night.

In the dream I'm a medic and out on patrol, walking along a dirt road with rice paddies on either side. We're all exhausted, and the midday tropical heat makes it difficult just to breathe.

Our platoon leader brings us to a halt about a thousand meters from a stand of trees. He's expecting trouble there and wants us rested before facing a fight. I drop my pack. The air hitting my back is deliciously cool.

Everyone is jittery. At either end of our line two guards squat back to back as they peer across the paddies. The rest of us are sitting or lying down, most puffing on cigarettes. There's little conversation.

A sharp yell from a guard at the front of the line, followed by a burst from his weapon, sends me diving into the water. Just as a grenade explodes in the middle of our group, the paddy comes alive with Vietcong in black pajamas. Our men fire nonstop while the radioman calls for air support. I must get to my pack to help the wounded, but I'm worried about getting shot.

Afterward we wait for dustoff choppers to evacuate our dead and wounded. Slick helicopters circle the area, sporadically firing into the paddies. The distant tree line is ablaze from falling bombs.

I stare at our casualties, sitting and lying in the road. One soldier's legs were blown off by a grenade, and they've been thrown into the rice paddy so he won't have to look at them. He lost a lot of blood before I got tourniquets applied, and I can see the pallor under the dirt on his face.

The soldier next to him has a badly mangled arm with a tourniquet just below the shoulder. His hair is matted with dirt, and I can see sweat streaks where his helmet straps were. Someone has lit a cigarette for him, and he's smoking with an empty gaze across the rice paddies.

A little farther down the line is a man with a bullet wound in his thigh and blood seeping through a stark white dressing. I know his leg will heal, and he'll be returned to the field in a few weeks. He's giving sips of water to a man whose whole right side is peppered with grenade fragment wounds, his chest wall suffering the worst damage. He might live, but he badly needs to get to a hospital. Next to them is a soldier with bandages wrapped around his eyes and chin, whose face will have to be reconstructed and who will never see again.

And at the end of the line is our pile of dead. One who took a direct hit to his face that blew off most of his head. Another with multiple gunshot wounds that ripped apart his chest and abdomen. One who stepped on a land mine while taking cover alongside the road and was blown to pieces. His arms and legs are laid on top of the pile to go home with him.

The first dustoff chopper lands, and our wounded are spirited away to the hospital. A second lands; the remains of our dead are slipped into body bags and flown off to graves registration.

I've agreed to speak about the war to a class of high school students on behalf of the Veterans Speakers Alliance, an organization formed to counter what students hear from military recruiters.

"Before I went to Vietnam," I tell them, "I firmly believed the Vietnamese people wanted us there. I didn't know those in power in South Vietnam were those who profited from French colonialism. I didn't know that Ho Chi Minh had helped downed American fliers escape capture by the Japanese during World War Two, or that he had requested our assistance in freeing his country from the French, or that he had fashioned their constitution after ours—some parts word for word. And," I admit, "I never stopped to consider how our burning and bombing their villages made the Vietnamese feel.

"I had faith in our leaders to risk our men's lives only for clear purpose and need and to use our military judiciously, to safeguard the world against tyranny and oppression. I had faith in God to show us the way, to protect the meek and reward the good, to care for all His creatures great and small. I had faith in myself to uphold the beliefs with which I was raised, no matter how hard that might be. And," I say, "I had faith in my countrymen to stand by their sons and daughters who served in war to preserve freedom.

"Whatever faith was left when I came back was lost thereafter, and losing it was so painful that I hope I never find it again." I look around at the classroom of eager young faces. "I'll never trust our government again," I tell them. "It is not all wise or as concerned with your welfare as it could be."

I wonder if I've reached them—if they can believe that war is not glorious but tragic. Their eyes are so clear, so different from the dazed eyes of warriors in Vietnam, though they are not much different in age. "That's why I'm here," I say, "to make you think twice about what we do as a nation. And to say if you don't like what you see, work to change it."

In my dream I'm shopping for clothes in Sausalito. Everything I look at either has bloodstains or is torn and dirty. Deciding something must be wrong with the store, I leave to meet my father.

We go together to a shoe store, where I pick out a pair of dressy high heels. But when I open the box at the counter for one last look before paying, I find a piece of bloody fatigue jacket in the bottom of the box.

My father has sent me a bronze replica of a woman in jungle fatigues, a miniature of the statue being debated over for inclusion at the National Vietnam Veterans Memorial. Supporters see her mission as twofold: to honor those wounded in body and spirit, as well as the dead, and to teach that women have served and died for their country in wars. She belongs near the wall, we say, juxtaposed with the "Three Fighting Men" and gazing at the names she knew in their final hours.

Not so, say some on Capitol Hill. A woman doesn't belong in a war memorial; it is inappropriate.

As inappropriate as the women whose names are on the Wall? we wonder. As the women POWs on Corregidor? As those who died flying cargo planes in Europe during World War II? Holding the little statue tight in my hand, I cry for all of us.

My mood is still depressed when I begin my recovery room shift this evening and take report on a new admission with a long leg cast for a fractured femur. It ends with the observation that the patient is extremely unpleasant, but that it's forgivable as he's a Vietnam veteran.

Fine by me. Anger will be a welcome change from all the whiny poor-mes we take care of. Maybe I can steer him toward a vet organization for help.

When he awakens, I begin the ritualistic questions: "When were you in Vietnam?"

"Nineteen sixty-eight."

"'Sixty-seven to 'sixty-eight or 'sixty-eight to 'sixty-nine?"

"What difference does it make?" he says shortly.

I shrug, bending to take his blood pressure. "Just thought we might have been there at the same time."

He looks at me suspiciously. "'Sixty-eight to 'sixty-nine."

"Where were you?" I check the circulation on his casted leg.

"In the mountains." There were no mountains in Vietnam; we called them highlands.

"What outfit were you with?" I ask, avoiding his eyes.

"The Two Hundred First."

"Funny," I say, "I never heard of it. Was it new in-country?"

"What difference does it make?" he says again, getting irritated.

"Just curious." I've finished checking him over and stand staring at him from the end of his bed. "Where did you go on R and R?"

"Look, lady, that was a long time ago. I don't remember."

"Where did you fly out from?"

"I said I don't remember. And I don't like being grilled!"

"And I don't like people that fake having gone!"

Propping himself up on his elbows, he shouts at me, "Are you calling me a liar!"

"Yes." I'm trembling with fury. "Anybody who went remembers where they left country!"

He makes a move to climb over the side rail. "Come on," I taunt. "Maybe you'll bust the other leg!" We glare at each other until he settles back on his elbows.

When I return to the nursing station, I tell his surgeon that he's no Vietnam vet.

"But it's written all over his chart."

"Then why isn't he at the VA hospital?"

He looks over at the patient, who is still glaring at me. "Good question," the doctor says.

I dream of a nine-month-old puppy, a springer spaniel with long, floppy ears and that special kind of bounce springers have.

His master enrolls the pup in a training school for hunting dogs.

The puppy is lonely and confused but gamely tries to keep up with the other dogs, most of which are older, bigger, and stronger. When the master comes to visit, he scolds the puppy for his poor performance. The puppy tries harder.

One cold, rainy day the dogs are being raced down a meadow. The puppy runs as hard as he can, but soon all the dogs have passed him. Unwilling to quit, he crawls on the ground, pulling himself with his front paws. He tries so hard he keels over.

Moving out of the sidelines, I go to pick him up, hug him, and tell him the race doesn't matter. But I'm too late. The puppy is dead, lying in the mud and pounded by the rain.

I'm sitting on my front porch when an old man, a Jehovah's Witness, appears. I say from the start that there is no way he can make me believe in God. He tries anyway. The point he keeps coming back to is that people blame God for their errors.

"Not me," I say. "I don't blame God because I don't believe there is one."

"Something very awful must have happened," he observes, "for you to have so little faith."

"Yes," I agree. "To many of us. In Vietnam."

His shoulders sag. "Oh, I'm so sorry." He holds out his hand to shake. I wish him luck, say I hope his message of peace reaches others.

As he retreats, something about his hunched shoulders makes me wonder if he lost a son in Vietnam. Maybe that's why he ended the conversation so abruptly.

I dream there has been a war, and the new government is a military regime. There are soldiers everywhere, looking for guerrillas. San Francisco has been bombed, but General Hospital still stands, and I still work there—and I'm still young. There's a street kid in the neighborhood whom hospital workers have more or less adopted, even though we know he works with the guerrillas. We don't help the guerrillas ourselves, but we don't support the government either.

One day three of us go to a favorite restaurant for lunch. The place is really busy, so I go back to the warmer where the day's freshly baked bread is kept. Grabbing what I assumed would be a loaf of French bread, I recognize it as the forearm of our adopted boy, the muscle split open the way a loaf of bread splits open along the top as it rises. I feel no horror or revulsion, just sadness that the boy is dead.

My dream is interrupted when the earth shakes. I snap awake and leap from my bed to run for the bunker. I'm standing confused and unable to remember which direction I should run when the earth shakes again.

It's not being attacked that terrifies me, but the fact that I can't hear the explosions. Have I gone deaf? Asking the question answers my confusion. It's not a mortar attack; it's an earthquake. I go back to bed.

I dream that I'm on duty in the emergency room at San Francisco General when an earthquake hits. Mass casualties start arriving shortly thereafter, and one is a Vietnam vet in a fatigue jacket. "Get him out of here," one of our doctors snarls.

I'm astounded and ask him why, just as two more vets are brought in. The doctor looks in their direction and snaps, "This is their fault!"

The wounded vets turn to leave, and I grab my purse.

"Where are you going?" the doctor demands.

"With them," I say calmly.

"But we need you here!"

I know that's true. A lot of the nurses are falling apart with so many casualties. "They need me more," I say, turning toward the door.

"If you leave, you're fired," the doctor says.

"And what about them if I don't leave?"

"They belong at the VA hospital."

I say nothing more, just walk out.

Casualties, all vets, are lying on a street near the freeway. Those less injured are scrounging up food, water, dressings, IVs, and blood. I don't know where they're getting the supplies, and I don't ask.

By afternoon there are hundreds of vets on the street. Uninjured vets, all wearing fatigue jackets, come to help. It's a good feeling to have everyone doing what he or she can to help, working together.

Late in the afternoon three police cars pull up. Someone asks who's in charge. When no one else steps up, I do.

"You'll have to leave," one policeman orders.

"Where will we go?"

"I don't know, but you can't stay here. This is a public street."

I look around. The buildings are collapsed, and there's very little traffic, even on the freeway.

"How do you expect us to move the injured?"

"That's your problem."

Vets are starting to move forward from behind me. The policemen become wary and touch their guns, but the vets don't back down. The police leave, but we know they'll be back. Some vets go in search of weapons. Others start building barricades around us. I'm nervous as I care for our wounded, but there's not a doubt in my mind that this is where I belong.

CHAPTER TWENTY-ONE

MAY 7 WEEKEND, 1985: The Canyon of Heroes, Manhattan

My father has stuck by me for almost two years now, staunchly defending me, even against my mother, who doubts that a war so long over could affect me as it has. Time and again my father has assured me that I'm a good person and strong, and I will be all right.

He's older and slower these days, but his big bear hug and "Hello, honey," aren't changed from when he picked me up at the airport so long ago. I've come for the dedication of New York City's Vietnam Memorial tonight, and a welcome home parade for Vietnam veterans tomorrow. Ten years since the war's end we're having our parade.

Mother and I aren't talking these days, but in spite of everything, she'd be hurt if she found out I was here. My father has arranged for me to stay with Lin, his friend who talked me through the Fourth of July last year, who lives in Long Island—within easy commute to Manhattan for the dedication ceremony tonight and to Brooklyn for the start of the parade tomorrow.

Sheila is here, too, staying at her sister's house, also on Long

Island. With her is another veteran to whom her sister has opened her home—Mike, a corpsman in Vietnam, known to Sheila from the Concord Vet Center.

We meet at Grand Central Station for the ceremony, wearing our old fatigue tops with patches. Converging upon the subway track must be thousands of vets in bits and pieces of their warrior uniforms. A policeman waves us through the gate, nodding and smiling, saying, "Welcome home." The atmosphere is as if we've just returned, and our country is celebrating. My heart swells with pride.

The train is packed with Vietnam vets, some already getting drunk. Everyone asks, "Where were you? When were you there?"

We jerk to a stop near Battery Park, and the conductor announces, "Welcome home!" over the loudspeaker just before he opens the doors. Our whistles and cheers thank him, resounding through the station as we spill onto the platform and ascend the steps into the brisk night.

Flags and banners ring the memorial. At one end the stark black and white MIA/POW flag flies above its honor guard of vets. To our left stands the unlit glass-block wall, etched with letters sent from warriors in Vietnam before they died.

All the laughter, friendly shouts, and banter among us stop. Tears streak our faces as the speakers, including Mayor Koch and parents of the letter writers, read excerpts from the glass wall.

When the reading ends, the area fills with Vietnam-era music blasting out of loudspeakers and accompanied by fireworks. The music—the Beatles, the Who, the Doors—evokes homesick warriors listening to radios in Vietnam, and the staccato bursts of fireworks bring back sounds of war—incoming, outgoing, a fire fight on the perimeter, an M-60, a howitzer. All around, old warriors identify them.

Less than a year ago I cowered at such sounds. Now that hardly seems possible. So Daddy is right. I will be all right.

The dedication climaxes with the lighting of the glass wall, illuminating the letters from within. Bold letters on one side read:

Mother
I am cursed.

AMERICAN DAUGHTER GONE TO WAR

I'm a soldier
in an age
when soldiers aren't in fashion.

An older man follows a letter with his finger, reading the words to his companion. A woman, slightly younger than I am, stands back to read another inscription:

And in that time when men decide
and
Feel safe to call the war insane. . . .

A middle-aged vet, unshaven and gaunt, touches the words tenderly. A black man who is the right age to be a Vietnam vet stands motionless for a long time with his hands folded behind him in parade-rest fashion.

"Are you Vietnam vets?"

It is early the next morning at a Long Island railroad station, near Lin's house and en route to Brooklyn from Sheila's sister's. The thirtyish woman who asks the question is wearing a conservative, expensive-looking business suit. Wary, Sheila and Mike and I instinctively close ranks as we nod.

"I won't be able to make the parade, but I wanted to add my welcome home." She smiles, holding out her hand.

Each of us shakes her hand numbly.

"I think it's terrible the way you've been treated all these years," she says. "I hope the parade helps make it up." Tears blur her image as she disappears to another part of the platform.

The train takes us to where the parade is starting, but we can't find the twenty-five women vets we're to march with in the milling mass of twenty-five thousand—in spite of where the checklist says they ought to be. We walk the length of the line of marchers forming up, asking if anyone has seen our group.

No one has, but all invite us to march with them. Tears well up when this warrior thanks us for saving his leg, when another says his buddy was hit and thanks us for saving his life, when one says his brother was in Army hospitals from Vietnam to Japan to stateside and is here today—thanks to Army nurses. All would be *proud* to have us join them.

We find a place on the sidelines and watch the parade from where it starts, to wait for our group and to cheer those who pass. The Marines lead, packed tight together. Then Army units with familiar patches—the 101st, the 173d, the 25th, the 1st and the 4th. Smaller groups follow, including one even smaller than ours, dressed in suits and marching under a banner proclaiming them as the CIA. Spooks. How strange to see them out in the open.

Our presence attracts attention; the crowd around us wants to know who we are and why we're here. One woman who can't be more than twenty-five asks if she can march with us. How could she think she has the right to march with us? Holding down my temper, I shake my head, turn away from her.

A TV reporter wants to interview us live, but we decline. Sheila doesn't trust what they might ask. I'm afraid my mother will see me on TV.

When our small band appears, it welcomes us with whoops, hollers, and hugs. We're a mixed group—civilian Red Cross and USO workers, military enlisted, and nurses, who include everyone from lieutenants when they got out to a recently retired colonel. One of the ex-lieutenants is trying to straighten our lines, singing cadence so we will march in step.

I'm not sure how to behave in a parade. I feel very self-conscious and set my sights on the Brooklyn Bridge, its spires barely visible over the treetops. When I finally venture past my awkwardness to wave at the crowds who are cheering us, I see warm smiles and exuberant waves. I take a deep breath. It's a mild, fresh-smelling day. Breathing out, I thank them silently for coming.

Men working on the bridge wave and cheer from overhead. I begin taking pictures. I never want to forget this day. When we top the slight rise at the bridge's mid-point, Manhattan comes into view.

Look at all the people! And *listen* to them! Still distant but distinct, carried by the wind in rolling swells, the cheers to welcome us home. Tears pour down my cheeks. We had worried that no one would come to our parade, that our welcome home would not be worth taking off a day from work! There must be tens of thousands here.

The closer we get, the more thousands we see, the cheering now a continuous drone that grows louder when we are no longer over the water. Every window in every building that lines our way is filled with onlookers. Through one window we can see a woman on a desk, doing a striptease.

The roar of thousands upon thousands applauding, shouting, and cheering bombards us from towering skyscrapers in the financial district—the "Canyon of Heroes." Ticker tape swirls from the buildings, spiraling into the street and turning into a carpet underfoot. Paradegoers overflow the sidewalks, spill out of doorways, crowd rooftops, balconies, and windows.

On the sidelines an on duty policeman who is keeping the crowd back recognizes a group of old buddies; it's the first time they've seen each other since Vietnam. Nor is he the only vet not marching with us. I've had several glimpses of jungle fatigue tops and boonie caps in the crowd.

By now I am infected by the spirit of our welcome home parade. Though I'm still awkward with the role, I wave happily at the people waving at me, and for the first time, I notice their faces. Most are jubilant, but not all. One young girl stands out for me— her face streaked with tears, serious and quiet until she sees our group and joins the thousands who wave and cheer. Her father, I think, must have been one of our wounded. Turning back for a last look after we've passed, I see her following us with sad eyes. My tears well up again. When they clear, it is to see yet more well-wishers with banners, signs, and newspaper headlines that proclaim, WE LOVE YOU. WELCOME HOME! It is our long-awaited dream come true.

After the parade thousands of us converge for a party in our honor on the aircraft carrier *Intrepid*.

"Excuse me."

Turning to face the voice, I find a man dressed in a three-piece suit.

"I noticed the patch on your arm and was wondering if you know someone who wore it."

With all the programs coming out on women vets, you'd think people would know women served there. "I did," I answer curtly.

"A nurse?"

I nod.

"Where were you?"

I look at him more closely.

"Saigon and Long Binh."

He nods knowingly. A vet in disguise. "Yourself?" I ask.

And so the ritual of when, where, and with whom begins, and I forgive his ignorance about women in Vietnam.

He looks wistful when he learns I was in the parade. "I didn't even go to see it," he says, "because it didn't seem important. But then I overheard some vets talking about it, and I really wished I had gone." He smiles at me again. "At least I made this party."

He's just beginning, I think. It's a long haul before he gets to where I am, and I don't envy him.

He's a 1st Cavalry vet, and our conversation attracts others from his old outfit. I slip back to the party, but I don't go unnoticed. What was it like for a woman? What was it like caring for casualties?

I shrink from the questions, the crowd. I'm not in a party mood. I'd rather be with my father.

Back at Lin's house in time for dinner my father greets me with some alarm. "Are you all right?"

Hugging him, I answer, "I'm fine. I just wanted to spend this evening with you."

"Well, it's about time!" he says with mock gruffness.

I think about the distance I've kept between myself and my parents for so many years—refused trips with them and made excuses not to go home for holidays. Like me, my father has waited a long time for me to come home.

"How was it?" Lin asks as I join them at the dinner table.

Before I can answer, my father adds, "We saw the early news. They estimate a million people were there."

Though he doesn't say it in so many words, I can see my father is relieved; the numbers vindicate his faith in me. After all, how could a million people be wrong about the same thing?

On the ten o'clock news veterans shout thanks to New Yorkers from the screen. When it ends, my father turns to me, his brow creased. "This must have been quite a day for all of you," he says.

Choking back my tears, I nod.

Lin gets up quietly to clear the dishes. Sitting back in his chair, my father crosses his arms and begins to talk about his war. Lin gives me a surprised look. Clearly I'm not the only one who has never heard these stories.

"I was on a mortar team, you know. The Army sent us to France on a troopship, then marched us to the German border. It was freezing cold, and supplies were scarce." He pauses. "At one point we had nothing to eat for three days."

His eyes are distant, looking back more than forty years. "I swore I'd never be cold or hungry again," he says, "and I never have been."

So. The memories never go away. They only hibernate.

"When we reached our destination, the krauts were giving us holy hell. We hadn't slept the night before, and I was so tired I could hardly see straight, but we were ordered to set up our gun before dark." He sighs. "That night was a bad one."

In my mind's eye is an old movie scene, a windblown snowscape with artillery explosions lighting the night sky. My father is gaunt in too-big World War II fatigues, warming his hands on the muzzle of the mortar between rounds.

He speaks softly. I lean toward him to be sure I don't miss anything. "That night the other guy on my team—a kid from Arkansas we called Big Red—got blasted with shrapnel when they blew up our position." His breath quickens in an attempt to hold back his tears. "He hung on for a long time. I did everything I could to save him, but the medics didn't get there until morning."

I can see them. My father has wrapped his coat around his buddy to keep him warm while they wait. Big Red leans against my father.

My father blinks away tears. "The next morning they told me

to pick up my rifle and fight with the infantry." He's quiet for a long time, still back in his war. Finally he says, "The war ended for me when I got shot in the leg."

When he says nothing more, I prod gently, "How long were you there?"

And I'm shocked when he answers, "Two weeks."

No wonder he can't understand how changed I am. He never reached the point of numbness and so never lost faith in his beliefs, in himself, or in his country.

I glance at Lin, who has said nothing, who leans against the kitchen counter. Neither of us speaks, not wanting to interrupt.

When my father continues, he speaks of his long months in the hospital in a different tone, in a lighter voice. These stories are smooth from years of practice. There're the ones that always get a laugh.

But I can read between the lines. I've seen the terror in a young warrior's face when the battle to save his leg is lost.

"I smelled so bad nobody wanted to come into the room." My father chuckles.

"I know." I don't smile.

He stops, gazing at me for a long moment. "Yes, I can see how this day must mean a lot to you." He nods slowly. "I wish it had come sooner."

I smile at the remark, so predictable, then notice how his body sags. It's late now. He's not young anymore.

Standing on my cue, he leans heavily against me as we walk to the door. His limp gets worse every year. And, I remember sadly, there was a day when he would not have allowed me to so much as offer him a helping hand out of the chair.

We embrace for a long while. He smells of Old Spice. Always has. "Welcome home, honey," he says, and kisses me good-night.

CHAPTER TWENTY-TWO

MARCH 1991:
After the Homecoming Parade

This is the first day of spring 1991. Tomorrow I will be forty-seven, and in three weeks my son turns five.

My decision to have a child as a single parent came soon after the homecoming parade. My biological clock was running out, and I was afraid to wait. The man I chose to be the father is a former boyfriend whom I still saw from time to time. He didn't want a child, and several weeks passed before he agreed to my proposal, on the condition that this would be my child alone.

I was five months pregnant when my father died, during Christmas week of 1985; that good-night kiss was the last time I saw him. He was excited by the prospect of being a grandfather, and more than once he jokingly said, "You'd better name him after me!" And I did.

My flashbacks stopped with my father's death, but the nightmares persisted—two or three a week. More and more their content changed from the past to the present. Instead of the war in Vietnam, my boy became the focus of my nighttime horrors.

The one time my mother saw "little Kenneth" was when he was three months old. I can see her now, holding him tenderly and saying with great delight, "He looks just like you when you were a baby!" After years of thinking she never wanted me, I realized then I had been wrong. Later, thinking about her life and how devastated she had been when my biological father left us, I saw that she had done what I had done for so long: pushed away painful reminders of the past, including me. She died in the summer of 1987, and her death hit me particularly hard because we were just starting to rebuild our relationship. She finally believed that Vietnam could affect me after so many years, and I finally understood how painful it had been for her to see me changed so much by the war.

After her death I thought little about Vietnam except when I was working on this book, and after two more years the nightmares abruptly slowed to once every five or six months. My last was a month ago, and it was triggered by a TV news broadcast about the Persian Gulf War—about an Iraqi soldier being buried in a shallow grave in the desert. In my dream there was a long column of Iraqi mothers dressed in black robes and veils, poking poles into the blinding white sand to find their sons' bodies.

I come back to the present and take a break from writing. I'm on a bench alongside the playground at Rocky Mountain Parent Participation Nursery School, named for a sheer red rock cliff on the far side of the grounds. The school is a private, nonprofit cooperative where parents contribute five days of work per month to staff the school. Many of us spend much more than the required time here, drawn to a place where we can relax with friends while our children play.

Right now Renee's dad is playing folk music on a guitar, accompanied by Noe's mom playing "Flight of the Bumblebee" on the piano inside. Another father supervises children modeling clay. The snack mom is setting up tables outside, so we can enjoy the reprieve from drought-breaking rains this week. Our teacher, Effie, sits in a big red tub, handing out long strands of red, white, and blue crepe paper. There's a brisk wind, and children run through the playground with their crepe streamers flying behind them. Ken is among them. "Hey, Mom!" he calls happily. "Look at my flag!"

For Ken, this is a close-knit community that softens the absence of a father and grandparents. For me it's a place to express openly how I think and feel.

When we went to war in the gulf, I talked about my horror over the around-the-clock bombing on Baghdad and what it must be doing to the people. I expressed my anger at the military's censoring the press that prevented the American people from being able to form an opinion about what we were doing there. Not everyone agreed with me, but disagreement is not synonymous with disapproval here—for either our children or ourselves—and no one accuses me of being unpatriotic.

Before this war in the Middle East, my biggest regret was that I had not had a child when I was much younger. Until it ended, I was deeply grateful that Ken is not old enough to be drafted. Now I dread the day when he will be.

Only once have we been separated for more than a day. That was shortly before Ken turned three, when I went on a three-day retreat for Vietnam veterans led by the Vietnamese poet and monk Thich Nhat Hanh. "You have seen many awful things, and some were by your own hands," he said. "Do not feel you are the only one responsible. You saw for the whole nation. You suffered for the whole nation." This gentle man watched his villages be bombed over and over again by our forces, yet he has forgiven us. And he gave us a way to forgive ourselves—the most important forgiveness of all. Through him and other Vietnamese at the retreat, I found the people I had glimpsed in a string of Christmas lanterns more than twenty years before.

I glance toward the snack table where Ken now sits, teasing a little girl. I can't imagine life without him. He fills me with a love I never dreamed possible and gives my life the purpose I had been searching for, without knowing it, for so many years. And he has brought back my old dreams of a house big enough for my mother's furniture, a yard big enough to play hide-and-seek in, and vacations together. Most of all, I dream of a big family, or friends

351

who feel like family, to fill our lives with all the different kinds of love.

I don't know if we'll ever have all these things, but I'm grateful for the dreams. Finally I can trust in happiness and in my right to have it.

As for Vietnam, these days I hardly ever think about it.